HOW TO KNOW It's HER | HOW TO KNOW It's HIM

A guide to finding your other half based on a true and inspiring love story.

JOHN and **ELLIANA REX**

ISBN: Paperback: 979 – 12 – 210 – 1492- 1

eBook: 979 – 12 – 210 – 1493 - 8

For enquiries and more information:

(+39) 3519123205 or

Send an email to:

howtoknowitsherhim@gmail.com

Table of Contents

DEDICATION

This book is dedicated to the concept of true love that seems to have faded away with the challenges men and women have faced over the years with finding their God-ordained life partners, and to every individual in search of their heavenly ordained assignment and purpose partner among the over seven billion people on earth. May you find true love and may true love find you.

INTRODUCTION

Not many people understand that love and the lack of it is what has steered the ship of life for centuries on the face of this earth and created the different situations that we all have been through individually, as nations and the world in its entirety. The burning desire to find the right person in the hearts of many is not born from the need to fill an empty space or close the chapter of searching as we usually think. If it was, nobody will be careful to make the right decision. In fact, as many couples as we have come by either while on the move or by a deliberate and scheduled meeting, have further helped us buttress the fact that everybody sincerely hopes for a happy ending. Nobody starts off a relationship and builds it into a marriage hoping to crash it and no matter how tough we seem to be, deep within, we all desire to find the one person that will love us unconditionally for who we are, that will be our best friend and confidant, that we can totally be ourselves with and even be silly around. That person has to be that special someone created from the beginning and destined to be your spouse. When you meet that person, your perspective about love takes a new dimension. From that instant, especially when both of you discover you are meant to be, love no longer becomes an external factor that you have been looking for, like a miner seeking precious jewels. That is when you begin to realize that love has always been in you because you were created in the image of God and if God is love, then you are specifically wired to give and receive love. You discover that all you should have focused on, if only you understood your genetic makeup as one created to think and act like our Father God, is to stay in the Father's love and keep perfecting who you were created to be in the place of prayers by allowing the Word of God transform you, in personal and character development. When you do, God will divinely orchestrate events to work in your favour and follow a certain course that will lead you to crossing paths with your significant other and I'm telling you, when you meet him or her, you will know! It will click. The complexity and uniqueness of your life's journey from the beginning will suddenly make sense and you will realize how incompatible you would have been with the other options you met earlier along the line.

God wants you happily married. This can be confirmed by the fact that finding Adam's perfect life partner was the first challenge He tackled for man from the day of creation. That is how important it is to heaven. God did not wait for Adam to become a billionaire, He didn't instruct Adam to acquire material things, dress to kill or use his skills to get her attention. As a matter of fact, they were naked and unashamed because they didn't even know they were naked so the physical state they were in didn't matter to either of them. Adam stayed in the place of purpose – in the garden, to tend it – which was his assignment. That was where he was when his wife showed up. God transformed him in that garden, put him to sleep in that garden and presented his wife to him in that garden. Find your place of purpose, that's where your wife is. As the woman, where you find the man, that is going to be your place of purpose! Halleluyah! In other words, what you find him fulfilling as his purpose is what you are meant to assist him do and if you don't find yourself synchronizing with his purpose, then you might not have met the person yet.

When Adam saw the woman God created, his thought was not if he had all it took to take care of that damsel or if he looked good enough, he simply followed his spirit and knew without a doubt that this was the woman for him – because they were always in the Presence of God and their flesh was not activated to impair their reasoning. He was certain, based on his closeness to his Father and creator that where he was at that moment was going to be perfect for her too. In other words, she was going to love and accept him just the way he was because they were both seeing things through the Father's eyes, their point of view had not been tainted by the cares of life, by other people opinions or the media's influence. Before I met my wife, I had been judged by what I had and had achieved by the previous women I attempted to date but when my wife and I met, she wasn't looking at where I was at that material moment. She had also developed herself to the point where she was mature enough to look through the right lenses, to look beyond what I had and see who I was, my love for God, my love for her and my passion and drive to become who God has destined me to be. Men, you must find yourself before you can find your wife. Finding yourself is different from acquiring things; it's discovering who you are and what you were created to do on the face of this earth. No man is worthy of being given the destiny of a whole human being in the person of his wife to lead, guide, direct and walk beside to a destination he doesn't even know.

Likewise the woman; you are designed to know he is the one, without asking for your girlfriends' opinions. I mean, how did Eve make that decision without a mother's or best friend's influence? Mind you, God didn't create her like a robot neither did He put her under a spell to accept Adam as soon as she sees him, free will had been given to man from the start. You might say 'but he was the only man available, she didn't have another option.' Well, ladies, I know that there are men you have met in your lifetime that if they were the only men on the face of this earth, you'd rather remain single! So, it's not about an only option, it's about understanding the revelation of how she knew he was the one; she found him in the presence of her Father and creator. She met him in that secret place, in that garden of fellowship, where Adam always went on a stroll with God Almighty. In that place of relationship with the Father, Adam and Eve's spirits were very much alive and bare before each other and they could see into each other's intentions and feelings and could tell that it was real, that it was genuine. Their hearts were like an open book to each other with nothing to hide and the love for their Heavenly Father and doing His Will was the atmosphere that surrounded them and the breath that made their chests rise and fall in constant adoration and passion for Him. Adam and Eve were not pastors, in case you think I expect you to seek out a pastor. They were simply two created beings, created in a pair to love and worship God as they helped Him execute His will and desire for earth as it is written in heaven in their place of purpose.

We highly recommend that you read this entire book so as to have an all-encompassing view of our story and our experiences according to our individual points of view. We are rest assured that there is someone God is keeping out there that is designed to perfectly match everything about you, to awaken hope and joy in you, if you have thrown in the towel over finding fulfillment in marriage, to keep searching prayerfully till you find them and most of all, to know that everything that has happened in your life from the time you were born till date is all working together for your good to bring you to a glorious end. And most of all, we pray that you are inspired to hunger for a deeper relationship with the Lord Jesus and to earnestly desire to know and follow His promptings in your spirit where decision making in your relationship life is concerned.

John and Elliana Rex

(How To Know It's *Her*)

CHAPTER 1
Life Before We Met

I love you! These are very rare words to come by or hear being said to you in the kind of home I was raised in as a child. Not because I had parents that were mean and uncaring but because they were raised in a generation where the cultural language of love was either considered an uncanny way of spoiling a child or could make a parent look weak and vulnerable where his or her relationship with their spouse or children is concerned. And so, love, rather than being expressed or communicated in a physical and emotional way, was communicated more in form of parental responsibilities in areas of provision of basic family needs and security.

Born into a middle income Nigerian home, I can't remember lacking in the areas of food, clothing and shelter as a child growing up, but, I also can't remember my dad giving me a fatherly hug or even as little as a handshake for a first son's good deeds or achievement among six siblings. His disciplinary regimental approach to raising a family or running a home even put my mother on the receiving end of the field missiles and mortars that further deprived us of her physical and outward expression of love in spite of her caring and gentle personality.

She was always meted out a measure of a grumpy and egocentric dominance from my father, that even as a child and all through my teenage and adolescent stages of life, I vowed I was going to pamper my wife to a state of stupor when I got married. I loathed everything about my dad's way of running the emotional side of his family that one day I promised my mom that I was going to grow up to be the direct opposite of him. She would always reply me by telling me that when that time comes, I should shower all the love she couldn't get from my dad on my wife and how lucky she knows the woman is going to be.

What baffles me the most about my mom was how understanding she always tried to be, excusing my dad's harsh and overtly unpleasant excesses. He never abused her physically but his quick temper always kept the house in a troubled and tensed state and one of our happiest moments as children was anytime he had to be away from home, most of the time, at his outposts as a civil engineer. This is not to say that I never had deep respect for him in a lot of areas neither was he a bad father but I craved his fatherly closeness, attention and outward expression of love toward me, my siblings and particularly my mom, which was a very necessary ingredient for creating a happy home and a balanced emotional state of health, especially for the children. Not until one day when my mom noticed how badly I wanted out from my own home as an eleven year old child that she had to sit me down and tell me the truth about my dad's past. The whole thing finally made sense to me to the point where I was moved to tears and began to feel pity towards him.

She told me how my dad lost his mother as a little child and was raised up by a wicked step mother in a polygamous family. She maltreated him so much until he was later picked up and raised by some Catholic missionaries which gave him the opportunity of being schooled up to the tertiary institution. That was when I realized **that love or the lack of it is transcendental through the chain of relationship and where not found, you must determine to be the one to break the chain.** The world can only be a better place when everything revolves around love, because God, who is the creator of the universe, is LOVE and expects us to translate His personality on earth starting from a small unit called *the family.*

At a very tender age of seven all through to my teenage years into adolescence, I was spiraled into a deep quest and search for a utopian love world. I would lay down on my bed for hours and dream of the ideal kind of home that I would love to have, a wife that I would be deeply and unapologetically in love with who would feel exactly the same way about me, surrounded by children that are being pampered with 360 degrees of different expressions of love and boy... did I get my utopia? In fact, I am swimming in it right now. "How?" you might ask. Because you will always get what you dream of. It all starts with a dream. But, I must tell you, that between that time and when I got it, a whole lot played out, a whole lot that I almost missed my utopia except for one person to whom I am greatly indebted and will forever be grateful to, the Lord Jesus Christ!

During my pre-university days, I dated the first girl at age fifteen. It was more of a teenage adventurous exuberance and at this point, my utopia was getting corrupted by wrong association and teenage peer group influence. It's what I can describe as more of an infatuation especially when the girl was the one showing more interest in me than I did in her. Not to mention the fact that I was inexperienced and not mature enough to handle a relationship; it was inevitable that I took her for granted. And was the girl hurt? Yes she was. It made her go into a rebound though I didn't have sexual relations with her, but the fact that she got her emotions too deeply involved made her take another wrong turn and got her hurt all the more this time. I felt very pained because it went totally against my resolve to show true love, especially where it had to do with a relationship with the opposite sex. But, here is where the mistake was; a teenager shouldn't be dating or dabbling with another person's emotions. Dating is a serious thing and should be for young adults who are psychologically and emotionally prepared. While there is no straight line defining when teenage dating should start, the chances of falling into sin or getting hurt emotionally is very high in early teenage dating due to the immaturity and inexperience of both parties.

Besides, at that point and initially, throughout my years at the university, the reason all my attempts to date never ended up in my love utopia that I had always sought after was simply because I was just at my very best what I can describe now as a young man trying to work his dream with his own self-righteousness. I didn't realize that finding true love starts with connecting to the origin of love. The Bible makes us to realize that God is love and you cannot love if you do not know God.

Beloved, let us love one another, for love is of God; and everyone who loves is born of God and knows God. He who does not love does not know God, for God is love. In this the love of God was manifested toward us, that God sent His only begotten Son into the world, that we might live through Him. in this love, not that we loved God, but that He loved us and sent His Son to be the propitiation for our sins. Beloved, if God so loved us, we also ought to love another. 1John 4:7-11, NKJV

If Agape love, which is the God kind of love, does not exist in us then we have not started the journey of loving or wanting to love anyone.

Let me quickly add that at this point in my life, I was looking for true love and someone to love truly but, my foundation was faulty, my philosophies had been tampered with by friends, peers, movies I watched, music I listened to, books I read, especially romance and love novels that are particularly misleading. I tried dating from all spheres of life, from a girl that came from a wealthy background to the one from a lowly background, to the ones I dated trying to hinge my love for them on pity and compassion. Then, I dated the one into sports thinking that because I was also into sports, it would make for easier match making. I was in a sea of total confusion where getting or finding true love was concerned because somewhere in my mind, in the hidden mental image and at the recess of my thinking was still that picture of building my utopian home with my utopian family but something was wrong somewhere that needed to be fixed.

I realized that I didn't even know what I wanted, I was game for the relationship haven I had always dreamed of but I didn't even know what I wanted in the woman for that haven dream. I couldn't even tell exactly how I wanted the woman other than the fact that she should be pretty and should love me in return for the much love I hoped to give her. Looking back now, I can answer myself swiftly saying 'how could I know what I wanted when I didn't even know myself and what my purpose in life was and how could I have known my purpose when I hadn't connected to my manufacturer.' So even if in that state I had gotten a relationship rolling that ended up in marriage, it would have been at its best a slightly better version of my parents and at its worst, have a marriage that ended even before it started. You need to understand yourself and your purpose in life before you hook up yourself into dating. And the only way I will advise that you do this is to get in touch with your manufacturer's manual through your manufacturer in the person of God, through His only begotten Son, Jesus Christ.

In the beginning was the Word, and the Word was with God. He was in the beginning with God. All things were made through Him, and without Him nothing was made that was made. In Him was life, and the life was the light of men. And the light shines in darkness, and the darkness did not comprehend it. John 1:1-5, NKJV

The Bible says in John 1:1-5 that all things were made by Him and through Him. His life is the light you need to see through the manual of your life in order to understand exactly who you are, what you want and what exactly is your purpose, why you are in existence among the over seven billion people on earth.

Let me just give a few examples of some philosophies of the kind of friends and company I kept before I gave my life to Christ and even while you are in Christ, you still need to be careful of the kind of friends you keep even within the church. Psalm 1:1 says blessed is the man who walks not in the counsel of the ungodly...and I have come to realize in my ministry walk, after I gave my life to Christ, that there are even ungodly people in God's house, the church.

Blessed is the man who walks not in the counsel of the ungodly, nor stands in the path of sinners, nor sits in the seat of the scornful; But his delight is in the law of the Lord, and in His law he meditates day and night. He shall be like a tree Planted by the rivers of water, that brings forth its fruit in its season, whose leaf also shall not wither; and whatever he does shall prosper. Psalm 1:1-3 NKJV

Philosophy 1: "Sticking to one life partner is like watching only one channel on your TV amidst a lot of other channels.

Absurd isn't it. Speaking from a marriage point of view right now, I can tell you how to watch several and as many channels as you want from your wife if you allow Christ to hold the center place in your home and furnish your mind with creativity in marriage.

Hear this one. It's a conversation between Christian male and female friends when I had already become a Kingdom citizen.

Male friend: "What exactly is next after marriage? The chasing and dating game is over and then boredom sets in"

Female friend: "you tell me, you're the guy and you should know better."

Male friend: "I think basically, married couples just make babies, attend a lot of weddings to add a little bit of fun to their social life, go to their jobs and wait for time to burn out for the remaining years of their boring lives."

Female friend: "yep. I think that's it, you got it properly summarized".

And they both chuckled with a sense of satisfaction in solving one of life's serious puzzles. I shook my head while being silent through the conversation, not knowing where to start helping their sense of lost identity and seeming hopelessness as tons of answers raced through my mind. I might have had a few questions I needed answered myself but I knew marriage was much more than this description they gave it. It was unimaginable to think that I was hanging with people nurturing such warped philosophies. In a case where someone is confused over the purpose of marriage, I consider this analogy by a group of Christian friends a case of being lost over a matter. Where on earth did the adventure of family vision run off to? What happened to the adrenaline rush of family goals setting and achieving them? Where have they hidden the unequivocal joy of seeking the face of God on the family altar? So many of such questions ran through my mind as I sat in between these two seemingly clueless friends of mine, thinking of what to do with them. Needless to say that a few months down the line, I disconnected from them till date.

One of our family's mentors and role models are Marcus and Joni Lamb and the entire Daystar Television family. Apart from the love and zest for propagating and enlarging the coast of the Kingdom through their media ministry, which is an area we have a call to too, their children and thier spouses are so immersed in the vision. Their children have grown up in the fear and knowledge of the Lord and they eventually married spouses who are God-fearing just like them, is that not the prayer of any parent? But, Marcus and Joni paid the price as a couple to set the pace and standard of their vision. Not just that, they are catching fun doing what they have been called to do as one big happy family. So who says marriage is boring. From this paragraph alone, I can give you some major points that can make a marriage work. No wonder the Bible says where there is no vision the people perish.

"Where there is no vision, the people perish..." Psalm 29:18, KJV

Paraphrased, I'd say where there is no vision, the family perishes and the marriage dies. What is your vision for your proposed marriage as a man or woman that feels ready to date toward marriage?

Philosophy 2: "Don't get too romantic, mushy and love struck with your spouse, else, she will take you for granted."

I have had cause to come across ladies in the past who stated categorically to me that they wouldn't want their men all too soft and all over them. They made it clear that while it takes away that masculinity they love, it also kind of makes them feel they (the women) are in charge of the relationship which they wouldn't want to be. Another lady once told me "I need a man, stern and hard on me sometimes, because I can be personally heady, stubborn and too strong-willed." Now in such a scenario, I think such women or ladies need help, perhaps they've been through some abuse in their past relationships that has impacted negatively on their psychological state of well-being. And then, for the guys who feel or think they will lose their self-confidence and masculinity by showing love and affection towards women, they also need to be helped and given a reorientation from wrong ideologies and philosophies they have acquired over the years in their growing up phase because the truth is, women are wired by God to receive love and affection.

Husbands, love your wives, just as Christ loved the church and gave Himself for her Ephesians 5:22, NKJV

Nevertheless, let each one of you in particular so love his own wife as himself, and let the wife see that she respects her husband. Ephesians 5:33, NKJV

Husbands, love your wives and do not be bitter toward them. Colossians 3:19, NKJV

In these scriptures, the Word of God instructs men to love their wives. Women are naturally and biologically engineered by God to receive love from their men and to be loved by their men. And so, where a woman is in conflict with what she is wired to receive, then something is wrong and she needs help. In a case where a man is also conflicting with the Word of God on what he has been created to give to the woman, there arises a big problem too. Sometimes, the root cause of these problems can just be as simple as wrong philosophies and ideologies, like I mentioned earlier, coming from wrong association.

Blessed is the man who walks not in the counsel of the ungodly, nor stands in the path of sinners, nor sits in the seat of the scornful; But his delight is in the law of the LORD, and in His law he meditates day and night. He shall be like a tree planted by the rivers of water, that brings forth its fruit in its season, whose leaf also shall not wither; And whatever he does shall prosper. Psalm 1:1-3, NKJV

Dr. Myles Munroe, who has gone home to be with the Lord, once said, that "we are all a product of those who have taught us, both great and small". Exposure to wrong teachings through wrong association can be fatal! I can state categorically from experience that where true love exists, you can never give or receive enough love and affection. Nobody says 'I've had enough' to love. Our Father God never held back His show of love for His Son, Jesus. Every time He saw it necessary, He would announce and brag about His beloved Son in whom He is well pleased. Jesus never fails to show us in scripture as well how much we are loved by the Father, how much we are valued and how much it is the Father's desire to give us everything we ask because of how much He loves us. As a matter of fact, some of the main issues we are faced with in the world right now are as a result of people's inability to connect to the thirst-quenching and eternally refreshing love of God bestowed upon us through His Son Jesus Christ. If only men and women can seek to taste and comprehend the depth of the Father's love for them, showing love and receiving love will come so easy.

Philosophy 3: A little harmless flirting with the opposite sex doesn't hurt, provided you are not sleeping with them.

Contrary to the right philosophy, I once stumbled on a write up on a social media page that stated that research have proven that 'harmless flirting in marriage can increase a man's life span'. That statement is coming from the pits of hell. Contrary to this home-wrecking philosophy, there is no such thing as 'harmless flirting'. The demon of lust that produces adultery at the end of this venture is the one that triggers the 'harmless flirting' from the start, with the intention of seeing to it that it culminates in the very act, giving suggestions like 'there's nothing wrong with it', that 'it's your life, you are only exercising your freedom to think whatever you want to think.'

We actually need to be careful in these times and days we're in, to filter what information we allow into our minds through the windows or gateways of our bodies and be extremely picky on the sources of the counsel we receive. Proverbs 4:23 warns us about keeping our hearts with a lot of diligence to avoid pollution to the serious and important matters of life, such as marriage and relationships. Jesus also clearly stated in Matthew 5:27-28 that a lustful look is as guilty as the act of adultery itself and in Matthew 6:22, He talked about the eye being the lamp of the body and the need to keep it good.

Guard your heart above all else, for it determines the course of your life. Proverbs 4:23, NLT

"You have heard that it was said 'You shall not commit adultery', but I say to you that everyone who (so much as) looks at a woman with lust for her has already committed adultery with her in his heart. Matthew 5:27-28, AMP

The lamp of the body is the eye. If therefore your eye is good, your whole body will be full of light. Matthew 6:22 NKJV

Guys, please be aware that flirting is an outright demonstration of the lustful desire of the flesh which is a sin before God, and most times, people get tempted to cross beyond the border line into the very act of sexual sins of fornication and adultery. The question I usually ask such people who let themselves fall into such acts of sin is, "where do you define the borderline, and how do you prevent yourself from crossing the boundary when the devil steps in, as you have already given him the occasion to do so?"

Let's break it down a little to the point where I was building up to how I met my wife before I digressed. I was talking about understanding or knowing who you are and what your purpose is in life and then the need to connect to your creator who has your manual with Him before you embark on dating and courtship. Dating, by the way, in simplest terms, is a superficial level and an early phase of a relationship that a man and a woman go into to get to understand each other better with the hope of finding out if the relationship has a future. Courtship or courting, however, is a level in the relationship between a man and a woman where they have only one goal in mind: marriage. At this stage, they are convinced, resolved and working toward a future together.

The truth is that we have no power on our own to be righteous, no matter how hard we try. No matter how much we desire to love somebody, we are most likely going to fall short of expectations somewhere. This is the reason why we need the One who created us, Who knows us, Who loved us eternally and sent His only Son to shed His blood as atonement for our sinful and imperfect nature so that through His own perfection and righteousness, we can now receive grace to become righteous, the grace to love deeply through the love of Christ Jesus and the Father. Only the Lord can reveal who you are to you. Only He can help you discover the purpose for which He created you and only in the steadfastness of character and faith that you now have through revelation will you be able to share a discovered purpose with another individual and take custody of her life and future and help her fulfill her own God-given purpose too.

Philosophy 4: There is always an exit door.

'The idea of being locked up in a marriage exists only in your mind. There is always an exit door when you need one.' This is one wrong philosophy you hear about marriage in these contemporary times. I have once had a conversation with a guy who strongly believes that if it's not working, then leave. I can't express my level of disappointment and disgust for such a philosophy and the fact that it came from him, especially considering the level of knowledge of the scripture he displayed when we were talking. I have also met a co-labourer in the vineyard who was very quick to advise couples going through challenges in marriage to get a divorce. Apparently, he had issues with his own marriage and was at the brink of one. Another terrible thing I've seen is spouses who are so quick to offer their spouses the option of leaving at the slightest argument or provocation. To this one I'd say, don't keep using such a deadly weapon of threat to scare your spouse, if you do it long enough, one day whether by accident or as a reason of continuous use, the undesired exit from the marriage will eventually happen. Anything that you don't want to see happen, don't bring it to life with your mouth. Your tongue is that powerful.

Guys and ladies, let me tell you the truth, if you go into marriage with the mindset of an exit door, the devil will present to you a hundred and one reasons why you should use that door and a hundred more other doors that exist that you can open too. Never go into marriage with a mindset of quitting if things don't work out as dreamed or as planned. Sometimes, the game on the field doesn't go as planned on the drawing board, neither does the battle on the field always go as drawn on the board in the battle room. God can still make any marriage work no matter how bad it seems to be going. He can bring out honey from that rock when we walk in obedience to His word. Besides, God hates divorce.

"But I would feed Israel with the finest of the wheat; And with honey from the rock I would satisfy you" Psalm 81:16, AMP

But not one has done so who has a remnant of the Spirit. And what did that one do while seeking a godly offspring? Take heed then to your spirit, and let no one deal treacherously against the wife of your youth. "For I hate divorce," says the Lord, the God of Israel, "and him who covers his garment with wrong and violence," says the Lord of hosts. "Therefore keep watch on your spirit, so that you do not deal treacherously (with your wife)." Malachi 2:15-16, AMP

So, when you make up your mind to step into that life time relationship called marriage, please lock the door behind you and throw the key away in your mind! That should be your mindset. It doesn't remove the fact that there are certain extreme marital cases that result in physical abuse and violence, and wreckless marital unfaithfulness that may give you a reason to look for a hacksaw or buy one to break the lock and exit your way into physical and emotional safety. However, violence and abuse in marriage is a large enough topic that can evolve into a book of its own, so, we hope to throw more light on it in the sequel to this book, titled, "Twelve Years After".

(How To Know It's Him)

CHAPTER 1
Life Before We Met

I was born and raised for the first nine years of my life in a little town called Kaduna in the northern part of Nigeria. These were the days when men were not given to the level of crime and the unthinkable measure of social vices we see today, so children could come out after school to form large play groups and play hopscotch and skip on the streets till sunset. There was only one television station in the eighties in Nigeria and every child knew that 4pm was the time to run inside and catch another episode of *Sesame Street*. Life was peaceful and simple, the environment was refreshingly green with vegetation and the serenity of the town couldn't make you feel more carefree and insouciant. I also grew up in a bi-racial environment with my Nigerian mom and Italian dad where I intermingled with a lot of expatriates who were family friends, however, I realized that the simplicity of life around my place of birth and mingling with my Nigerian friends, cousins and relatives had rubbed off on me in a way that I never looked at myself or the people around me with the eyes of color. I can say that I grew up well socialized and unbiased about people, with a sense of non-attachment to material things that people would naturally gravitate to, maybe to a fault. I remember visiting my

Sri-Lankan friend and spontaneously following her to a birthday party her parents had planned to take her to before I arrived at her house. At the party, there was a conglomeration of almost all the Caucasian and expatriate kids in Kaduna town. I was wearing bathroom slippers, as we refer to flip flops in Nigeria, and a dowdy outfit without a single feeling of awkwardness or inferiority complex. My ability not to care about some of these petty things, as I will call it, has stuck with me ever since and given me the confidence to make friends and build relationships without a single care of the outward material status of a person.

I also remember being very inquisitive about life and asking questions about things that I didn't have to try to understand at my age. I was just curious about anything and everything and I especially could understand people's emotions far beyond what I should have at my age. This continued into my teenage years and made me want to be able to explain why people behaved in certain ways.

At age nine, my family had to move from the simple life and friends that I had grown so fond of. We were relocating to Abuja, the capital city of Nigeria, the center of affluence, governance and beautiful architectural structures in the country. It was going to be a new start for me culturally and environmentally. We moved to the heart of the city, a high-class and ritzy environment where a large number of the high commission buildings were situated. The transition was smooth and easier than I expected, not even with the beauty of the house we lived in that captivated me so much and filled my day with exciting adventures around the premises especially with the new Italian friends I made next door and a Bulgarian neighbor who didn't have children of her own and so, grew very fond of me. A few months down the line, my mom, my cousin who had been living with us from a very young age and I started attending a Pentecostal church that held services at the Hilton Hotel just a walk away from where we lived. I accepted Jesus into my heart there and began my spiritual journey right there at the children's church.

In no time, the hunger to know God grew so strong within me that I began to filter everything I saw or knew through that desire. I wanted to understand this new feeling I was experiencing, of never wanting to leave the church premises after the service was over, I knew being in church brought gaiety and warmth to my heart but I couldn't tell why. I couldn't explain my disinterest in the children's church either. It was so bad that it would make me plot sneaky escapes from there into the adults' church where the preaching was undiluted and designed for mature minds. I was supposed to enjoy listening to Bible stories, singing nursery rhymes and eating as many cupcakes as I wanted but not Elliana, something in me craved deeper knowledge that was reserved for 'grown ups'. Once I had successfully gotten in, I would tuck myself in between the rows on the floor and most times, close to the feet of church members who were like family to me, or next to my cousin who was in the choir. The ushers had gotten used to my constant trespass; they just knew where to find me and it constantly resulted in my ally pleading with them not to throw me out.

Can I stop for a moment to say that we are in a dispensation where knowledge has increased, and that includes spiritual knowledge. It will only be unfair to the total and balanced growth of our Christian children for us to treat their spiritual lives as irrelevant and incapable of expansion. Our children have always had the ability to comprehend spiritual things, we just never thought it possible because we have been trained to view it as too weighty for their young minds. If all the teachers of the law in the temple could be astonished at Jesus' understanding and answers at age twelve, then, I guess we are supposed to learn something from that. The Bible says in Luke 2:40;

And the child grew and became strong in spirit, filled with wisdom; and the grace of God was upon me. Luke 2:40, NKJV

There's no better proof that spiritual growth begins or should begin from our childhood and children have the ability to become spiritually strong and equipped to deal with spiritual issues if taught and trained. So, I'll put it this way; to the cupcakes and dramatized Bible stories, let us add some teachings on praying in tongues, spiritual warfare, intercession, water baptism, Kingdom authority, the spirit realm and angels, discovering their purposes and assignments for God, the end of the age, the second coming of Jesus and other foundational teachings that can help them grow in wisdom. As a Pastor, Sunday school teacher, a parent or a guardian, you can trust the Holy Spirit to help them understand these things as you gradually introduce them to a closer and deeper walk with the Lord.

The Still Small Voice

As a slim, pretty, mixed-race young lady in my teenage years growing up in a part of the city made for the rich, I began to see suggestive displays from both young and older men. There were unanswered questions in my head about the hormonal changes taking place at that time in my body at that time but the most I got when I asked questions was the "birds and the bees" story with an African twist to it. In this case, one was taught that losing their virginity was a big disgrace to the entire family and an unwanted pregnancy would lead to being thrown out of the house or disowned. It may sound silly to expect clarification over this as a child but that's how the mind of young children and teenagers work. It helps when parents learn to break such topics down in a calm and loving discussion than to dish out bullet points of strict rules and the consequences of breaking them. In my case, I didn't have a problem abiding by the rules; my love for God and the teachings in church produced the boundary lines, not the stern one to two sentence discussions over the subject. I was just the type of child that also wanted to understand things in detail with an explanation to go with it, sadly, nobody had the time to teach one how to deal with youthful exuberance, teenage peer pressure and even meeting material wants. Like I said, two factors came to my rescue on this; the teenage church where the youth ministers did the best they could to keep us in the straight and narrow and my undying love for the things of God. The indwelling of the Holy Spirit from a very young age was my saving grace. I had a very special way of being led by Him. The still small voice of Wisdom in my heart would not only tell me what to do or not to do but would break down the consequences to me ten steps ahead progressively. He also taught me ethics and manners even before learning it from anyone. Wonderful counselor!

Incidentally, even as adults, we can identify that spontaneous small voice or knowing, as some refer to it, in our hearts saying something like "this guy is only after sex, don't take him seriously" or "he's lying". Sometimes it's as if an alarm of restlessness goes off in our heads warning us of danger ahead even without any visible sign of it. That is the Holy Spirit trying to save you from a lot of trouble. Unfortunately, people let such things slide and treat it as mere thoughts or imaginations only to remember afterwards that they sensed it or saw it coming, for some, they realize it after they have fallen victim of the enemy's trap.

Lies versus Truth

You are a product of the people who have taught you in life, either great or small, according to Dr. Myles Munroe. The people you listen to can make or mar you. It is important to listen to or get counsel from people who have succeeded or are succeeding in the area you wish to succeed in. Where courtship and marriage is concerned, please do not listen to everybody. A lot of people desire to help and feel they can proffer solutions because of their age or status, however, interestingly, the best way to know if someone is worth listening to is if the person's home and marriage is exemplary and worth emulating. To follow a mentor on social media, you have to also be careful to tell that their lifestyle behind the scene, without the cameras, the spotlights and the stage is worthy of emulation and is a true reflection of the type of person you want to become or the home you want to have.

In retrospect, I was my own guide to life and decoding of complex matters along the way. Yes, there were uncountable moments of sitting together with my mom and her relations, having loud conversations in Igbo, my mother's native tongue, about indigenous tales, myths and real-life stories. A lot of times, the real-life stories were centered around or would build up to relationship matters and everyone who was older would give their various opinions on what dating and marriage should be. Interestingly, I observed that they all shared something in common, their philosophies about marriage was the same. It could only indicate one thing; that they had all been feeding from the same bowl. My cousin who would counsel me every now and then was also feeding from this bowl so her mindset was already being formed based on what she was constantly hearing. They would discuss their past relationships, those of friends and how they were dealing with the current ones. My mom would throw in a final thought on these matters and would seize the opportunity to advise everyone on the right thing to do. Their concept of love and dealing with relationships made me see dating, courtship and marriage as something for the tough, the dogged and shrewd. I saw marriage particularly from the light of a venture with an end result that can never be predetermined from the beginning. It was made to look like a battle that you needed to dress up in armour for, part of your ammunition and artillery would be a pair of binoculars and a secret observatory where you could monitor your partner from, in case he goes rogue all of a sudden then you would have to launch an offensive with the rest of your ammunition. Chances were that the battle would result in a pyrrhic victory anyway, leaving you worse than when you began. I was further thrown into confusion, I knew the type of marriage I had envisioned from a very young age but all of a sudden, it felt as if I was living in a world of fairy tales, as if I was joking or lying to myself to think that some happily-ever-after existed. Their stories were so disturbing that I wondered what good was in this thing called marriage besides childbearing. I wasn't sure if I had what it took to handle marriage as they described it. After such hyped exchanges had taken place, all I could take back to my room were examples of very unstable love stories and clever nailing-the-culprit approaches to running a home that I couldn't wrap my mind around. There was no room for a single heart to heart talk with mom, one was expected to count themselves privileged to partake in these group chats, they felt they were passing down age old wisdom and expected it to be enough to guide anybody. Something in me rioted with all that information but I didn't have any other to compare it to. Here are some lessons they taught that I'll list out as lies about marriage.

LIE #1: ALL MEN CHEAT

One mindset they all had painted so clearly the fact every man was made to look like it was impossible for him not to cheat on his spouse. Men were made to look like cheating ran through their veins and only an 'iron lady' could tame a man or could have the strength to tail him and give him a hard time doing it. I was given the impression that every woman would just have to live with the fact that it would happen sooner or later. In other words, trust could never be found in any relationship. That was their belief, in a nutshell. That belief, we all know, is a disaster waiting to happen because there's no friendship, relationship or marriage that can make it beyond the starting point without trust. Even if it looks like all is well, in a short while, the true and sickly state of that relationship or marriage will reveal itself.

LIE #2: FINANCIAL SECURITY IS GREATER THAN LOVE

I was also given an impression that financial security was supposed to be number one on the list of what to look out for in a guy. The lesson of 'no money, no love' was taught with countless stories of how a woman would have two suitors, one wealthy and the other poor. She would eventually choose and marry the poor guy because she was in love and years later, she would find herself in a mess, wallowing in poverty and regretting her decision. The lesson was that financial security was greater than love. In the financial security lesson, their concept was that the man was supposed to be able to shoulder the needs of the woman's extended family members. This point makes me laugh every time I think back on when I was in the university and one of my spiritual fathers, Apostle Yemi Adefarasin, asked me what qualities I was looking for in a potential husband. The question was impromptu, just a few minutes after I stepped into his office. I scanned my head for an answer and I didn't know when I blurted out

"I need a man who can take care of me...", he stared at me intently as I continued "...and my entire family". I watched his expression change suddenly as he vigorously shook his head in outright disapproval. He seemed thrown aback by my archaic mindset and couldn't even speak for a few seconds after my statement. I was completely embarrassed, I knew this theory was coming from what I had been fed over the years by those long hours of fruitless group discussion and old wives' tale and I also knew that I never accepted this theory but where did it pop out from? I never knew that the seed of that counsel was in there until I said what I said, that was a lesson for me on the power of upbringing and consistent influence. Garbage in, garbage out, they say. Eventually, he recommended a book to me and that was all the relationship counseling for that day. He probably felt that I was lost where priorities were concerned and didn't know where to start the reorientation from. My mind needed renewal with new knowledge before he could even start any counseling.

So, the lesson I was always learning from these stories was that a woman needs to find a man with a fat bank account if she wants to be happy. Secondly, trust is never guaranteed, so, one was to expect a spouse to cheat at some point and thirdly, don't forget that a man is meant to be able to carry the entire extended family members' needs on his shoulders. This could not be any farther away from the truth.

I know you might be asking; so is it a bad thing to find a guy with a good job or enough money to care for me? Absolutely not! My question to you in response to this would be "What if you found every good quality a good husband should possess in a life partner and all that was left was the money part, what would you do?" I guess I should also be asking "Do you know what to look for that can ensure that you have met the right person and do you know the order of priority it should be arranged in?"

It is the idea of making financial security the first thing on your list of priorities that is faulty. No man wants to be the family cash cow or cash dispensing machine. Nothing makes a guy more disinterested in a relationship or frustrated in a marriage than discovering that he is only a means to an end. It is a relationship nightmare for a man or woman to be in a relationship knowing that their spouse's family will continue to choke them for the rest of their lives. Be rest assured that a man or woman genuinely in love with you will naturally want to make you happy, so let's say that in marriage, a need arises to help someone in your extended family, if he or she can at that moment, they will, because of you and because they know that it will make you happy. But, it shouldn't be used to overburden them neither should it be a requirement for them to be able to win your hand in marriage. If he or she decides to marry you despite their knowledge of your attachment to your family members and your desire to make them part and parcel of your home, thereby overwhelming your spouse with extended family needs and presence, based on my experience with a number of people I have had the privilege of counseling on this same topic, I can assure you that it's only a matter of time before you will have to choose between them and your family. You would have also succeeded in helping him or her develop an escape plan or route ahead of the marriage. An example of how it affects men would be; staying away from the house as much as possible, not necessarily because of the wife, even though some of that frustration may get transferred to her, but just to avoid conflicts and the irritation that wells up within from having too many hangers on in his home. This is an area where a lot of African women need to be corrected and further enlightened. It is a dreaded situation for men and this can singlehandedly create disappointments or what I'll like to call a near-success-syndrome in dating relationships. There's no doubt that there are spiritual reasons why people find it hard to get married or sustain a lasting relationship, which require strategic prayers to break the hold of the enemy, however, most of the time, the prominent reasons for disappointment in relationships revolve around character flaws, exaggerated demands and requirements expected of a husband-to-be (of course it could be vice versa), misplacement of priorities and influence from cultural orientation. In some cases, character issues like anger, lack of trust or self-control will also require prayers, in addition to renewing the mind through the Word of God. I can assure you that by the time you are done reading this book, you will be equipped to make a well informed decision about a life partner, whatever the given circumstance around your situation.

When I look back, I remember that the few times I attempted striking up a conversation with my mom about dating, she would tell me that she'd rather not know. It gave her more peace of mind to assume I wasn't dating or thinking in that direction. Who, then, was going to answer my questions about life, love, men, marriage and sex? This can be a very dangerous position for a young person to be in because the devil always takes advantage of such situations to mislead that person into the hands of a wrong counselor and other opportunists. My mom certainly did not have the best approach to the subject of relationship and guiding a teenager but I can't blame her because she didn't know any better and like a lot of parents in that generation who are a product of a harsh upbringing and the tough unloving parental relationship they grew up to accept as normal, she did what she felt was right in her eyes.

A Vision of a Perfect Match

As I grew older, ready to get into the university, I knew that there was something faulty about the picture of not being able to find complete happiness in marriage. I knew there was something discouraging, unappealing and creepy about thinking that I could end up with a man that might change, all of a sudden, and reveal that he was pretending all along, and the thought of either being hooked for life or going through the trauma of having to run for dear life was frightening. The stories scared me to my bones. I shivered deep within thinking that I could become a victim of such a gloomy future.

I knew in my heart that I wanted a certain type of marriage and home that I had imagined, dreamed about and nurtured in my heart. All my quiet observations of those around me made me picture the way I was going to love my husband and the way I wanted him to love me, the way I wanted to relate with my children, give them all my time and attention and be there for them. I visualized my husband doing the same. I knew I wanted to meet someone that would love me beyond measure, someone that would love me a hundred and fifty percent; because I knew that I was going to love him with reckless abandon. I wanted someone I would be so in love and compatible with that we both would be able to tell what we were thinking without saying it, that we would love each other so much we would want to shout it out from the mountain tops. I wanted someone who would be so perfectly matched with me that even his weaknesses would further make me know that he's designed and crafted for me and vice versa. I desired to be with someone I could let down my guards around a hundred percent and be free with, who would also feel the same way, someone I could do the craziest things with, laugh hysterically with and live without a care in the world around, someone who would become my best friend, a confidant, someone that if I were to be stuck in a room with forever, I wouldn't miss any other thing. I began to ask myself if it were possible to meet the man that I could consider God's perfect will, the man that I could boldly say was my soul mate, my other half. I longed for it and I ended up after several conflicting thoughts, based on all the clashing ideologies I had in my head, choosing to believe that I could find the ONE.

Every young lady has, at some moment in time, imagined and desired a man that will love her unreservedly. This is because it is possible. If this desire was not possible or let me put it this way, if it weren't possible for a man to love a woman totally and genuinely, the scripture would not require and demand that a man loves his wife, sacrificially, just as Christ loved the church (Ephesians 5:25). And according to Psalm 37:4, God gives us the desires of our heart, because we are made in His image and the fullness of life we are supposed to experience through His Spirit is what triggers a hunger for such a beautiful, almost fairy-tale like love life because everything, including your life partner, that God gives is good and perfect and adds no sorrow – and it's for everyone. Over time, I had heard the love stories of a few people I hold in high esteem and I was able to draw my conclusion that true love was not only desirable but that it exists and is achievable. There are people that have experienced it and are currently experiencing heaven on earth in their marriages. Are they any more special than others or just lucky as some people would say? No, not at all. It was a result of applying the right principles in the process of decision making and properly arranging their values in the right order. Most of all, I know that it has always been God's plan for us from the beginning, He made it clear to us when He made a perfect match for Adam;

"At last!" the man exclaimed "This one is bone from my bone, and flesh from my flesh! She will be called 'woman', because she was taken from 'man' Genesis 2:23 NLT

The result one gets in different spheres of life is largely determined by what one values or prioritizes. When you focus on something, the other things around become defocused, therefore, it is very important that you are conscious of what you focus on or think matters most to you in the man you want to marry because it will become the first thing you observe whenever you meet someone new.

(How To Know It's Her)

CHAPTER 2
The Quest for Purpose

In 1996, while I was serving in National Youth Service Corps, a compulsory one year community service done in Nigeria after graduation from the University or any tertiary institution of learning, I gave my life to Christ and this happened through a family friend. That singular encounter redefined the next phase of my life's journey. At this point, my quest for love and the search for my utopia took a totally different turn as a regenerated man. I totally forgot everything about dating and relationship in my first few years as a Kingdom citizen, as all I lived for was my new found love in Jesus Christ and desire to please and know Him more. Consequently, most of the teachings of the branch of The Redeemed Christian Church of God where I was fellowshipping further helped in rearranging and reshaping a lot of my philosophies and concepts of life, love, dating and marriage through the Word of God, especially as I began to find serving in the house of the Lord exciting through participation in youth programs, camps and conferences. That was when I realized that the first place to start loving from is the agape love of Christ; the unconditional love God has for mankind and man's willful expression of such love back to God and people. First, you just have to come to terms with loving everybody around you without any hidden motive or selfish intention. This is what I call freeing your mind toward everyone around you and just loving them the way they are.

Let me put it clearer His way. Before I knew the Lord Jesus, I loved a lady with the intension of wanting to date and marry her, with the intention of making her fit into my utopia. But, when I encountered Jesus and my mind started getting renewed by the Word of God, I realized that I don't even have to want to date a lady before I love her with the love of Christ. I just love her because she is first of all my sister and then my friend. This could only be made possible for me because my mind was being renewed through the transformation of the Word of God.

And do not be conformed to this world, but be transformed by the renewing of your mind, that you may prove what is that good and acceptable and perfect will of God. Romans 12:2, NKJV

It is important before you start dating or going into a relationship that you reinvent yourself through the Word of God. In addition, for intending young Christians who want to embark on the journey of seeking their life partners, it will be important to choose a life partner from the household of God; somebody you are sure is from the household of God. Based on the book of Romans 12, the truth is stated clearly that the philosophy of the world system is totally and completely different from that of the Kingdom of our Lord. I will be shedding more light on this in subsequent chapters. In Genesis 24, Abraham made his servant to swear to him that he was going to get his son Isaac a wife from amongst his family rather than allow his son marry from amongst the Canaanites. In God's Kingdom, ruled over by our Lord and Saviour Jesus Christ, we are all members of one big family regardless of race, tribe or nation. The Blood of our Lord and

Saviour Jesus Christ run through all of us and since the Old Testament Bible is a shadow and a type of the new, Abraham's standard of getting a spouse for his son is the same that should be used as Christians in God's household today. That means, find a wife from within the Kingdom family.

Back to my track again. So, I immersed myself in the house of God (church). I loved going to church so much that when service was over, my friends and I, better still, my brothers in the Lord in the youth department and I, would stay behind to pack up chairs and clean up the church. We would then sit back and enjoy the residue of God's presence during the service. It would have to get to evening hours before we would return to our respective homes. At this point, I had my true identity in Christ but my purpose was still kind of unsure. I was in the security department and, at the same time, the prayer department. I never liked missing out on evangelism, so they co-opted me into the evangelism department too. I was hand picked by my pastor to join in the church planting exercise called 'go-a-fishing', a program organized by The Redeemed Christian Church of God where new church branches are created. I was part of church building projects time and time again; I'm talking of practically joining the manual labor work of the building project. Guys and ladies, one of the best things you can do in your Kingdom journey especially as an unmarried or single person is to find yourself useful in service in the house of the Lord. There is so much it does in the life of a believer spiritually and physically that time and space will not permit me to exhaust in this book. However, I will briefly enumerate some or a few of the things you stand to benefit through service in the house of God. As a matter of fact, one of the tips I will give my Kingdom committed and purpose driven and searching readers, who are passionate about locating their clones is this; using the Old

Testament's shadow and type as a template here, the 'Holy Place' can be likened to the workers unit. That is, those who have decided to take it a step further from just being nominal or lukewarm Christians, to becoming workers in the Lord's vineyard; employees of Jesus.

Working in the Lord's vineyard is a conscious, reasonable and voluntary service that not only elevates you above the other believers physically but it places you on a higher pedestal spiritually in your relationship with God. It gives you the privilege of becoming a co-laborer with the Lord Jesus in His vineyard.

For we are God's fellow workers; you are God's field, you are God's building. 1 Corinthians 3:9, NKJV

So, imagine where the Old Testament tabernacle is used to describe the church. If nominal believers are in the outer court, then the workers and ministers will be in the Holy place while the priests will be in the Holy of Holies. This means, all things being equal, the character and personality of a worker should reflect more of Jesus than those in the outer court; those who are just nominal Christians, though there are always exceptions due to several variable factors. But, the Holy place will be a better place to search for any serious minded purpose driven Christian or Kingdom citizen. Being of service to the house of the Lord exposes you to and brings you into a closer contact relationship with the priests. And the oil of the priest or high priest who goes into the Holy of Holies will certainly rub off on you. Moses' oil of leadership rubbed off on Joshua. Elijah's oil rubbed off on Elisha. I am not surprised that I am running my own ministry today as an independent minister. I was in the place of service as a worker in the Redeemed Church branch called 'Strong Tower Sanctuary' Lagos, Nigeria. When I was selected amongst a few to go and officiate at the first *Holy Ghost Festival* which later became *Holy Ghost Congress*, and on getting there, I was selected to join the General Overseer's elite VIP Protection Unit. This brought me in close working contact with Pastor E.A Adeboye of The Redeemed Christian Church of God for close to six years. I remember how, after most Holy Ghost Congresses, when he was done with his prayer and counseling sessions, he would always bless and pray for us before retiring back to his house. How could I forget the several "God bless you" he pronounced on me every time I was privileged to be the one to get his car door for him as he stepped out for ministration, or the close body protection we gave him to avoid the crowd pressing in on him when he tried to make his way in and out of the different places he went to minister. It was a great privilege and opportunity to work so closely with such an anointed servant of God.

Perhaps I should give you more practical stories why it is good to work in the Lord's vineyard. I had the privilege of once having to drive the wife of one of the highly anointed men of God in the same Redeemed Christian Church of God by name J.T Kalejaiye back to her parish after she had finished with her ministration in our branch of the church. When we got to her destination, just before she alighted from the car, she asked me if I was married and I told her that I wasn't. She took out a few minutes of her time and rained down some quality and powerful prayers on me where marriage was concerned. She particularly prayed that I marry the right woman. Why am I not surprised that a few years down the line, I got married to the best woman in the world and that would not have happened or been facilitated by the men of God I made contact with if I was not in my place of service in God's house. I didn't and couldn't doubt it then that it was God's visitation for me on that day because I was actually in the middle of a thorough search for a woman to marry at that period when I encountered Pastor Kalejaiye's wife. Another priceless encounter I had was with her husband, Pastor J.T Kalejaiye himself when he came to minister at our branch church and I got the door for him as a worker in the protocol department. As he walked through the door, he paused and looked at me and began to shower some heavy prophetic blessings on me that I will not tell you in detail, hehehe... my point is, it is good to serve in the Lord's vineyard. A lot of times even our deliverances come from the place of service to the Lord in His house.

Service helps you discover your purpose. A lot of times, from the very beginning of our relationship and walk with God, which starts with receiving the Lord Jesus as one's personal Lord and savior, or as growing Christians, we really don't know what we are called to do in life or what our purpose and assignments are. In fact, a lot of people at this point lack vision. But as we engage ourselves by working for God in His vineyard, our purpose starts getting clearer especially when we have a servant of God close by who is always ready to help with directions. In 1Samuel 3:1-18, the Bible recorded Samuel's position as the altar boy under the priesthood of Eli and despite the Lord's displeased disposition toward Eli, where his sons' misbehavior in ill-treating the holy things of God was concerned, it still had to take God using Eli's experience to teach the boy Samuel how to hear God, which was the first step he needed to take, to step into his ministry calling. I was just everywhere and all over the church with lots of energetic excitement. I wanted to learn everything I could grasp from every department. The only department I didn't step into was the choir and that was simply because I felt I didn't have a strong singing voice and I thought a person of my tall stature would look out of place there. Interestingly, in all these, little did I know that on the smaller scale, God wanted me to step into the media industry and on the bigger picture, there was a pastoral calling upon my life.

It was in the course of my exploration, with a lot of joy and excitement, of all I could do in the Lord's house that, one day, a brother approached me with a very wonderful proposal of us setting up a drama department in our local assembly. And wow!! Was I blown away! It was one of the most joyful moments of my early Christian walk, and to think it was one of God's humorous ways of setting me up along the path of my life's purpose and destiny. It was a golden opportunity that was going to unlock a lot of my gifts and build my life's experiences till date; It was a door that took me on a journey where I saw the good, the bad, the ugly and the beautiful side of life. If it were possible to re-live life on earth after this one, I'd still walk through it again; a door that produced the woman of my dreams.

I was all grown up, a graduate with a bachelor's degree from the University of Ilorin, Nigeria and I had just completed my National Youth Service. I went visiting home just that period. I was sitting in the living room one evening with my parents and siblings and we were all watching a Nigerian movie together popularly referred to as 'home video' back in Nigeria. Suddenly, like a flash of a flood light bursting into thick darkness, I caught a vision of exactly what I wanted to do with my life. I told my dad I wanted to go into the television media. With a serious stern look on his face, he turned sharply and asked "to do what?" I replied that I wanted to pursue a career in television and film production and of course, become a movie star. To my utmost surprise and with a calm and relaxed voice, he seemed to recline into a more comfortable position in his chair and answered "okay, if that's what you want". I was actually surprised because this was totally unlike my father who gave me a tough time when he made all attempts to dissuade me from joining the army some years before then. His dream was for me to work in the banking industry, after he realized early enough, while I was in high school, that I wasn't cut out for sciences, meaning that I was never going to become an engineer like him. That was the next best thing for him. Over the years, I realised that I had always had a strong sense of creativity and vivid imaginations. As a child growing up, my mother was apt as a lecturer in educational technology and curriculum studies to notice this and she further helped to reinforce it by buying me lots of book, several Marvel and D.C comics, Asterix and Obelix, Tin-Tin. Later on as I grew up into a teenager, I would save my allowances to buy myself more comics and novels. I read James Hardley Chase, Sydney Sheldon, John Grisham, Stephen Kings and a whole lot. I lived in a world of comics and books; it helped provide an escape route for me into my own world, away from the tense ambience around me that was mostly jump started by my dad. I'm bringing up my interests from childhood to you because I want you to look back and see yours as indicators too. They very well can serve as a guide to what you have been called to do.

And so, as a graduate of sociology, I could think of no better place to have a career than where I could express my own world, my own stories and my bottled up ever flowing tap of imaginations; the audio-visual film and television industry was the perfect place for this. My only dilemma was when and where to start from, and the church provided me an answer by giving me a platform through the drama department. For me it was an answered prayer and a dream come true. And the beauty of this was that I never had the faintest clue that my wife, somewhere in the nearest future, even before we met, was also going to be media inclined and become a TV host, at some point, of a musical segment of Christian Broadcasting Network, One Cubed.

I have always counseled guys around me and one thing I never fail to mention to them is that there are two major factors that determine a man's success in life beyond all other secondary factors such as hard work, planning, commitment, focus and so on, and these two factors are; marrying the right woman and making sure that where you work is your place of purpose and vision. It could be a career or a business, not necessarily a ministerial calling. When you are working the wrong job, no matter how much you earn, you can never find fulfillment, but, if your dream or vision becomes your job and becomes what you do, no matter how little you earn, it will only be a matter of time before the satisfaction and happiness that comes from doing what you love push you into the big 'bucks', your desired level of wealth. In the same manner, if you marry the wrong woman who is not God's perfect will for you, you might just have gotten yourself a lot of work to do before you can enter the train of life's success.

Let me share a revelation with you guys that might shock you a little which I'm going to still talk on in one of the subsequent chapters. **God has your clone out there in a feminine body. Please do all you can to look for her. Marry your clone!** One of the ways to know your clone is when a woman you intend to court and marry is passionate about your vision, regardless of whether she is into the same field or not. People are different and so are our senses of taste and choice. Do you know that if your lady does not as much as like what you do for a living, no matter how holy she is, there is a high chance that you are about to build on a faulty foundation. I love the way the New Living Translation of the Bible puts Amos 3:3, it says:

Can two people walk together without agreeing on the direction? Amos 3:3, NLT

At the time I made a decision to tow the path of film making in Nigeria, the entertainment industry was still struggling to find its feet for two reasons. One, because it was still a new terrain of unnavigated waters where there was very little corporate or government involvement and support. Producers independently sourced their funds to make films and the chain reaction was that actors were paid peanuts, and thus, were living a broke life, except for a few who had alternative sources of income or were from rich parental backgrounds. Secondly, film and video piracy was a gregarious monster on top of the food chain preying on producers' and film makers' sweat. And so, it was considered a very broke industry with no clear cut future, even before it took off.

Now imagine the guts a young lady will need to pitch her tent and destiny in the hands of a man with a vision on this path; it would be like dating a man planning to set up a coffee shop in the middle of a desert. Better still, it will take your own clone to believe in such a crazy dream to travel that path with you.

My first journey to finding a date in the church at this point ended up in a painful disappointment. We were both in the ushering department and then we became close friends. I had shown my intentions to date her and she displayed a measure of interest only to discover later that she was also seeing another brother at the same time who happened to be the head of the same ushering unit I was in. And guess what, she lied a lot. She seemed more interested in the other guy because he had a job that gave her a sense of security. Well, we parted ways and the guy never ended up marrying her anyway because she was running after the superficial. Guys please don't get into a relationship with a lady that is more interested in your status or financial security rather than your true personality. I know this sounds like something we all know but as familiar as it sounds, I still see many young men falling into this same today.

There was this case of a brother who was working in an oil firm and had a very attractive pay package. He dated a lady and got married almost immediately. Then, unfortunately, the unthinkable happened. He lost his job because the company downsized two days after his wedding. In less than two weeks from that time, his wife left him. This is why I emphasized earlier; marry your clone, just the way a man's shadow is stuck to him, a man's clone, in the person of his wife, is part and parcel of him.

At this point, I would like to correct a misconception. From my experience in the Kingdom, I have come to discover that we expect perfection from everybody else but ourselves. When it comes to dating and relationships, some part of our mind casts blames of imperfection so easily, making it look as though the other party should have known better or been a better Christian. Have you ever heard statements such as 'I thought that sister was a Christian, how could she condescend so low' or 'she has a serious temper issue and yet she's a worker in the church, didn't the pastor notice that in her?' How about; 'she is such a materialistic and worldly sister'. There is no perfect man or woman in the church. We are all 'work in progress'. One of my fathers in faith once described the church as a laundry where dirty clothing are being made clean through a process of the washing by the Word. And, unlike the case of a regular laundry, this washing is not achieved in a day in the church. Yes, no doubt about it, we are the righteousness of God through Christ according to the book of Corinthians but our minds and flesh still need to be worked on by the Spirit of God through our regenerated spirit.

"But of Him you are in Christ Jesus, who became for us wisdom from God – and righteousness and sanctification and redemption." 1 Corinthians 1:30, NKJV

I am making this clearer because sometimes as guys in the Kingdom, we have a notion that any sister in the church is good to go. Yes, a genuinely born again sister in the church is good marriage material, but maybe not for you. Brothers can still get a broken heart, even in the church! If this does happen, it is not a reason to quit searching in the church and go to 'Egypt' to look for a bride. Egypt here represents the world, the world system, the secular environment and the non-Christian community. This still brings me back to the need to 'search for your clone'. The Bible says that

He who finds a wife finds a good thing, and obtains favor from the LORD. Proverbs 18:22, NKJV

Finding starts with searching. There is a finding to be done, so, get ready to work the process both physically and spiritually, which brings me to another point that I would like to emphasize on here; **you must know what you are looking for**.

You must have a mental picture of the type of woman you want to spend the rest of your life with; her physical, spiritual and emotional qualities. Marriage is more carnal than it is spiritual. So, as much as you would want to focus on a woman's inner beauty, which we Christians like to make a cliché out of, the physical beauty according to your taste and preference is also very important. As a matter of fact, men are usually more visually inclined and the physical appearance of a woman usually makes the first striking impression. So, please guys, let's not hide under the cloak of religion and miss our the right person. I have a friend who got married to a woman who was in no way appealing to him sensually but because he felt God strictly told him to marry her. Now, we have to be very careful with how we interpret hearing God when it comes to the issue of making a choice in marriage. One thing that I know for sure is that God knows you well and loves you so much that He will always give you the best. In other words, He will not impose on you someone you will not be attracted to physically. A few years down the line, the woman left the marriage on the grounds that he was always giving his attention to church activities and the ministry. According to what she told him, she felt excluded from his major interests. Oh, did I forget to mention that he is a pastor. Obviously, he was hiding under the cloak of ministry to stay away from home, because he wasn't physically attracted to her. Marriage has a lot to do with the carnal part of man, always remember that.

After my first attempt at dating in the Kingdom went sour, I decided to give myself some time to stay off dating, which is a very important relationship rule. The no-relationship time gap, geared towards evaluating your values and visions, what you really seek in a woman and in a marriage, and reengineering yourself to be who God has called you to be, in the place of prayer and study of the Word, has so many innumerable benefits. Interestingly, even after this time gap given to work on myself, I still encountered a number of failed relationships before I finally met my wife. Now, the fact that I had more failed relationships did not mean that the time gap was in any way wasted, neither did it mean that I had not developed myself. It just had to do with the fact that searching is a process and a failed relationship does not spell the end of the road; you just have to continue searching carefully and prayerfully. If we were meant to meet our clone at the flick of a switch, the Bible wouldn't require us to *find* a wife as previously quoted in Proverbs.

I am going to briefly use some of these failed dating attempts to teach you guys how to prayerfully identify someone else's clone and quickly move on without wasting too much of your life's most valuable gift and resource, which is Time. In addition, I will guide you on how to let go easily and not force the relationship to the altar and end up ruining your life. In my season of searching, I met a variety of sisters that taught me very valuable life lessons. My various attempts to kick off a serious relationship with each of them failed, but my encounter with them helped me recognize that each of them represented a certain category of women. I will also use this opportunity at each point to highlight my own mistakes and lack of sensitivity to the Holy Spirit. Permit me to label these wonderful sisters according to what they represented.

The 'Be my option 'B' Sister: I kicked off friendship with this particular lady who was a chorister in my church and a medical student. Everything about our friendship seemed perfect. Her body language and the buildup of communication between us gave me good hope of a relationship that was going to work out into dating, courtship and perhaps marriage. I would travel kilometers within Lagos State in Nigeria just to get her groceries or gifts and spend time with her. I was enjoying the friendship building up gradually between us that I didn't feel a sense of urgency to formally make my intensions known, intentions of wanting to date her. She had drawn really close to me, she acted very fond of me that I felt we had something going already, even without officially asking her out, until one of my evening visits to her room at the University of Lagos Teaching Hospital where I got my bubble busted. I met a guy with her, whom she introduced to me as her boyfriend and a fellow medical student. I felt so hard hit that I didn't know if I was to cry or just walk out. I eventually walked out quietly anyway.

The following week, even after all that happened earlier, I made another trip to see her and to make my intensions officially and verbally open to her. She told me how much she liked me but that she was already in a relationship with the other guy. She expressed her desire for us to continue our relationship as best of friends! In my heart I was like 'No, She didn't just say that to me!' I mean, she just broke my heart after leading me on and what baffled me the most was how much we had become intimate as friends that one would assume we were already dating, not knowing she had somebody on campus all along. Did she not know I had intensions to date her, with all the visits, gifts and body language? Well when I asked, she told me she did but that the other guy was already in the picture.

Guys, my advice, don't push such relationships any further or waste your time still hoping she will change her mind – because I did try to continue due to the emotional attachment I had developed over time with her and it only further led to a more painful heart break when one day I walked into her room and met her in a very compromising position with the guy. Do not compromise or settle for the option 'B' position no matter how much you have invested emotionally, physically or materially. Learn to let go and move on. If she is your clone, you will be the only option for her.

Now my mistake; I did not at any point in time ask her if she had somebody she was dating or in a relationship with. I didn't also bother to let her know verbally what I felt towards her and what my intensions were. I just assumed that the coast was clear based on her body language and entire emotional disposition.

The Soul-tied Sister: I met this lady at one of our church members' birthday party. We got together and actually started dating especially when I realized she was from another branch of the same church where I worshipped. She was also a university roommate and friend to the celebrant's daughter who happened to be a very prominent and outstanding Christian family in the church. It all looked so perfect in the beginning until I realized how strongly attached she was to her past relationship. Then, I noticed something shocking, which she admitted to, that wasn't looking good at all about the whole thing. She had sexual attachment to the guy which, today as a pastor, I refer to as 'sexual soul tie'. She did confess to me later that she didn't want the guy as much as he didn't want her anymore, but, she couldn't stay away from the sexual bond to him.

Guys, this is why the Bible is strictly against premarital sex. It can lead to a serious soul tie that may prove difficult to break out from except by God's mercies and I recommend to anyone reading this book and going through a similar problem to seek deliverance through a deliverance ministry immediately. What you are going through is called an unhealthy evil soul tie. There will be a few prayer points addressing evil soul ties at the end of this book that can also be used to break the enemy's hold over your life. There is more to sex than unwanted pregnancies and contraction of sexually transmitted diseases. I am working on a book coming out soon that will unravel the mystery of soul ties and give deep insight on premarital and extra-marital sex.

A soul tie situation is a very delicate and serious matter to deal with. It requires a spiritual and psychological approach by experienced ministers and therapists. If you are not sure you have a leading from God that you have found your clone, my advice is to get her help as much as you can and move on because forcing your way through such relationships into marriage may lead to a greater hurt or turn out catastrophic.

My mistake; I passed my perception of her through the filter of the people around her as my motivating factor to commence a dating relationship with her rather than seeking God's face to know if I should commence the relationship. Remember I mentioned that she was a friend to a fellow church member and she belonged to a sister branch of my church. That wasn't enough to make her the right person. Secondly, I didn't give myself enough time to get to know her well as a friend first before asking her out on a date. To be honest, my decision to date her was completely ruled by the flesh. There was never a time I remembered praying to God or bringing the Holy Spirit into it till I got hurt and broke out.

The Mother-Controlled Sister: There is nothing wrong when mothers get involved in helping to guide their children in the right direction when it comes to dating and relationships. But, when the mother now wants to make sure her daughter or son goes with her choice, then there is a need for him or her to draw the line. In this lady's case, the dating couldn't take off because as much as she would have wanted to, her mother was not in approval. This lady and I were in the same church. She is from a tribe in Nigeria where names of affluent families matter to them where marriage is concerned, and incidentally, I was the son of a 'nobody' as far as my surname was concerned, how much more not being of the same tribe.

You can only push, as a guy in this kind of situation, to the extent to which the lady is ready to push with her parents and stand her ground. If she truly loves you enough and she truly sees you as her clone, there's nobody in the world that will be strong enough to stop her, not even her parents. This same situation almost played itself out when I later met my clone and we started dating but because she knew what she wanted, she told her parents that it was either me or no one else. She stood her ground in an undaunted manner that I will be highlighting in one of the subsequent chapters.

The Rebound Lady: I met this lady who came for a youth love feast fellowship we had in my church. She was a very committed member of a sister branch of the church I attended then. I got introduced to her through a well-respected friend in Christ. We got close under a short period of time and before long, started dating. I was very fervent in my faith and was very cautious of any action like sexual intimacy that could jeopardize my faith and walk with the Lord. When I started dating this sister, I became a little restless when she was always trying to get all touchy and physical. I felt we shared the same spiritual values but I guess I was wrong. I also remember she was always reminiscing about her past relationship like someone who had not gotten over it. I mean she sounded like a broken record with her constant sessions of 'he did this' or 'he said that' and she obviously liked how physically intimate she had gotten with him and desperately desired that I continued from where he stopped. Well, I wasn't ready to do that and I knew she was disappointed. One fateful day, I went to visit her early in the morning and met her absence. Her neighbor who seemed excited at a golden opportunity to expose her told me she went to her ex-boyfriend's for the night. Her neighbor said to me that if I was in doubt, I could wait a little longer for her to return and ask her myself. A few minutes from then, she strutted back and met me where I stood talking with her neighbor, and so, I had no other choice but to confront her about it. Apparently she informed them herself that she was going to his place so she couldn't deny the allegations.

My mistake: I also jumped into that relationship almost immediately after my last attempt to date didn't work; and that means that I was also on a rebound. It is totally unadvisable and risky to jump into a relationship out of hurt from the previous one without allowing yourself to heal first. It is equivalent to going on a blind date. Now imagine what a disaster we were in for when the two of us were in the same wounded emotional state. I will always advise that you space out your relationships; the hurt experienced in the previous one could lead you to making grave mistakes you ordinarily wouldn't have made. There's nothing greater than getting into a relationship emotionally whole and complete, not needing anything, but rather having so much love to share.

The Jezebel: This lady was the straw that broke the camel's back. She is one lady that I had to testify and I keep testifying now of how grateful I am to God that I never married her neither did I fall for all her seductive attempts to get me to sleep with her while we were dating. I had almost given up hope of ever finding my dream woman; I almost felt it was never going to happen because the disappointments from sisters were getting beyond control. When I met her, I knew quite well that she wasn't born again but I felt I could share the gospel with her and get her to start a relationship with Jesus and then make her start going to church. Thankfully and interestingly, I actually succeeded in getting her saved but the problem now became how to verify the genuity of her salvation. I wasn't sure if it was born out of her desire to date me because she liked me or because she was new in town and based on this, she could have been flowing with the salvation thing so she could find a companion in me, in an attempt to make friends with a good guy who knows his way around town. Then I thought maybe she actually genuinely gave her life to Christ but needed more time to grow in faith. Oh, but this lady was a handful. She quietly and persistently began to do everything in her power to change me into the guy she wanted me to be. She said I was too skinny and needed to eat more, she complained about what I did for a living and kept painting a picture of how wonderful I would look in a suit going to work in a bank or some corporate organization. She as much as wanted me to change the way I spoke, the way I dressed and where I lived. In addition, she complained that I didn't appreciate her physique or consider her beautiful. She expected me to have sex with her as a proof that I was physically attracted to her and as my proof of affection towards her. Consequently, she tried to set up situations for such to happen. For example, staying at my place till late and saying she was scared to be on the road at night alone, that she would leave in the morning. How I resisted her that night was by God's mercies. I insisted I didn't want us to have such intimacy and I gave up the bed and slept on the floor. Based on these types of advances and manipulative actions, even if she did genuinely get born-again, there was no trace of regeneration in her soul and flesh; it had not begun in any way. That girl had the capacity to shatter a man's psyche and make him a shadow of himself. In spite of all that, she was milking me financially like she was the only one with cares in the world. Eventually, some friends told me how they had observed her movements with several other strange guys that weren't me.

In this case, I will highlight my mistakes and some life-saving moves that I made that I want every guy reading this to keep to heart. Guys, always listen to the prompting of your heart. I still remember not feeling quite right about her, I lost my peace and was under constant pressure to please her. Those were enough signs that it wasn't meant to be but I continued, because all my friends were getting married and I felt I needed to bring the search to an end and settle down too. My mother had also never reacted to any woman I was dating like she did to this lady. I was shocked at her expressions and kept it to heart. Then, when my friends told me about her escapades, it confirmed all the disturbing dreams I had been having about her that I didn't share with anyone. A disastrous and belligerent home is an understatement when trying to describe the mistake of marrying this type of woman. The desire to get married should never pressure you into hurriedly settling for the next lady you see because the devil specializes in capitalizing on our desperation to send the wrong person so they can turn your life upside down, crash it and turn you into a traumatized and sad man whose life is in such shambles so much that he wouldn't remember if he ever had a vision or purpose. The Bible says:

If the foundation be destroyed, what can the righteous do? Psalm 11:3, KJV

Do not be unequally yoked together with unbelievers. For what fellowship has righteousness with lawlessness? And what communion has light with darkness? 2 Corinthians 6:14, NKJV

Please don't start a relationship on a faulty foundation. Getting a lady saved is good but good judgment is required to check out her overall character as it also negates scripture to move with the notion that maybe if you get a lady saved, she will become who you want her to be. If two people meet when both of them are not saved, get married and one of them eventually gets saved, there's grace available for that saved spouse to pray for the salvation of the other. But, in a case where you are a believer and unmarried, you have no business being unequally yoked with an unbelieving life partner. You know, when I met this lady and knew she wasn't saved, that alone was a good enough reason not to date her let alone conceive the idea of marrying her.

Besides all my mistakes and shortfalls, I realized at some point that there was something totally missing, something I had not gotten right in my search for true love. Among the ladies I dated or tried dating, I couldn't put a distinct similarity to their physical looks. In other words, I had not sat down and asked myself what exactly I wanted the woman of my dreams to look like, what qualities and character traits I wanted in my true love besides just being a kingdom citizen and beautiful. How do I know exactly what I'm looking for and know when I've found it if I don't know how what I'm looking for should look. The Bible says categorically 'he that finds a wife...', in other words a search is involved and you must have a clear image or mental picture of the "wife" being searched for. That was when I realized that **when you get it right in your mind, heaven will be ready to start work on your behalf.**

I had to go to God in prayers and tell Him exactly what kind of woman I was looking for. It is important we tell God our heart's desires so that when He strategically brings the right person our way, we can spot our answered prayer according to the desires of our hearts. At this point, I sat down and thought deeply and it dawned on me that I had always desired from my childhood to marry a white woman or a mixed race, where the physical attributes or qualities of the woman is concerned. I realised that I had picked interest in that race when my dad would interact with lots of white men by virtue of being a civil engineer by profession. They seemed naturally drawn to him and we had quite a number of them as family friends. However, in the passing years, we migrated to another part of the country as a family and somehow, he lost contact with almost all of his expatriate colleagues. As I gew up and faced pursuing my education and visions in an environement with less foreigners, my dream naturally looked impossible and I had to face the reality of what was available which, of course, with time, I got used to.

And so, I drew out my list and tabled it before God in prayers while I told myself that I was completely done trying to date outside of this vision. I resolved that it's either my dream or I'd rather remain single. I forgot about dating and relationships and immersed myself deeply into the work of the ministry, holding unto the scripture that says:

Delight yourself also in the LORD, And He shall give you the desires of your heart. Psalm 37:4, NKJV

Your life's vision must be inclusive of your marriage. **You must have a clear vision of what you want your wife to look like and the qualities and character attributes in her**, beyond just finding a child of God or a worker in the house of God.

(How To Know It's Him)

CHAPTER 2
The Journey to School

I tried to gain admission into two universities in the North-central part of Nigeria. I made every effort, wrote every examination required but there was no head way. I craved an admission so badly because my mates had all started going off to further their studies, and I didn't want to feel left out. However, in my own little way, I had learnt to let go and let God so I wasn't that perturbed over it. When the option of going to study in Cotonou, Benin Republic came up, I remember fasting and praying for God's will to be done, I never imagined that He was about to lead me through an exciting and life transforming journey.

Importantly, in the midst of trying to know what God's will for me was concerning my traveling, I didn't hear anything specific, I just felt a rest and excitement in my spirit about the whole thing, as if there was an adventure set before me and the unknown was exhilarating.

It wasn't long from then that my mom got the admission details we needed to travel and off we went crossing borders into a new territory to get my life into the next phase. In one day my mom had made payments, we picked International Relations as the only preferable arts course available at the time in the absence of Mass Communication and paid for my accommodation in the hostel. The journey was too far for us to change our minds just because I didn't get the course I wanted and the environment did not meet my expectations architecturally, the stress of travelling, the money spent on the admission registration while in Nigeria was not going to be in vain as far as my mom was concerned. The family friend that introduced this new university to us was well known and trusted so we moved at her word. The only thing that could have made us return home, especially for my mom, would have been if we had seen a different establishment at the address, met an empty space at the location or discovered that we had been defrauded. We got there. It was a school. That settled it.

In 2003, Houdegbe North American University was young, I believe it had only churned out a set or two of graduates. Upon arrival, I couldn't help but notice that the entire campus was still looking like work-in-progress with just three structures scattered within the bare and sandy premises. My heart sank as I looked around to make out the purpose of the pale looking high rise buildings I saw. I had just turned nineteen and I wondered if I had the ruggedness required to navigate through life away from home, in a new terrain miles and miles away from my comfort zone, a new culture, unfamiliar currency, a French-speaking country, all by myself. Besides going to church and a few family outings, I was never an outgoing type so being away from home was a big shift for me. I wasn't sure anymore if it was the right thing to do but there was no turning back. As much as uncertainty and the fear of the unknown gripped me, there was a subtle tiny seed of courage and confidence lying within. I could sense the Holy Spirit filling me with peace to move forward. In that moment, I knew everything would be alright.

If you can pause for a minute to examine your life's journey so far and other situations you've been through, when you look back carefully, you will find a thread of God's guidance and Presence helping you. You will be able to realize that God is not unaware of the twist and turns in your life, as a matter of fact, He has been turning the things the enemy planned for evil around for your good such that your life story has become intertwined with the challenges you've been through and you begin to realize that you couldn't have become who you are or gained the experiences you have without them. All of a sudden, your story seems incomplete without them. He is indeed a master strategist. He knows how to turn stumbling blocks into stepping stones. If there's one thing I know, you will come out stronger, wiser, mature and experienced enough to guide someone else who needs help.

God wants to see you happy, He loves seeing His children happy and fulfilled. More than any earthly father, His desire is for you to meet the right person that will become one with you in spirit, soul, body, vision and purpose and if it will take Him relocating you outside your country or state, or orchestrating an event that will ultimately lead you to meet the love of your life, you can trust Him to do so. He takes pleasure in giving you the best.

Take delight in the Lord, and He will give you your heart's desire. Commit everything you do to the Lord. Trust Him and He will help you. Psalm 37:4-5, NLT

So if you sinful people know how to give good gifts to your children, how much more will your heavenly Father give you the Holy Spirit to those who ask Him. Luke 11:13 NLT

I can categorically conclude by my experiences that my inability to secure an admission within Nigeria which led to a friend's suggestion of a school somewhere in a different African country was not a coincidence. God was setting up the perfect meeting point for me and my other half.

Your Time Is Your Life

There is something important you must always remember and that is God's unfailing love for you. If you have made mistakes up until this point or have experienced trauma and heartaches so far, just know that God can and is willing to fix it. He is not responsible for all the pain and hurt. Usually, a continuous crash in the journey to finding the love of your life indicates a spiritual cycle that requires prayer attention. There are forces of darkness from the demonic realm that are afraid of the greatness in you and the impact you were created to make on the face of this earth. Now the enemy understands the power of a family as designed by God to bring the agenda of His kingdom on earth as it is in heaven just as much as he remembers that the Bible says that one shall chase a thousand and two put ten thousand to flight (Deuteronomy 32:30) and so, he will do anything to fight it so you don't come to the full experience of becoming nine thousand times stronger when you become joined to your spouse. Some of his strategies include creating so many disappointments in relationships that will make you lose hope in ever finding love or ensuring you make a mistake by marrying someone that is not the real deal.

The thief does not come except to steal, and to kill, and to destroy. I have come that they may have life, and that they may have it more abundantly (John 10:10 NKJV)

That has been his strategy against every child of God and he uses relationship issues as a weapon especially against women. There's no woman who experiences such that will not feel confused and frustrated, disoriented, less passionate about life and possibly serving God. And if by God's mercies she is able to pull through and regain hope and faith, the process of retracing her steps will waste a part of the time apportioned to her on earth for destiny fulfillment. You might not be in this situation but believe me it is happening to a woman somewhere right now even as you read.

The devil's sole goal is to ultimately waste people's time; his goal is to waste your time. We know that as human beings, we have limited time on earth and we also know that there is a time frame, a blossoming phase as ladies when finding a life partner is easiest. Once that phase has been crossed, getting into a relationship can become a major issue and a prayer point. A man at age forty is not the same as a woman at age forty. Our biological clocks tick differently. A man does not usually have issues looking youthful, attractive or getting a woman pregnant at forty. In a woman's case, however, except she immerses herself into a lifestyle of exercise and good diet early enough, which only a few are disciplined enough to achieve, she begins to age visibly and lose her body shape. Based on a research published in year 2000 by the *The New York Times*, fertility begins to drop from when a woman is in her thirties. At age 35, she is already considered to be of 'advanced maternal age' and by age 44, the chances of spontaneous pregnancy approaches zero. The fact is, her eggs decline in number and quality and the chances of miscarriages and complications are higher – except in a case where God intervenes supernaturally. A doctor I was chatting with in the past once mentioned that his advice to women is that they get married in their early twenties because uterine fibroids can wreak reproductive havoc as they can occur in women older than thirty years, especially in women who have never been pregnant. And so, you think that the decision to delay marriage and achieve financial independence first, or to be extra picky with an outrageous list of what you are looking for in Mr. perfect, or maybe your choice to be a 'no-nonsense' woman that will not compromise anything for any man who will not meet your standards is not an idea from the pits of hell that you have bought into? If you don't wake up and change your perspective about men, relationships and marriage, you will only succeed in assisting the enemy in wasting your own time. Unfortunately, the people who also encouraged you to be an 'independent woman' will turn around and push the blame back on you when it backfires as 'late marriage' or 'no marriage'. Surprisingly, they'll say 'she's just too picky' or 'she's too proud' or "money is not everything!'. Don't be shocked when the same people say 'why will a woman be so focused on making money and not know where to strike the balance between money and family?' Don't follow what people think, please I beg you. Follow what will move your life forward and keep you in the center of God's agenda for your life. Follow the right path as a woman. After school, a career should not be the ultimate thing a woman seeks. Don't allow that 'career woman' concept mislead you. Whether you get a job immediately or not, after school, let getting married be the next paramount thing in your heart, except if you deliberately decide that you want to stay single for life, then that's a different scenario. Eventually, you will find something doing, a job or a business, that will put money in your hands.

Marriage to a woman is what financial success is to a man. It is a launch pad into the next phase of life and purpose fulfillment. There is an age a woman gets to that, like I said, except she deliberately decides to remain single, she begins to feel unfulfilled and restless no matter her level of success in her career or finances. She begins to desire the glory of being a wife, a mother and also synergizing with her husband to fulfill a unified vision. Before that age of restlessness, the enemy would usually come up with suggestions of finding success in her career. It becomes so enticing and she begins to enjoy the power of being self-sufficient and the accolade, so much that she does not realize that she is losing her youth. So many women out there have ended up unmarried, not by choice but because they took the bait and never discerned this demonic strategy early enough to stay focused. Some encountered challenges with men and decided to channel all their energy and focus on their careers rather than tackling the repetitive situation of disappointments in prayers. Eventually, later on in life, they realize that their careers mean nothing to them after all, because there's a vacuum for love and companionship that a job or money cannot fill.

Take Your Husband By Force!

The devil specializes in hiding behind our ignorance. The Bible says;

"My people are destroyed for lack of knowledge..."Hosea 4:6KJV.

A problem known is a problem half solved, they say. The less you know of the enemy's deceptive strategies, the less you will see him in the detail. The less you associate a problem to spiritual causes, the less you will apply the appropriate prayer necessary to deal with the root cause of that problem, that's if you even think it requires prayers at all. The devil does not mind playing this cat-and-mouse game until it becomes too late for much to be achieved with the time left. Then, the individual realizes that at 45 or so, they finally settle down, as if the battle suddenly eased off. Well, think about it for a second. The enemy feels comfortable to hands off because he has succeeded in wasting precious youthful years when a couple could have maximized their strength for maximum productivity and done mighty exploits in their calling together. They could have also had more children if it was part of their desires. At this point, it usually seems that God has just been sitting back and watching your life get ruined but in the real sense of it, He has been waiting on you to maximize the authority given to you over the power of the enemy, to engage heaven in the affairs of your life. You have the power to determine the course of your life. Through prayer, you can change the outcome of events, you can stop the trend of late marriage or divorce in your family line, you can facilitate the process of meeting your husband and you can pray for his safety wherever he is before you both meet.

Experiencing battles does not mean that you have lost your salvation. We are in a constant war with the kingdom of darkness because the enemy hates the children of God and what we stand for. Even if you choose not to fight, they will come after you so you might as well follow the advice given in Ephesians 6:11 to put on the whole armor of God and fight the good fight of faith from a victorious standpoint. When you discover that you might just be a victim of enchantments, demonic manipulations, marine spirit attacks or generational cycles and curses, it will require a tenacious application of the Word of God, warfare prayers, and fasting. When the disciples asked Jesus privately about why they couldn't cast out a demon in Matthew 17:14-21, Jesus answered them and said;

So Jesus said to them, "Because of your unbelief; for assuredly, I say to you, if you have faith as a mustard seed, you will say to this mountain, 'Move from here to there,' and it will move; and nothing will be impossible for you. ***However, this kind does not go out except by prayer and fasting.*** *" Matthew 17:20-21 NKJV (emphasis added)*

Demonic issues require prayer and fasting. Believe it or not, the demonic realm is real and listen to me, the marriage institution has been one of hell's blacklisted institutions ordained by God. Because marriage is of God, because it is symbolic in representing Jesus' relationship with His bride, the Church, and it is God's way of depicting how the unity between the Trinity works. The home and family is the heartbeat of any healthy society and the devil will stop at nothing to ensure that he destroys God's perfect plan for humanity. But God in His infinite mercies has never allowed the devil enjoy the pleasure of victory over His children. At the end of this book, a number of prayer points will be enumerated, addressing some of the different spiritual causes of relationship and marital challenges so you can also claim the victory that is yours and enjoy heaven on earth in your marriage.

(How To Know It's Her)

CHAPTER 3
Stop! That's My Wife!

In the year 2006, my younger sister got admission into a University in a neighboring country, Benin Republic. Interestingly, it took me a lot of effort to convince her to take the offer and go. She had wanted to travel to the U.S or South Africa to school rather than a neighboring West African country. I told her God has a purpose for everything that happens to us in life and that she could always leave and go to her dream school anytime she receives an offer from there. Little did I know that I was not just pushing her toward God's ordained school for her but my destiny was tied to it too.

On her first semester break back to Lagos, she came over to my house to have a chat with me on how she liked the school after all and how she was having so much fun in her school campus fellowship of Christian students. She told me about their school's fellowship pastor and his assistant pastor, a very pretty mixed race who happened to pick so much interest in her, and then, my heart froze. Honestly, till date, I can't still tell how the revelation hit me so strongly. All I can remember was that I just shouted out so loudly, excitedly and with conviction "Stop! That's my wife!"

Proverbs 3:5-6 was one of the top three theme scriptures that ruled my heart as a single young man trying to chart the course of his life's destiny and purpose and Don Moen's gospel song on that scripture further helped in creating a theme sound track with the scripture for my mind.

Trust in the LORD with all your heart, And lean not on your own understanding; In all your ways acknowledge Him, And He shall direct your paths. Proverbs 3:5-6, NKJV

My kid sister took my sudden outburst of interest in her campus fellowship assistant pastor who later became my wife as half joke and half fantasy as she went back to school and continued her excited life as a fresher in her new University, almost completely forgetting my discussion with her on arranging a meeting between me and her assistant pastor. I continued in my fervency in the Lord's house and at this point, I had since left The Redeemed Church by the Lord's leading to an independent ministry called City of Refuge in Lagos. I had already become the youth pastor/president of my church's youth fellowship. I was also the armor bearer to the Senior Pastor and founder of the ministry who took out his time to identify God's calling upon my life and mentored me thoroughly in the dynamics and evolvements of churches, church growth and ministry. He took out time to develop the teaching and preaching grace upon my life, which was first identified by a fellow pastor and very close friend that God used to help me identify and bring out a lot of the hidden gifts in me. **The company you keep can decide, define or reshape the course of your life's destiny.** If you want to be on course in locating your clone, it is my advice that you keep a good company of friends in the same faith with you.

Blessed is the man who walks not in the counsel of the ungodly, nor stands in the path of sinners, nor sits in the seat of the scornful; But his delight is in the law of the LORD, and in His law he meditates day and night. He shall be like a tree planted by the rivers of water, that brings forth its fruit in its season, whose leaf also shall not wither; And whatever he does shall prosper. Psalm 1:1-3, NKJV

In the cool of a certain evening, while trying to catch a nap, a phone call came through from my sister in the North American University, Benin Republic, telling me to get ready to come on an official invitation to preach at their campus fellowship. It felt like our patriarch father, Joseph, being remembered in prison. Two major excitements ran through my veins instantly and one was even more dominant than the other; the excitement to teach and preach outside of my familiar territory and the excitement to see my 'wife' for the first time. I am sure you can already tell which the greater excitement was.

Cotonou is the capital of Benin republic and it's one of the biggest commercial hubs of their country and West Africa. It runs on a stretch of about 125km from Lagos state Nigeria, an approximate journey of about three and a half hours with the given traffic in that area. The excitement of being on this route on that beautiful morning was one I am never going to forget. What seemed to be a fairly long trip, especially coming out of the Lagos traffic along Badagry express way looked far less than a thirty minute drive to a nearby ice-cream store. The excitement that gripped my heart on this 'trip of faith' coupled with the ministration ahead of me created a strong feeling inside me that couldn't be described in any other way than a feeling that my life was about to change and a new chapter had been opened up in my book; the book of my destiny written in heaven.

Amidst the several thoughts and questions that sped through my head, just the same way the palm trees along the shores swished past us in the vehicle in a rush leaving a cool refreshing ocean breeze and view of calm waters, I had butterflies in my stomach and at the same time an adrenalin rush while questions such as 'what does she look like?', besides a vague description of her that my sister gave me, questions like 'what if she's already in a relationship?' and 'how do I get to know her in a short trip as a guest minister?' and so many others that flashed even faster than I could process them. Somewhere deep within me, I felt peace. I felt so much peace that can only make sense to say it came from the Holy Spirit.

Guys, when she is your woman, when she is your clone, you cannot but feel peaceful about it. I'm talking about the God kind of peace that the Bible describes in Philippians 4:7 that surpasses all understanding. Why, because the blessings of God makes rich and adds no sorrow.

Then you will experience God's peace, which exceeds anything we can understand. His peace will guard your hearts and minds as you live in Christ Jesus. Philippians 4:7, NLT

The blessing of the LORD makes one rich, and He adds no sorrow with it. Proverbs 10:22, NKJV

A protocol team that included my sister was sent to pick me up on arrival to the campus fellowship house where I met the fellowship pastor, a very pleasant young man who gave me the warmest reception and took me to a nearby hotel that had been booked for me. I kept my eyes darting back and forth as I hoped to see my 'wife' pop out from a corner but guess what, SHE WAS NOT AROUND!!! That was the biggest shocker I got from my sister as soon as I settled in my hotel room after the campus fellowship pastor left and I was alone with her. "What do you mean she is not around?" That was the only question that I could spill out in the shock I was in. She let out a loud laughter and said, with a cheerful tone of amazement, excitement and mischief at my appearance of being love struck and disappointed at the same time, "Man of God, are you here to minister to us or to pick a wife?", she asked. "Both!" I replied immediately. "Well, she went on a trip to Nigeria today, probably as you were leaving Nigeria for here" she explained. "To do what?" I blurted out with a tone and expression of shock that triggered loud giggles from my sister again. "She needed to go attend to something important back in Nigeria and you had better get yourself together because you will be ministering in a couple of hours" my sister responded grinning from ear to ear.

The ministration was nothing short of an explosion of the power of God through the Word, it was my first ministration outside the shores of Nigeria and I gave it my best preparation spiritually and physically. According to my sister, days after I returned back to Lagos, the atmosphere was still pumped, the message was still ringing in the air and the excitement could still be felt among the fellowship members. I know that a residue of the Presence of God from the program must have lingered on; there's no greater fulfillment as a minister of the gospel than knowing that you were able to get people to see the truth about a specific subject; all that excitement meant the word of God had given them new insight on who they were in Christ based on the message preached. For me, the joy had no limit too as the trip did not only indicate a new step into a greater height in ministry, but also a new beginning into the next phase of my life. In spite of not getting to even meet my wife at that time, I felt a strong air of change taking place in my life and in the realm of the spirit. I knew beyond feelings that I had begun a journey into marrying the woman I had always prayed to God for.

As Christians, we must learn to develop a keen sense of understanding of the times and seasons in the realm of the spirit. In first Chronicles 12:32, concerning the sons of Issachar, the Bible says that they were men who understood the times and knew what Israel should do. Up till date, I still can't describe exactly what I felt all through my two-day stay at the campus. She was literally everywhere around even when she was physically not there. I had looked forward to seeing her so much that it felt like she was watching me all through my ministration. And at a point, when their fellowship pastor and a team of sisters who made up the fellowship's leadership decided to treat me out to lunch and show me around town the following day, I felt strongly like someone I had known all my life was missing from the team. My heart was divided between the reality of the people around me and the mystery lady I was longing to see, so much that at some point, I felt a strong need to pray for journey mercies for her return back to school.

Back in Lagos, the sudden realization of the dawn of a new season that was about to take place in my life made me also realize that I had to play my role in bringing into manifestation in the place of prayers, whatever God was about to do in my life. Quickly, I tagged along with a friend and a brother in the Lord to go to a prayer camp ground to seek the Lord's face.

The devil hates and disdains the marriage institution and he will do everything to stop you from either getting married or at the very least make you marry the wrong person. Anytime people decide to go into a relationship and get married, it always looks like all hell is let loose and this is where it becomes very important to engage in warfare prayers when you find your clone, God's perfect will for your life.

I remember how the Lord gave me victory about two weeks before my invitation to this said trip I made, to preach at my wife's campus in Benin Republic, over what would have been an unfortunate incidence. I kept having these series of repeated dreams of man slaughter some weeks before the incidence and it got to the point where I had to get some of my church elders to join me in prayers until suddenly, one evening, I was returning back to my uncle's place where I went to spend some time with my cousins and the brakes of the Mercedes V-Boot saloon that I was driving failed on the peak of descending down a flyover bridge in a very rowdy part of Lagos called Oshodi. In the bid to stop the vehicle by brushing against the dual carriage divider, the car was sent on a faster spiral down the bridge rather than being stopped from further movement. How I avoided crushing the retinue of the heedless busy sea of pedestrians, until today, remains one big miracle in my life. It literally felt like an invisible hand was clearing the people away from the path of my speeding and down-sloping uncontrollable vehicle. At this point, the engine had gone off, the steering wheel had self-locked and the horn of that model V-boot usually would stop working once the ignition was off. And so, there was no way of alerting the crowd all the way down the bridge of the looming danger coming behind them as they were all mostly backing the on-coming out of control vehicle I was struggling to bring to a halt. If I had killed or maimed people that evening, I don't think I would have been able to honor an invitation that would have led to finding my wife.

My counsel and advice, guys, please pray like it all depends on you when you are searching for your clone, pray after you've found her and keep praying as you are planning your wedding. Even in marriage, keep praying for your marriage. Pray without ceasing.

Never stop praying. 1 Thessalonians 5:17, NLT

About a month after I took my first trip to Benin Republic, the campus fellowship pastor gave me a call concerning a discussion we had earlier toward having my senior pastor's wife , Pst. Mrs. Ugochi Ossai, come to minister at their next program organized for the ladies in their campus. Of course, with gladness I asked him to come over to Lagos and personally give her an official invitation. I didn't know that this was another divinely arranged opportunity for me to finally make contact with my wife. Prior to this time, I had collected her number from my sister and their fellowship pastor respectively. My aim of getting her number from him was to register with the pastor that I officially had her number and to make it obvious that I planned to get in touch with her. We spoke on phone a few times as we got acquainted and had an opportunity to also discuss the upcoming program involving my pastor's wife. Speaking with her was such a thrilling experience that I lack the appropriate words to describe the feeling, knowing deep in my heart that I was speaking with the woman I had always dreamed about and prayed earnestly for as a wife.

We fixed a date and I picked him up at the motor park upon arrival. As we were about to start heading for my senior pastor's house, he asked me if we could go and pick sister Elliana first at Dolphin estate. He explained that she had something crucial to do in Lagos and had gone a few days ahead but he thought it would be good to have a female go with him since it's my pastor's wife we needed to go and see in preparation towards a ladies' program too. Of course, at this time, he had not known my hidden interest so, the moment I heard her name mentioned and the idea of going to pick her up to go along with us, it felt like I was suddenly and unexpectedly thrown into an ocean of excitement that I couldn't recover from throughout our less than one hour drive to the island side of Lagos.

"Pastor John, meet Sister Elliana our campus fellowship pastor and this is Pastor John, the man of God that God used to minister greatly to us about two months ago". These were the first words that came out of Pastor Niyi's mouth, immediately after she had the door opened for us to come in. And standing right in front of me waiting to welcome us by the door was the prettiest, sweetest, angelic looking heaven's master craft I had ever set my eyes on. She was a perfect match for the beautiful voice I heard on the phone when I couldn't stand the wait to meet her anymore and had to sneak in a few calls across to her to introduce myself and open up a phone chat with her. Guys, sometimes, you need to be a little more aggressive and proactive in going for what you want. I had thought to myself that delay could sometimes be dangerous especially when I didn't have an inkling of how soon I would be seeing her. But here I was, finally face to face with my clone. If I could, I would have screamed out "Alas! This is bone of my bones and flesh of my flesh!"

Listen to me guys and ladies as well, every time a potential suitor turns you down or leaves you in tears of disappointment, please just tell them 'Thank you. Thank you for giving me an opportunity to meet with a better person ahead'. That was one big lesson the Lord taught me in my sojourn and search for my utopia. God will give you the one that will make your previous relationship or relationships look like trash. He always reserves the best for His children. Our marriage is over ten years now and every time I look at my wife, I wish I could see all the previous ladies I met before her and thank them sincerely from the depth of my heart for not marrying me, for whatever reasons best known to them. I remember driving home from work years back when I was in Lagos and I was thinking about a certain lady I had met earlier on in the day and how I knew she could never be mine because she was going to be leaving the country for the U.S in a couple of days, and then I heard the Lord speak to my heart telling me not to be down cast because He was going to give me the best among His daughters when the time is right. And truly, I can say without an iota of doubt today that I married God's very best.

Trust in the LORD with all your heart, And lean not on your own understanding; In all your ways acknowledge Him, And He shall direct your paths. Proverbs 3:5-6, NKJV

(How To Know It's *Him*)

CHAPTER 3
How It All Began

By the end of my first academic year, I had located the campus' Christian fellowship and was eager to be a part of it. I heard that the fellowship was held in a building outside the school premises, I had seen the fellowship pastor a few times from a distance and he looked approachable and welcoming. At that time, it was still a very young group and because I had experience with running a number of groups and the youth choir in my church back home, I thought it would be great to make my impute, no matter how little. I desired to offer part of my time in school for the expansion of our Father's Kingdom on Earth. Within a short period of time, with a lot of extensive commitment into the Vineyard, I got ordained into the office of the assistant fellowship pastor. Something I learnt from the leaders that preceded me was that once appointed or ordained into an office in the campus fellowship, it was the duty of that leader to find someone they could pour out their knowledge into and groom to replace them. This was because we were all in a school environment where we would all graduate after a given time frame; we were expected to find someone we could pass the baton of leadership to. It was primarily the duty of that leader to mentor his or her protégé spiritually, train him or her and develop the passion and capability in them to keep the torch of God's work burning.

I began to prayerfully seek someone I could confidently say was sold out to God enough to handle the enormous responsibility of managing the spiritual welfare of several students from different backgrounds. The responsibility of overseeing the choir and the ladies fellowship was on me, I oversaw welfare severally until we got someone to handle the role. I was programs coordinator along with the head pastor and was open to other tasks assigned to me. I had all these responsibilities to shoulder and needed to find someone who could wear these multiple shoes at the same time. I had a lot of sisters under me but had not seen anyone yet that I could run with side by side.

It was the first semester of my third year in school, a batch of freshers had just come in. Usually, we would evangelize to them, host them to a school welcoming and orientation dinner where we would introduce the fellowship to them and hope that they would accept our arm of invitation to be part of the fellowship. The ultimate goal was to get them to meet the Lord in the process and start their own personal journey with Jesus. Among those we welcomed was a young lady who moved into the hostel just a floor above mine. For whatever reason, she caught my attention. I paid one or two visits to her to personally get to know her and also offer a few tips on how to best enjoy her stay in school. I got to know that her name was Yvonne and she promptly mentioned that she would be spending just an academic year because she had plans to move to another school in another part of the world. Knowing that she wasn't going to be with us for long, I felt it would be nice to just get to know her a little better and give her some good memory she could always make reference to anytime she remembered our school, especially as I was only a floor away.

My visits became a bit more frequent as our friendship grew exciting. She told me a little more about herself, her walk with God and passion for the Kingdom and that was my connecting point. She showed me pictures of her entire family and gave me a vivid description of her parents' and siblings' personalities. I remember that she spoke so fondly of her eldest brother and would take more time to describe the qualities she admired in him and how he had influenced her greatly. Incidentally, she had had previous ministry experience in the church she was coming from in Lagos, Nigeria and there was a lot to talk about and relate to. Interestingly also, a lot of her ministry experience was in the company of her big brother, and of course, consequently, his name was always popping up every time we discussed church stuff.

I understood every single thing she said earlier about not being able to continue her education in our school, it was already preplanned from home for her but I couldn't help the feeling of wanting to mentor her. I discerned the connection I felt with her as a strong enough reason to want to impart the knowledge I had gathered over the years with her. As much as I knew she was meant to leave, the one thing I was sure of was that no knowledge is wasted; it would come in useful tomorrow wherever she found herself. I chose to make her a protégé in my heart, as if she was staying. I hoped that she would decide to remain in our school since there was still a very slim chance, from the way she spoke, however, I planned that I would raise one or two others just in case her plans worked out as initially arranged.

I would never have imagined that she was going to be instrumental in bringing my love story together, It didn't even cross my mind to picture her as a piece of the jigsaw puzzle of my life. I never in my wildest dream connected the dots that I was already getting introduced to my future in-laws and husband when she spoke extensively about her family. I never knew that God rerouted her schooling just so I could meet her brother, my husband, and that all the time and energy I invested in her was Holy Spirit led because she eventually would not be leaving as we all thought, both for my good and hers. The pull to draw closer to her was key to shaping my destiny. Now that I am married to her brother and she is my covenant sister, I can look back and be amazed at God's matchmaking skills that are beyond human comprehension. I mean, isn't it staggering sometimes when you try to wonder how God brings two individuals who are worlds apart across each other's path in the most unlikely location. He is that reliable and amazing! With Him ALL things are possible! He can and will deliver on the job if you can trust Him with your relationship requests or challenges.

At the point when Yvonne came into my life, I wasn't looking for a relationship. All I wanted to do was to develop myself, discover and understand my purpose better and grow in my knowledge of God. I wasn't sure for how long I was going to be in this phase but I was sure of one thing that God was going to lead me to the best days of my life. I knew that I was determined to carefully and purposefully step into the next relationship and I wanted it to be one worth the wait.

The Invitation

Yvonne had obviously grown fond of me too, she respected me as her pastor but we related as friends. I suspect that she had thought to herself that it wouldn't be a bad idea to have a sister-in-law she can be good friends with. She must have pictured us becoming one family long before I imagined because the frequency with which she spoke about her eldest brother could only suggest someone who was trying to buy a share of my mind in that regard. She knew that it would interest me to know how deeply rooted he was in the things of God and she didn't fail to inform me that he was also a youth pastor in his church. She mentioned how much of a strong calling he had, the several hospital evangelism they had ministered in together with astounding healing testimonies. Without any doubt, it sure caught my attention but because I had conditioned my mind not to be searching at that time, the stories only raised my respect level for him. Moreover, after seeing his picture and hearing so many wonderful stories, I thought to myself that there was no way a man like that wasn't engaged or at least had all the youth fellowship ladies swarming all around him; 'he has so many options around him', I thought. It was one of those fast thoughts that would speed across your mind and you quickly moved on to reality.

A few weeks later, the lead pastor over our campus fellowship, Pastor Niyi Osadare, told me that he was considering inviting Yvonne's brother, John, to minister at the fellowship. I wasn't surprised at all that Yvonne's campaign had reached Pastor Niyi too and that he had bought into it because as a youth group, we always tried to stay innovative, bringing in activities and guest speakers that would keep the fellowship fun, exciting and buzzing with something new to look forward to. At that time, our purse was not very large so if we could also have a guest minister who would be willing to come because of their passion for ministry and not necessarily considering the size of the honorarium, it was always a win-win situation for us. I personally liked the idea of having someone familiar with relating to young people come around and a new face we hadn't invited before that we could vouch for through a trusted member. So, we fixed a date and made necessary arrangements to bring him over.

Prior to the arranged invitation, I had been working on securing a new visa to travel to the U.S.A for the recording of the youth oriented music television program, One Cubed, which I started hosting in 2004 under the auspices of Christian Broadcasting Network (CBN). I had also planned a visit to Abuja where the CBN regional headquarters for Africa was located to sort out travel documents that would be needed for the interview. My trip to Nigeria couldn't be cancelled; I had people waiting for me to discuss pressing matters concerning the scheduled recording. At this point, I knew I was going to miss out on John's visit and the opportunity to meet the much talked about elder brother and youth pastor but sadly, there was nothing I could do about it. I also knew that it wouldn't be his last visit to our fellowship so I was already expectant of the next visit. Incidentally, my trip out of Benin Republic was the same day that John was expected to arrive. One could say we missed seeing each other by a hair's breadth.

The First Meeting

I was back before the next weekend. By the time I returned, I couldn't believe my eyes. Everyone in the fellowship was looking excited and pumped. It looked as if a good wind had swirled everybody around and given them a new focus and helped them hit their stride. The atmosphere was energized and I seemed to be the stranger that was gliding through the crowd in silence and amazement because I couldn't relate with them on the same level. It was as if our fellowship members' pulse had been taken up to a certain rate and it never came down after that. The name of the visiting youth pastor and the message on vision and purpose fulfillment that he preached was all I was hearing on the lips of almost all the fellowship members I came in contact with. The brothers went on and on about how motivating and powerful the message was while the sisters, on the other hand, were falling head over heels for this young pastor. A number of them, as I heard, had seen their dream man and some described him as tall, dark and handsome with an athletic build. A tall, good looking man who is also anointed? What more could a woman possibly need to get swept off her feet! Pastor Niyi was part of those ringing it into my ears that I had missed out on an anointed ministration. I could only afford a grin on my face that made me appear lost as I looked at his face. It was obvious that this was certainly not the last of him we would be seeing.

Yvonne, of course, was all giggles, releasing doses of overflowing happy expressions and laughs every now and then as she beamed from ear to ear. Every one that knows her easily describes her unique and untroubled laughter as one that draws out yours. I could read from her sense of satisfaction that she delivered on her word and was thrilled that the program had the impact it did. She had also hoped that her brother would meet me because she mentioned that she had told him about me and he had the intentions of meeting this pastor of hers that she had grown so fond of. In a brief meeting with her and my lead pastor, I was informed that everyone was looking forward to his return, which had been concluded before he left. In addition, Yvonne had also informed our fellowship pastor that the senior Pastor's wife, Mama Ossai, as we fondly referred to her, was a fantastic speaker who would be delighted to give spiritual and relationship mentoring to the ladies within our campus. This was a much welcomed idea, it would help satisfy the hunger and expectations built and further bless the lives of the youths. Before John left for Lagos, they had discussed the possibility of having Mama Ossai grace our fellowship with her presence and as Bishop Ossai's armor bearer, John was in the best position to know his pastor's wife's itinerary and give an idea of how feasible it was.

While we waited for John's call on this, I was told that he requested for my phone number so he could say hello, since I was the only member of the fellowship's leadership team that he didn't get to meet. No sooner than later, he called. He was very cheerful and sounded very excited to meet me. I appreciated him for making out time from his busy schedule to visit and expressed how much the message blessed our members. He seized the opportunity to mention that he planned to return soon to our fellowship and had successfully secured a meeting for us with his pastor's wife in Lagos to enable us set our plans in concrete, which he eventually related and planned with our lead pastor privately.

In less than two weeks, we had gotten the call from John to come over. I also had the U.S visa interview I was working on to attend in Lagos at about the same period which gave me a reason to partake in the visit and official invitation to Mama Ossai, which ordinarily, Pastor Niyi would have easily travelled alone to handle and conclude on. He, Niyi, also felt that since it was a ladies' affair, it would be nice to have me there as a representative of the fellowship's ladies and just in case Mama Ossai needed information on private gender related matters. I headed out a little earlier, on my own to meet up with my scheduled visa appointment. I would usually stay at my aunt's place whenever I was in Lagos. I had also given the address of where I was to my lead Pastor so he could meet me up, and from there, we could move together to attend the long anticipated meeting.

I tidied up my interview the day before our visit to Mama Ossai. My aunt lived in a high rise apartment in an estate on the Lagos Island and was already off to work by the time I woke up on the day of our appointment. I was expecting Pastor Niyi that morning and I got myself prepared waiting when my phone rang. He was downstairs and told me he had a guest with him. I requested that they climbed up while I hurriedly sorted myself out and crosschecked if I had picked up everything I needed. To my amazement, my lead pastor walked in with John. I should have expected or guessed that he could have been the guest but my thoughts never ran in that direction. That would also be our very first physical meeting and what a pleasant surprise it was indeed. We greeted each other cheerfully with mutual respect built from our little acquaintance over the phone as Pastor Niyi gave a formal introduction.

He did fit into the description that the ladies back at the campus fellowship had given him. He was stunning! Six foot plus, an athletic build and an upright posture that reminded me of the US marines garnished with a charismatic personality and a very pleasant disposition. I knew a fine looking man when I saw one. As much as I appreciated his good looks, I had been in church leadership for a while and in my few years of experience, I had been taught by a few respected mentors what was right and what was not. I had also met so many guys within the church setting to know that it wasn't every good looking guy or pastor that was meant for you or to be desired. It wouldn't be realistic or responsible to look at every good looking single male figure one sees from a perspective of a potential husband. Even if one was 'searching' and was just being vigilant not to let a good opportunity pass by, that attitude is a reflection of desperation and tending towards obsession, if not done with care. Besides, as a pastor or someone occupying a spiritual office, it would be a disaster, a total catastrophe not to be able to exercise self-control or know where to draw the line between one's love life and showing brotherly love to the tens or hundreds of people that one will meet in the place of carrying out ministerial functions. Rules and ethics of life demand that we respect ourselves first before expecting it from people. This kind of knowledge along with my personal decision to stay off dating temporarily made me restrict myself from seeing him as anything other than a well-respected pastor.

To strike a balance however on being able to determine that a believer in church who's born-again might or might not be the right man for you even though he is saved requires putting your ability to sense and pick up little signals that indicate turbulence or smooth sailing ahead into consideration. Don't ever make the mistake of accepting a guy by face value or because he professes to be born-again and belongs to a department in church. This is because you are expected to study him carefully, to know if he is allowing the Presence of God regenerate his mind and old ways of doing things, you must seek to know the depth of his love for God, if he is submissive to his pastor and willing to be corrected. Never assume that he has it all together because he goes to church.

I am strongly of the opinion that a brother in church is by far a better option than an unbeliever and these are some reasons why; being born-again means he is now a Kingdom citizen - a member of the household of God. Therefore, he has been given the gift of the Holy Spirit, the transforming, regenerating, resurrecting power of God, the ONE who can lead him into all truth, convict him of sin, counsel him and guide him – you cannot trade this for anything else. Any man that is far from God is a tool and a slave in the hands of the devil. The enemy can twist and turn his life in any direction he pleases without any hindrance; he is, in fact, like a puppet in the hands of demonic forces who will manipulate his destiny to make sure he becomes the very opposite of what God intended for his life. Unfortunately, a man without Jesus will find it very difficult not to yield his members to the desires of his flesh. However, a brother that has a relationship with the Lord is under authority, both God's and man's, that means he understands what is right and wrong according to the Bible and is in a position where the Holy Spirit can reach him and change him. He is also accountable to his pastor and other church leaders. If caught in a dicey situation, you can be sure that he will consider what God thinks or how it will affect his walk with the Lord first, and what will happen if his pastor or spiritual father finds out before taking a step.

I know that the days we're in have become horrifyingly evil, there have been several gory stories associated with 'Christian' brothers and pastors that make it hard for anyone to vouch for someone based on a mere title or position. You cannot allow yourself live in fear or be incapacitated by all this; evil will only keep increasing in this world we live in till the day the Lord comes for His elect. The only way to navigate through these times we're in is for you to work on your relationship with God as well so your sensitivity and discernment can be sharpened. You should be able to test all spirits and know people by their fruits, the Spirit of God at work in you will bear witness with your spirit when you meet someone operating a familiar spirit and living a life of lies and deceit, if you're willing to listen. Consequently, the works of the flesh, the false fire and false glory on that man should be like a repulsive smell to your spiritual olfactory lobe, you should be able to sense that something is wrong somewhere, no matter how much he poses as a good person; something should make you uncomfortable deep within. But, you see, it all depends on how much you develop your senses and once you begin to see that something is not adding up, that there seems to be a contradiction between his words and actions, that his character does not match what a genuinely God-fearing man should be, you owe yourself the duty and favor of leaving without looking back. At the end of the day, his Christianity or integrity is his to worry about and he will stand before God someday to give account of his life. You, however, cannot expect the dating world to be devoid of evil men whether you meet them in the higher institution, at work, at a decent social event or in the Church. Yours is to watch and pray, to walk circumspectly and be in tune with the Holy Spirit so that you are not deceived.

I offered them a seat as they stepped into my aunt's living room. This was a special moment; to have a pastor and guest minister visit, I had to pause and honor him by sitting for a bit to chat and familiarize briefly before getting my shoes and rounding up my things for us to start heading out. As we rode in the car, it was a very friendly atmosphere where most of our conversations were centered on ministerial experiences. We drove all the way to Mama Ossai's home where she was already expecting us and with warmth and delight, welcomed us. Our meeting yielded a much desired result and all that was left was the date of the event which John would correspond with us over, as soon as possible. Throughout the entire trip from my aunt's place to Mama Ossai's place, to when we stopped to grab something to eat, I couldn't help but notice that John was particularly friendly. He loved to engage me in every conversation, even when I withdrew every now and then to check up something on my phone or observe something in the surrounding, he would try to get my opinion on every topic in an attempt not to let my mind drift away for too long from the talk. He was all smiles, as if the entire meeting and visit was all about me. He seemed so drawn to me but I was restricting myself and being careful to think that he was attracted to me. We were to keep in touch till the much anticipated ladies' seminar materialized.

We travelled back to Cotonou that day happy with the outcome of our meeting and I couldn't get the activities of the day we all had together out of my head, it was fun and exciting in a gratifying way. We had our seminar date fixed by the end of the week and off we were to work to make adequate arrangements towards the event, expected to hold in three weeks from then. So, here we were, Mama Ossai's visit was less than a month away, John, being so close to his Bishop's family and having had the experience of navigating his way from Lagos to Cotonou during his first visit, was in the best position to accompany Mama and also offer protection across the very busy and sometimes volatile Seme border.

Just like every other program involving a guest minister, the preparation phase was very crucial and critical. We had been through this type of phase severally to know what to expect, there is usually an adrenalin rush that builds up as the days draw nearer and as the organizing team see to it that every necessary thing required to make a guest feel welcomed and comfortable is done. John, on the other hand, had the responsibility of corresponding with us on his pastor's behalf and as if speaking to Pastor Niyi about any concerns or needed information was not enough, he would call me as well to include me in the matters discussed, on a lighter note of course, with a lot of pleasantries and digressions – digressions like wanting to know my likes and dislikes, finding out what my visions were and what my future plans were. I didn't mind talking to this extent with him because he felt like family now, I mean, with his sister being a rooted member of the fellowship, his closeness to Pastor Niyi, our newly built relationship with his pastor's wife whose invitation Apostle Yemi Adefarasin long approved before we went ahead to invite her, we felt connected spiritually. Apostle Yemi Adefarasin was the father in faith our campus fellowship was submitted to. Majority of our fellowship members belonged to one department or the other in Action Faith Chapel, where he pastored at that time. I was a member of the choir there too because our fellowship services were on weekdays. I remember clearly how he laughed as he called out her full name when we informed him of our desire to invite her to minister at the campus fellowship. He told us how she and her husband were good friends of his and even counseled us on making sure we gave an honorarium as a way of honoring her, no matter how little. So, there was a web of connection that was built that made it easy for my friendship with John to grow.

(How To Know It's *Her*)

CHAPTER 4
How It All Began

Our journey into friendship started at this point. We all had a fun-filled day navigating our way through the Lagos traffic and the blazing heat all the way to my senior pastor's house at the edge of the mainland. Heat? Lots of it! Especially when your car's air conditioning is not working and that was my case at that time as a hustling young man in Lagos. But did anybody notice? We were all engrossed in the magical moment of our newly found friendship that felt like we had always known each other for years. It was such a beautiful moment that was completely devoid of artificiality and superficiality. Even in that short moment shared together, we were all bonded in the sweet simplicity of the agape love of Christ that sees the other person better than themselves, even as we agreed and disagreed on a lot of issues and topics in the kingdom and as our conversations varied from everything good to everything great. Please, I would like to plead with you that if you are reading this book right now and you are still single and searching and also a citizen of the Kingdom of God through Christ Jesus, don't get a spouse outside the fold of the house hold of God. And if you are not yet a citizen of the Kingdom, it's not too late, the gates are still widely open for you right now to accept the

Lord Jesus as your personal Lord and savior. Confess your sins to Him and forsake your old ways and voila! You are in the Kingdom!! All you just need from here is to find a Bible believing church near you and begin to fellowship with God and the brethren. Commit your heart daily to studying God's Word and to service in His house, the church; He wants and has reserved the best for you, trust me.

My senior Pastor's wife's acceptance of the invitation to travel over to their school to minister put the icing on my day's cake, especially knowing that she wouldn't travel without me. I knew my Bishop, her husband, would never let her travel by herself either and there's nobody else he would have nominated to go with her if not me; I was his closest aide, I was also very close to his family and so he knew he could trust my judgment and ability to be of assistance to her. Furthermore, they both knew I had been there to minister previously, which means that someone trusted already knows the way there. For me, it was going to be another big opportunity to get to meet with my dream lady and get to spend more time with her again as friends. However, I had made up my mind that I was going to just go ahead and make my intentions and desire for us to date known to her.

No matter how certain you are about a lady being your future wife, no matter how much you feel you heard from God or got a prophecy from a man of God, please learn to follow principles and precepts. Life is all about established principles and precepts and one of the principles of establishing a good and healthy relationship is to start as friends with your wife-to-be. I disdain hearing about brothers who walk up to a woman for the first time and dump their fears at her feet on the platform of "Thus says the Lord". Fears of not wanting to go through the routine of wooing a woman, their inadequacies of not being bold enough to strike up an intelligent conversation with her till they hit the topic of dating and not being able to handle rejection has made some men in the kingdom misuse the words "Thus says the Lord". This is the cheapest and most cowardly approach to dating and courtship. Hello! You say "Thus says the Lord, you're my wife" to a lady you are walking up to for the first time? And you know what, you will be held accountable by the Lord for every word you speak. I have seen a number of Christian marriages crash on this wrong premise, some which probably wouldn't have if only the right principles were applied from the beginning. I have also seen where fathers in faith, I'm talking about ministers of God, out of love for their sons and daughters in the Lord, try to match make or find spouses for them. I had a personal experience on this which I will be talking about in the next chapter. Dear ministers of God, it is dangerous to play 'God' with people's lives especially where marriage is concerned. **Be your clone's friend first**. It's very important to get to know them first. "Thus says the Lord" can be a scary and confusing position for any woman to be in, It's almost as if you are forcing her into the relationship using the name of the Lord as blackmail. It's actually wicked to do so.

In continuation, within the weeks that passed, while waiting to commence my next journey with Mama Ossai back to Benin Republic, our friendship built up stronger in spite of the physical distance barrier. We stayed in touch on phone and through our conversations, I got to know more about her family, her temperament and personality traits, her likes, dislikes and her visions. I realized how much we had in common and how compatible we were going to be, and of course, needless to say that I also used the opportunity to sell myself too. You can call it advertising or 'customer focused selling' and it is required, in dating, to make her see what you both have in common, if you truly do, and how genuinely interested you are in her interests. You should also, when she asks you questions about yourself, take advantage of the few seconds to tell her about yourself, where you are now and where you are going. I say 'few seconds' because you are not expected to steal the show, give her as much time to speak about herself and give her every inch of listening ear you've got. One of the memories I will not forget during this period was how comfortable and relaxed I was being myself around her. When she is the right woman or better put in my concept, clone, when she is your clone, I guarantee that you will have a feeling I can best describe as 'home'. You will feel at home around her, be it on the phone or in every one-on-one contact. I am not superimposing this statement over the natural feeling you get as a guy who is around a lady you've just fallen in love with such as the butterflies, the natural poise of being the best you and putting your best foot forward and some other natural feelings that come when a guy is around a woman he cares about. I am talking about the non-pretentious and non-exaggerated you. The feeling of being brought back to a relaxed state by the woman's simplicity and interest in you as an individual without putting you under pressure, even when you feel uptight, nervous or a need to perform and display your qualities to her, is a sign you must look out for as your indicator of being on the right path.

Making My Intentions Known

Most assuredly, I say to you, he who does not enter the sheepfold by the door, but climbs up some other way, the same is a thief and a robber. But he who enters by the door is the shepherd of the sheep. John 10:1-2, NKJV

These were the exact words of Jesus that I quoted to open up my conversation with the campus fellowship pastor when I sneaked away from the counseling session my senior pastor's wife was having with the ladies after her wonderful ministration on that fateful day, to go and make my intentions known to him concerning my desire toward his assistant pastor. After all, it was more of a women's affair and my presence wasn't really needed, so why not make better use of my time. I told him how I had fallen in love with Elliana over the period and how I would love to take his permission and blessings to date her towards marriage. Guys, let's learn to follow principles of the Kingdom where we have our citizenship. If you truly love her and you have her best interest at heart, then, **go through the gate. That is the only way she can truly become yours.** The gate is any authority instituted around her. It could be her parents, foster parents, pastor or other relations. Not going through these routes makes you unserious and irresponsible over the relationship. It means you are going through the window and scripturally, it makes you a thief and she can never be yours because you stole her. Stealing her leaves a loophole for the enemy to come in and break or strain that relationship.

The route I went through was that of getting her pastor involved because he was the nearest authority around her at that point. It is important to get a responsible third party involved in the picture of what you are about to embark on. It could be your own pastor or unit head, or even hers if she belongs to a different church. It could be her older sibling or even her trusted friend. Tell somebody you can hold yourself accountable to, it will go a long way in making you respect and treat her nicely. But, if you go through the window to steal her, you may end up at some point thinking you don't owe anybody any explanation on what you do to her or how you treat her.

"Thank you, man of God, for giving me this honor and privilege. Elliana is one of my best hands in this campus ministry and right now I don't think she's in any relationship because of her desire to stay focused on God's work here. If there's any way I can best describe her; she is a very good, God-loving young lady and I give you my full consent and blessing, although there is still someone higher than me I would love you to get across to, if you can, to also get his blessing, our father in the Lord, the senior pastor of Action Faith Ministries here in Cotonou", explains Pastor Niyi. "And who could that be?" I asked. "Apostle Yemi Adefarasin". I took a brief pause and took a few seconds stare at the graceful and gentlemanly face of Pastor Niyi as I let out a loud giggle. "What is funny man of God?" as he asked with a perplexed and inquisitive look on his face as to why I bursted out laughing. It all looked suddenly to me like a case of Isaac's bride Rebecca being picked from his father's kindred. Apostle Yemi Adefarasin has always been a very close friend to my father in the Lord, my senior pastor, Bishop Oscar Ossai and they both are sons in ministry to Bishop Duncan Williams. Pastor Niyi couldn't help but stare in amazement as I thought to myself, how much God orders the steps of His children.

The steps of a good man are ordered by the LORD, and He delights in His ways. Psalm 37:23, NKJV

First, I wasn't going to have any problem about looking like a stranger to Apostle Yemi Adefarasin and secondly, once again, it felt to me like I was just about to pick a bride from my father's kindred. I remember a few months down the line when we had started dating and Apostle Yemi Adefarasin came to minister in City of Refuge Ministries, which was my home church then, my father in the Lord, Bishop Ossai, was walking him to his car after the ministration while I followed them closely as his armor bearer, I was by his side and he made a joke to my pastor saying "this is the young man that came to steal my daughter away from me" and all we could simultaneously do was to give it a big laugh as my Bishop told him that he was fully aware and in the picture of it. Guys, relationship and courtship is a serious thing and can be so beautiful and pure when you do it right. Just do it the right way.

All these put together, for me, were strong indications that the hand of God was in the whole arrangement and much later, during the preparation towards our wedding, when the enemy tried to come in as a flood against us through the several financial challenges and human resistance we encountered, it helped give me an inner sense of peace that God who is behind it all will finish that which He started. As a Kingdom citizen in a relationship, when you can't feel the hand of God with you, give it a pause and isolate yourself to pray and seek God's face further. It's very important to know God is with you all the way. In Exodus 33:15, Moses speaking to God said *"If your presence does not go with us, do not bring us up from here"*. Guys and ladies, this is a life time journey, you need to be sure God's Presence is with you.

Back to the campus, no sooner than we had gotten back to the hotel where we were lodged did I get my sister Yvonne to go help me call on her assistant pastor, letting her know that I would like to have a little chat with her. With a fixed mischievous grin on her face, knowing what I was up to, she hurried down stairs, back to the fellowship house which was not too far from the hotel, and with my senior pastor's wife a few doors away, it was going to be one of the most decisive moments of my life.

Hope deferred makes the heart sick, but a dream fulfilled is a tree of life. Proverbs 13:12, NLT

This was the scripture that gave me the confidence and boldness to have the prettiest angelic handiwork of God sit opposite me on the visitor's seat in my hotel room that fateful day while I opened up my heart and poured it out to her. And of course, I had prayed to God for favor with her just before she came in. Oh, you think that wasn't important? Well, if you have ever been in a relationship that went sour beyond your control, you will understand that it feels as if there are forces manipulating outcomes that you can't see but are almost tangible. These forces are responsible for the highest percentage of marital failures, broken homes and relationships. Have you experienced telling your partner or spouse something and then you discover that he or she was hearing something else? That is just one of many evidences of those forces of darkness at work, misrepresenting you and misinforming your partner. So guys please don't stop praying. Pray even when you don't think it's necessary to pray. Take charge of your life's affairs and environment in the place of consistent prayers.

Back at the hotel room, I told this lovely angel, now my wife, how love struck I got by her from the very first day my sister mentioned her to me in Nigeria and how I felt it so strongly in me that I have just finally found myself the woman of my dreams, even when I hadn't seen her. I told her how I had always had a good ability to be first in knowing what I want right from my childhood, which explains why I rarely waste time shopping even in the supermarkets. I told her how beyond her angelic beauty, I saw in her my soul mate and life's vision partner that would travel with me into greatness. While she was still staring at me with her keen, innocent sweet and naïve look, with a tint of indifference reflecting a quiet 'I don't know what to say' kind of expression, I made it clear that I would know no greater joy than to spend the rest of my life with her into eternity but, meanwhile, I was not asking her to walk down the aisle with me right away, but to give me an opportunity to date her. I remember letting her know that I was not the 'Thus sayeth the Lord, you're my wife' kind of minister, but I knew that just as the Spirit of God bears witness within us that we are the sons of God, I was so convinced in my spirit by the witness I had deep inside that I was finally home.

By the time I was done, we were both staring blankly at each other for a couple of seconds. The only words that came out from her mouth to break the silence were "Thank you for telling me how you feel about me, I'll go and think about it and get back to you". This answer that she gave me, even though with a flat and non-expressive look that was so difficult for me to read through, gave me a feeling of hope that got me all excited and singing all the way back to Nigeria in a way that Mama Ossai couldn't help asking "so how did it go?". She was aware of my mission before we travelled. Little did I realize that the journey had just begun, and so did the battles too.

(How To Know It's Him)

CHAPTER 4
A sign from God

The day finally came. I particularly looked forward to this event because we had never had a female guest minister in our fellowship before. Pastor Niyi had been on the phone with John a few times that morning getting updates from John as they progressed in their journey. Their last conversation was at the Seme border because the Nigerian telecom network on John's phone would lose its network coverage inside Benin Republic. When Pastor Niyi couldn't reach him on the phone anymore, we knew that they had successfully crossed the border and would be arriving in no time. I quickly dashed into my hostel to get something done when Pastor Niyi called me to mention that our guests had arrived and that he was in front of *Hotel Quinze Janvier* where we had booked rooms for them. I hurriedly left what I was doing to join them. The hotel was right across the street, opposite the University building. As I came out of the campus gate, crossing the very sandy street almost in slow motion because my shoes were sinking into the thick layer of sharp sand that stretched across the coastal city, especially the area where our school was located due to its proximity to the beach, I observed that John was standing in front of the hotel and was looking in my direction. I didn't see Mama Ossai when I looked up but I knew she would have been taken upstairs to her room as soon as she arrived. The ten foot or so stretch of road felt like forever to cross, knowing that someone was staring at me as if asking quietly "can I come and carry you across?" I felt watched, admired, like I was in a beauty pageant and my every step and body movement was under scrutiny. I couldn't keep my head up for too long walking on that road as my shoes sank into the sand at different depths with every step, giving me a very wobbly and unbalanced movement. As students, we were all used to this. My eyes were mostly on the ground most of the time and I would look side to side and forward, quickly in between. For every time I looked up, I would still see a smile in the distance beckoning to me and eagerly awaiting my arrival.

As I stepped up to the entrance, the smile on John's face got even wider, we gave each other a modest side hug as I smiled back and welcomed him. I could tell that if given the chance, he would have wanted to probably lift me off my feet and spin me, it was written all over his countenance. Pastor Niyi and a few of our fellowship leaders had been inside the hotel putting finishing touches to ensure our guest minister was comfortably settled in. They stepped out to where we stood to let John know that she, Mama Ossai, requested to see him. Pastor Niyi and the other leaders headed back to the fellowship house while John and I climbed upstairs together to the room as it was my intention to welcome her too. He knocked on her door and told her that I was also there to greet her. She asked us to come in, gave me a warm hug while I expressed how pleased we were to have her. She got John to help her with a certain task and politely requested for some privacy to pray and prepare for the first session of the seminar that evening. As we stepped out and went down the stairs, I informed him that I would also need to go immediately to get dressed and to ensure that my area of responsibility was not being neglected. I let him know that those in charge of welfare would also be bringing their lunch over soon, which he thanked me for. He watched me as I walked away on a more solid path by the edge of the road hardened by the constant pedestrian use. Knowing what I know now, he certainly would have longed to walk with me to the fellowship house and partake in any task I needed to handle as long as it earned him more time with me.

We ended the program at about eight o'clock at night. It was indeed a powerful session, our sisters were excited but I didn't have time to partake in anything going on around, my focus was to ensure things ran smoothly. The next session was scheduled for the next morning so as to afford John and our guest minister time to travel back early enough. A few of my co-leaders were heading the welfare team and their services were required at that point not mine so I had no business going to the hotel. Yvonne did try to get me to come with her but I was too busy sorting out the program for the next day to consider it. The morning after was going to be a life transforming one, not just for our fellowship members but for me as well; something I never expected happened that changed the course of events in my life. A seed was sown by the Holy Spirit that was going to germinate in months to come and grow into one of the most inspiring love stories written by God Himself.

We all came in early for the second session of the seminar. In no time, the hall was filled to capacity. Everyone took their seats as our guest minister stepped up to the podium to continue from where she stopped the night before. She paused to ask for a moment of privacy with the ladies from the few gentlemen who made up the administrative team in the house as the discussion was about to get up close and personal with the sisters. John was not left out. He was ushered into another room which we had converted into a mini-library and Book Club. The fellowship building was a duplex and was built in such a way that the top floor and ground floor were two separate apartments consisting of separate kitchens, living room spaces and ensuite bedrooms. It was designed in a way that it could be occupied by two different residents. The entire building was mostly occupied by fellowship members while the living room spaces were used for our services interchangeably. The dining room downstairs was demarcated with plywood and converted to the book club where John went into, to afford the ladies some privacy to talk. Like any other house, the dining room could be accessed through the kitchen and the leaders particularly liked to move in and out of the building through the back door which was still connected to the kitchen. It was a route I always took to quietly get things done without distracting any service in session. While the meeting was on, I had paper work to pick up from the library which made me take my usual route. As I stepped in through the already opened door and spotted John, something beyond the ordinary happened. It was as if time stood still. A gush of enthusiasm overwhelmed me, filling me with joy, excitement, butterflies, insight, certainty, satisfaction and an adrenalin rush all at the same time. All these feelings accompanied by a wave of calmness and joy in my spirit flooded my entire being. In a split second, my eyes scrolled from his black cowboy boots to his long stretch of Jeans met by a tucked in blue lumberjack shirt bridged at the waist by a black leather belt. John was standing tall and looking at the books on the bookshelf before him with rapt attention and was unaware of my presence. His sleeves were rolled up half way as I noticed him trying to pull out a book that caught his interest. It felt like time stopped in that moment, like I had been transported into another realm. There must have been angelic singing in the background that I didn't hear because it felt that glorious. Sparks were flying deep in my heart as another wave of something I had never felt in my entire life welled up within me; it was pure undiluted love. I got a witness and a knowing inside me. As if I was speaking to myself, I felt my heart say "this is the man I want to marry, this is my husband". Despite being glued to a spot in silence as I looked at him in a new light, probably for just a few seconds that felt like hours, he immediately turned his head swiftly realizing he wasn't alone. He gave me the most welcoming and captivating smile I had ever seen; he always welcomed me so happily that I felt celebrated every time I was around him. This time, the smile had a different effect on me. I snapped out of it as quickly as I could and asked if he was comfortable, with my usual courteous but serious minded look, as I walked towards the table where the documents were. I asked if I could get him something to drink which he politely refused. He went on to compliment the hard work and dedication I had put into the success of the event that he said he admired. I thanked him and quickly dashed out for fear of not being able to conceal my emotions any longer. There was no doubt, something supernatural and special had just happened to me that I had never experienced before. I walked out of there so fast that I was sure he would have wondered what was going on with me. I couldn't understand it myself. What I felt was like an awakening, it made me want to leap for joy. I had never seen a guy and thought of him as my husband, ever, nor had a man brought such a strong magnetic attraction and conviction to my heart. The entire incident was all that occupied my mind even after I returned to the service. I couldn't explain what had just happened, I was trying to make sense of the sudden transition and astronomical speed with which my emotions switched from a neutral and carefree mindset to an overwhelming deep experience of love that filled me with such excitement.

Should I Say Yes?

The event rounded up on a very high note, everyone was caught up in the euphoria; even after the seminar, they all hung around chit chatting away within the premises. Our ministers were driven back to the hotel to freshen up and prepare for their trip back to Nigeria. Pastor Niyi and I climbed up the hotel stairway a little later after we were sure that our guests had eaten lunch and rested a little. John dashed to and fro the hotel hallway trying to get their entire luggage down to the reception. I stood aside as I watched him move swiftly like a man on a mission. I still remember myself savoring the scent of his cologne that rose into the air as he walked past me. I remember taking deep breaths of a sea breeze fragrance that blew on me from the white track suit with sky blue trimmings he had changed into. I couldn't believe what was happening to me, I couldn't believe I was thinking and acting like this.

Pastor Niyi had joined him to move their luggage into the vehicle waiting at the entrance. After a while, John walked back in my direction alone and requested to speak with me in private. Pastor Niyi had obviously taken a stroll down stairs, intentionally. Apparently, he was aware of everything, which I found out much later; John had opened up to him on his intentions towards me and sought his blessing as the shepherd of the house to ask to date me. I consider that an honorable step a proof of his seriousness about his intentions. He proved, by that singular action, to be a man under authority and who respects authority. For a man to respect and open up their feelings for you to any form of authority over you, be it pastoral or parental, is one way you can know a man who is not out to play games. This is not the only prerequisite that proves a man's feelings for you, however, it is a sure way to know how serious he is about being with you and how much you're worth to him. If a man truly loves you, he will tell the world about you and will want to get formally introduced to authority figures in your life. When he is not out to play games, he will prove his pure motive and seriousness by coming after you through the 'front door'. Any guy that leaves you guessing what he feels towards you because he can't seem to be straight forward about where the relationship is headed is not ready for a commitment. Do not waste a second of your precious time on him.

I learnt something simple but profound growing up and that is; "don't do anything you don't want to remember". You ought to be calculative when going into relationships; too many trials and errors will only leave you emotionally drained. It will also leave you with too many bad memories that will be a part of your story for the rest of your life. If you end up in bed with him as well, you can't pretend to yourself that it didn't happen; you can never erase that memory. And you know what, we live in such a small world, much smaller than you think; the chances of crossing paths with someone you have not only dated but had an affair with is very high. In fact, in the future, you will be so glad you didn't build relationship memories with so many guys when you met them because now they have become colleagues, friends of your friends or unavoidable in some work or church environment. Choose who you date as if your life depends on it. Don't date because you want to gather experience, you don't need it; you only need to find the right man and he'll be worth more than a thousand failed relationships. So you want to make sure you see seriousness in him, a clear vision of where the relationship is headed and his ability to tell spiritual and parental authority around you about the relationship. Despite all this, your personal sensitivity and ability to discern is still key in figuring how genuine he is.

I went into the room with the door ajar behind me. We both sat and down and I listened as he opened up the conversation. John was in love, there was no doubt about it. He mentioned how he was attracted to me and blown away by everything about me. He also told me in the sweetest way ever how he wasn't planning to beat around the bush, how he gets into a relationship with marriage in mind as the ultimate goal and how he had seen everything he wanted in a wife in me. He was direct, he wasn't joking; he wanted to marry me. I guess I was stunned by his resolve so much that the things that had been embedded in my subconscious concerning men began to rear their heads up. I began to question his show of sincerity. I began to raise an eyebrow at how much he expressed his love for me, I asked myself if he was pretending or if he had a hidden motive. I remember learning as a teenager that when a guy is acting like he is very much in love with you, that is when you should suspect him. How much further away from the truth could that be?! So how else should a guy show that he loves a woman before she can believe him? Is it easier to believe a man who is proud and haughty, giving her a taste of his love in little pea sizes? Unfortunately, a number of women, African women especially, find it hard to receive love because they never grew up around openly expressed love. I've heard that a number of women actually prefer a tough guy who doesn't smile much, who doesn't get all mushy and over affectionate; they feel being an 'over pampering and sweet' type of guy means a man is weak. Well, what do we call that? I'd suggest you choose a man who will treat you like a queen a million times over. With the overwhelming experience and sign I had a few hours earlier and the type of person I had observed him to be, I should have known what questions to ask myself but out of nowhere came the seeds of lies that had been planted years back which I never confronted and dealt with. Now I know better, that is why I chose to write this book. Even if it's just one person that gets it right and ends up finding their perfect match by reading and applying what they have learnt in this book, I will be fulfilled.

Guess what, after almost having an out of body experience when my eyes met John in that library, I still gave him some flat response to his proposal; I told him how much I appreciated his openness about his feelings towards me and that I would give it a thought. Women! We are something, aren't we! I look back today and wonder what was going on in my head and why in the world I was cold to his request when I was sitting right in front of the man I felt like making my husband just some hours ago. Here he was, openly declaring his love for me and instead of being a little more receptive, that was the least I could do even if I didn't want to give it away very quickly that I felt the same way, but all I could say was "thank you for sharing your feelings with me, I really appreciate your openness to me. I'll think about it". I'm bringing it up because it is very important that we address the situations that make us stiff-necked as women, the reason we play hard-to-get to the detriment of our own marital success and progress. It is understandable that most of the time, it is because we are trying to protect ourselves from making a mistake. However, the root cause is a mental stronghold of limitation over the years and thought patterns that have become instilled in us about relationships and how to deal with them. We learnt even before we realized that we were learning that men can never be trusted. We learnt that we had to put up our guard by not showing how we feel or else we stand the chance of being taken for granted. We learnt to always keep the backdoor open or at least let the man know that the backdoor is unlocked in case he messes up and one needed to jump out. The Bible says:

Do not be conformed to this world, but be transformed by the renewing of your mind, that you may prove what is that good and acceptable and perfect will of God. Romans 12:2, NKJV

We must unlearn these things. We must allow the Holy Spirit to change the way we think and break the strongholds of the world's philosophy of what a relationship should be like and how we're meant to build it. The world's way can never be God's way. The new age way can never be God's way. They may come close in some areas but there will always be erroneous beliefs, doctrines and philosophies that contradict the Bible. There are quite a number of entertainment stars who have something to say about relationships, a lot of Christians listen to them and some try to apply their lessons but if we weigh the overall statistics of their failed marriages and the rate of infidelity within that clique, those are enough signs to show that they are not getting it right and what they are preaching is not the truth you need. If you choose to listen to old folks and family members too, you might be in danger of receiving counsel and philosophies built on an inductive approach to every relationship issue, where broad generalizations are made based on one experience. So, if one man cheats on them, it means that all men cheat. If they experienced past hurt, pains and a broken heart, then all relationships will end up like that. Unfortunately, the problem here is that they never got totally healed from the experience they had and they failed to discover that no true and lasting healing takes place outside of God. The power of God is the only force that has the capacity to pull down mental strongholds we have due to negative memories or past unscriptural philosophies (see 2Corinthians 10:4-5). What you ought to believe is

His opinion about you and the situation. If truth is not one hundred percent based on the Word of God, it has become perverted and will not yield the result of freedom that the Word of God promises. Besides a few exceptions, these same old folks grew up in an environment where love is expressed as a tough tool of discipline. They, consequently, grew up with an inability to be lovingly expressive, to let down their guards around people or even apologize when they are wrong, which they take pride in and consider a show of emotional strength. They grew up viewing it as normal and didn't realize that things could be done differently. Don't waste time blaming them for who you have become today, knowing now that they didn't know any better. Rather, no matter the cause of what you are going through right now, take out time and think of the solution that can bring the change you need and begin to practice it daily. Choose to focus on the solution, not the problem. Break that evil emotional cycle and tell yourself that all mistakes in your family stops with you in Jesus name. Choose to be different, choose to be flexible and pliable in the hands of the Holy Spirit, choose to open up yourself to learn how to love and receive love. There's no better way to learn to love than by getting a revelation of how much LOVE loves you. He is Love and you need to ask the Holy Spirit to reveal the love of the Father to you, for you to become whole. If you don't allow God to work on you, it will hinder you from bringing out the best in your relationship and instead of walking beside your beloved, you will find yourself on a watchtower with a rifle waiting for a wrong move from him. With this mindset, the relationship had already ended before it started. If your fiancé has opened up his heart to you without the fear of being vulnerable or taken for granted, then you owe it to him to appreciate that character trait so he can be assured that his heart is secure with you. You want to be able to reciprocate using words of affirmation and other love languages that are within the confines of what is Biblically acceptable – because if you encourage such behaviour, he will keep it up, even in marriage. There's nobody who, when applauded and complimented for a specific thing they've done, will not be encouraged to do it again; because we are beings drawn to praise, thanksgiving, appreciation and celebration just like our Father in Heaven. Your fiancé is, consciously and unconsciously trying to establish a pattern of actions and behaviours around you. If you approve of and celebrate him for something he did that made you happy and excited, he will want to repeat it again and again because, except if he's not the man for you, it brings a man pleasure and joy to do the things he knows will make you love and respect him more.

My attitude on the day John opened up about his feelings towards me was as a result of things I had learnt about men growing up and other poisonous counsel gotten from here and there. I am not saying that I should have jumped on him and said 'Yes' at that moment; the issue wasn't necessarily about my physical response. The chain of thoughts that went through my head while he spoke, that shaped my attitude when I responded, was a sign that I had absorbed and internalized the very information I criticized. How open I was to these counsels was primarily my choice, then, how much I let it influence my decisions was also my choice. You cannot stop negative information reaching you, we're almost being drowned by it in today's world, but you can limit it drastically by restricting your contact with its sources and choosing what's right, if you know the right tool to filter information through. If I had known that the Word of God was the only filter I needed, I would have long crosschecked what I heard against what God's Word says and would have duly discarded what was wrong before it found a foothold on my mind. But for the mercies of God, these ungodly counsels came close to thwarting my marital destiny. In summary, the need to distinguish between the right information and the wrong should be priority when seeking your life partner in order to ensure that you are positioned to make the right choice and follow God's leading. I know now that it was the Holy Spirit that was behind the spontaneous feeling in my heart in that library, but I had a bigger giant to contend with; the information in my head.

(How To Know It's *Her*)

CHAPTER 5
Is This The End?

Back home in Lagos, we continued as friends through phone calls and text messages. I didn't push nor put pressure on her for an answer to my proposal neither did she also make any reference to it. We would rather pick on different topics that would help us know more about each other, that was when I was able to share my passion and vision in the audio-visual media with her, and only to discover that she also had a passion and a calling in that area too. To cap it up, she hosted a couple of CBN's music segment known as One Cubed and was partly working with the media unit in her home church. For me, this was a further confirmation from God on our compatibility, especially against the back drop of how I had had to endure a few heart breaks from my past relationships majorly because of my choice of career path and vision. It was so bad at some point that I felt my choice of career and vision were jinxed. Suffice to say it was at the point when the Nigerian movie industry was trying to buy a share of the people's interest and find its footing in the country's economy. It was a volatile field to be in that required a huge price to be paid by anyone, this could only be described as somebody taking a vow of poverty.

Guys, every man must not necessarily have to date a woman in his line of career or vocation, but it is very important that the woman you want to spend the rest of your life with is someone who loves what you do for a living or better still can comprehend your vision of where you are going. Amos 3:3 says can two walk together without agreeing? I remember in a past relationship just before I met my wife, the lady was trying to manipulate me towards getting a job as a banker, and meanwhile banking was one of my worst nightmares for a choice of career even while I was in the University. And this brings me to the point on why you need to know each other considerably well before advancing towards the altar. Be sure nothing is acting as a smoke screen that could mislead you or your partner into making a wrong hurried decision. I can imagine if I was from a financially privileged home while trying to pursue a career in film and television production, chances are, one of those girls in my past would have gone ahead to get married to me without thinking twice because of the comfort and not necessarily because she loves my choice of career or vision pursuit as a film maker. And that would have been akin to one of those parables of Jesus in the Matthew 7:24-27 that talks about not building your house on a sandy foundation where the rains descended and the floods came and the winds blew and beat on the house; and it fell. Build your relationships on a solid rock! Not just the solid rock of God's Word alone but also the solid rock of truth about yourselves.

Beware of Friends

A couple of weeks after my trip to Benin Republic, while having one of our frequent telephone conversations, she told me she was going to be travelling home to Abuja briefly en route Lagos as usual and of course, I didn't wait for her to ask, I quickly offered to pick her up from the bus park arrivals to any place of her destination. Every opportunity presented for me to see her at that time could only be described as a rare privilege of taking a trip to paradise and back; she was and is still my paradise on earth till Jesus comes. I have always told her that if God gives humans ten life time opportunities to live and make different choices in each lifetime, I will still choose to marry her over and over without wanting to ever discover what a relationship could be with another woman.

I got to the bus park on that sunny and humid afternoon and found her standing and waving frantically at me as I was trying to locate her beautiful face and complexion from the crowd of travellers just arriving Lagos from Benin Republic. I quickly dashed over to where she was standing to give her a warm greeting and pick her luggage into the vehicle only for me to notice a young lady standing beside her with a smile on her face too that was obviously sending a signal to me that they were together, even before she got introduced as her close friend and also a travel companion from school to Abuja. I took the hand stretched out and pleasantly exchanged greetings with her as I picked both of their luggage and we all headed for where I parked my car. While on our way to her friend's cousin's place where they were to sleep over before proceeding on their journey to Abuja the next morning, I picked up a feeling on her friend that wasn't quite pleasant. Besides the irritation she was causing me by her continuous interjections on my every attempt to strike a conversation with my queen-to-be, she was so domineering in a way that made me feel sick. It looked like every conversation was more between the two of us that just met each other a few hours back, for crying out loud, rather than Elliana. She barely gave my angel an opportunity to talk right from where she was seated at the back seat or even hold a straight conversation with me. I instantly sensed it in my spirit that she was going to be trouble, I couldn't figure out exactly in what way but I saw in her, a friend who had a more domineering personality than my gentle and soft spoken wife-to-be. I saw someone who could be a strong influence on her decisions, especially where dating each other was concerned and I could only hope and pray that it was not going to be a negative one. And later on down the line, my hunch and feelings about her were proven right.

We arrived at their destination late into the evening hours, after wasting almost two hours of driving time heading in the wrong direction, thanks to the third party dominance that couldn't even allow us breathing space to communicate, and to think that she was the one meant to give directions because it was her cousin's place. Anyway, by the time we located the house, Elliana was too tired to hold any private conversation with me, which I was looking forward to because before she left school, we had agreed over a phone conversation that we would have that talk when I would get to hear her answer to my proposal. And so, we said good night and farewell with a promise that she would call me and give me an answer when she got to Abuja. Little did I know that the devil was buying himself time to set to work.

Listen guys and ladies particularly, don't let a third party into the details of a relationship you hold in high value at an early stage, no matter how close you both are and no matter how much you trust him or her. And even when you need to do that, pray about it before you do so. Sometimes, the devil lurks around looking for any available vessel to use to scatter a good relationship that is headed for the altar.

For a couple of days after Elliana arrived Abuja, we kept our communication going, more via text messaging and I avoided putting further pressure on her to get an answer to my proposal, after all, I was still enjoying the relationship between us the way it was anyway. I had no idea that the turn of events was about to take a different dimension. I usually would go to spend the weekends in my uncle's house with my cousins at this period and on one of those weekend trips while I was in the living room with my cousins watching a TV show, the familiar ring tone I customized to her number caught my attention. I quickly picked my phone and dashed to the room where I could get some privacy from my cousins, and thank God I did because that evening turned out to be the darkest day of my life as I couldn't help walking into the kitchen where my aunt was preparing dinner to lean over her shoulder and cry. She knew immediately that something was terribly wrong and it had to do with Elliana. She knew the entire story and was believing with me that things would work out. "It's okay, don't worry, I know, she gave you a NO, right?" she said. I nodded a yes as she walked me into her room to calm me down and hear me out well enough on how and what exactly she said. That evening, I remember clearly how it felt like a part of me left me and how it felt as if life was never going to be the same for me again. I sat down with my auntie and narrated how our phone conversation went, how Elliana told me she wasn't prepared to go into dating anyone then and she didn't think she was going to be prepared anytime soon from that time. Besides, she had a different picture of the kind of man she wanted to date whenever she felt ready and didn't think I fitted into that picture. My auntie who had been looking with intense concentration took a serious long stare at me and calmly said, "she's been distracted by something or someone. She will come out of it and come around, don't worry". "And how would you know that, mummy" I asked. I called her mummy because of her age and motherly figure but we related more like friends. My aunt was a romantic at heart. She never wasted time to ask me about my relationship life and my plans to settle down in marriage when we met after having not seen each other for years because she believed in one finding their true love and also believed I wasn't married because I had not found 'the one' yet. We could sit down for hours and talk on relationships and love and how she met my uncle and how much they were in love with each other. She would tell me how she let go of a relationship she had because of my uncle. She was just a sweet motherly figure who was very fond of me, which explains why she was interested in my relationship with Elliana, especially when she saw how in love I was with her. "It's too sudden" she said. "You two were getting along so well for this sudden and abrupt shift. Besides, if you didn't fit into the kind of man she wants to be with, she wouldn't come this far with you" she added assertively. " A woman knows from the very beginning when a guy wants to date her and from the way you described her, she is a good girl and wouldn't waste your time coming this far with you as a friend without an intention to have you date her" she continued. "Something happened and we can only pray for God to reveal it and bring her back on track, if she's meant for you, which I think she is". After a little pause, my aunt concluded "she will come back". "I will join you in prayers" she said with so much love and concern coming through her voice.

The importance of family cannot be overemphasized. One of the reasons people experience mental and emotional breakdowns in life is largely due to their self-isolation away from their families. When all the chips are down, church sometimes is not even your nearest place of finding succor and comfort. In fact, church can sometimes be the cause of your hurt. Family is always your best bet and could be your last wall of defense. I have seen people who turn their backs on their families over relationship matters and when they get hurt or abused over time in the name of relationship, they have no place to run back to seek help and support from. Do not abandon your family; they could sometimes be your last wall of defense to fall back on.

It's Not Over Till You Win

"John, where are you?" came the familiar calm but assertive tone of my senior pastor's voice, Bishop Ossai, as I picked my call the following morning. I had barely caught enough sleep from the heart break I got the previous day, as I kept tossing and turning on the bed with a lot of sleep hallucinations and countless dreams. It probably would have been worse, but for my good hearted aunt's motherly and comforting words and prayers. "In Festac town Daddy" I replied my pastor. "Festac town doing what?" he enquired with a surprised tone. "How soon can you get here, we need to meet and get prepared for a journey to Enugu State tomorrow". For a period of time, he had been talking and preaching about the need for Christians in Nigeria to get more involved in governance and the polity of the nation and so for him, an opportunity had just presented itself to contest for the House of Representatives under the federal constituency in Enugu State. As his armor bearer and personal assistant, I had to tag along. For me, it was an opportunity to embark on an adventure into the world of politics. It was also a much needed distraction to get my mind off Elliana.

My stay in Enugu State, located in the eastern part of Nigeria was for about a month. I was lost in the intriguing world of Nigerian politics that I did not make any effort to call or check on Elliana for two straight weeks. The memory of our last conversation always brought back the feeling of a part of me being severed and I saw this trip with my Bishop as an opportunity to heal from the pain. It was my first time of getting up close and involved in the dynamics of political campaigns, party meetings, coordination of different groups, meeting with village traditional rulers and different stake holders of partisan politics within the constituency. We were virtually busy round the clock with an almost incomprehensible movement from one point to the other in such a way that made me respect my Bishop's level of energy, drive and determination.

In all these activities, however, I realized that there was a feeling of emptiness and void somewhere in the cold recess of my heart. I couldn't but tell myself the truth that it all had to do with Elliana. It got so cold and lonely in there that I couldn't help it anymore but to give her a call by the third week of my stay in Enugu State. The familiar sweet edge on the tone of her voice on the evening I called brought back a sudden rush of memories that made me realize how much I had missed her. By the end of our conversation, which was nostalgia driven on my part, with a pounding desire to divulge all my recent adventures with Bishop Ossai, I felt a ray of hope and light at the end of the dark tunnel I had been going through and somewhere in my heart I felt strongly again the machinations of the devil at work and the need to pray more concerning our relationship. Guys hear me, the Bible says that;

For though we walk in the flesh, we do not war according to the flesh. For the weapons of our warfare are not carnal but mighty in God for pulling down strongholds, casting down arguments and every high thing that exalts itself against the knowledge of God, bringing every thought into captivity to the obedience of Christ, 1 Corinthians 10:3-5, NKJV

That is why we need to be sensitive to the Holy Spirit at every point in our lives, which includes even when dating or trying to get the right woman for your life's purpose journey. Beyond being a Kingdom citizen, one must make a conscious effort to become friends with the Holy Spirit. The Bible says that He will guide us into all truth. We need Him, we need the Spirit of God to guide and navigate us through life.

In the following two weeks that succeeded the campaigns, the elections had come and gone and we were on our way back to Lagos. My pastor and the entire aspiring candidates in the political party he belonged to had all lost out in the election that was clearly rigged with assorted and sophisticated methods of sharp electioneering malpractices by the ruling party. I had Elliana on my mind almost throughout the long stretch of hours on our return journey back to Lagos. We had only communicated a few more times after I put my first call through to her in Enugu State and then, on one of those calls, she told me she would appreciate it if I stopped calling her 'angel', a pet name I had gotten used to calling her since we became friends. I couldn't understand what was happening, I couldn't comprehend what was pulling her heart further away from me. It drove the feeling of hurt and pain deeper when her statement made it glaring that she didn't want me to draw closer to her beyond just a friend. At that point, I began to consider letting go, calling it quits in my heart and disconnecting my emotions from her. I told myself that I wasn't going to call her again and when I got to Lagos, I was just going to find a way to get busy with my visions and allow time to heal me, like it had always been with the other ladies I met before her. And almost as if my Pastor could read my thoughts where he was sitting next to me in the luxury bus we were traveling in, he suddenly interrupted my thoughts with a reminder of his upcoming investiture into the office of a Bishop in the next couple of weeks and how he would like me to meet a nice African American young lady who was one of the ministers in Bishop Willie Blunt's church. She was going to be among the entourage from the United States for his investiture. Instantly, I felt a jolt of joy and excitement rush through my body like a sudden transmission of electricity wave. At least, I thought, for my pain of losing Elliana, God seemed to have provided me with an instant replacement. So it seemed until some days later after we had arrived Lagos, then it dawned on me that clones are not that easily replaceable.

Back in Lagos, life continued as usual except for one thing, a feeling of an empty void deep inside of me that gave me a strange sense of incompleteness and no matter how much I tried to shake it off or how much I pretended to be happy and to move on with my life, it was just still there waiting for the littlest iota of sobriety in me to take over my soul like the dark clouds of a heavy rain about to fall in the middle of a thick dark night. The more I tried to draw away from Elliana by pushing her to the recess of my mind, the more it seemed like drawing away from my own self. I had never found it this hard in all my past dating experiences to push the thought of relationships that couldn't work away from my mind like this one. In fact, if anything, I had always made boast to my friends that when it comes to letting go of a relationship that wasn't working, I had the grace of letting go easily. But this was totally different and I didn't know what exactly it was that was making it so hard for me to even shake her off my mind.

I came back home from work on one of the afternoons, after a few weeks had gone by without a word of communication with Elliana despite always carrying her around in my soul every day from dawn to dusk. And just as I was about settling down on the bed to catch a little rest from the day's exhaustion, I heard the still small voice of the Holy Spirit right inside my heart tell me "If you miss this God's gift for you

– because Elliana is God's gift to you and your wife from the foundation of the earth – and if you miss her, it will take you another cycle of time to get someone close to her, not even exactly but at least close to her". "Why are you giving up so easily", He said to me. "I have seen you pursue other goals with so much tenacity and courage, why is this one any different?" This moment I had with the Holy Spirit marked the second time in a long row that I will be hearing something very close to an audible voice right inside my head. It was small, still and quiet but yet audible and clear. The first time I heard the voice of the Holy Spirit in this manner was when I had to change churches from The Redeemed Christian Church of God to City of Refuge Ministries International. I needed to hear such a clear instruction from God to move and now, this time, concerning Elliana, I didn't waste a second too. Immediately after that encounter, I picked up the phone and called Elliana and to my greatest amazement, the excitement I heard in the tone of her voice that day marked for both of us the beginning of an experience of what I can only describe as "Heaven on Earth".

(How To Know It's Him)

CHAPTER 5
Love is Deliberate

I have never believed in love at first sight, I have never believed that love is blind too. I believe that even if you get attracted to someone physically on your first meeting, you should be smart enough to tell yourself that you need time to get to know this person. I am also of the opinion that we can willingly choose to overlook some faults that we feel are too small to stop us from having a relationship with someone we love, especially if they are inconsequential in the equation of what we should be looking out for in a potential life partner and what we have on our 'priorities' list. It's more understandable to say you chose to overlook than to pretend that you cannot see the faults. Pardon me if I sound too direct but it's the way some women have pretended to themselves that they can't see the giant red flag in front of them warning them and then they go ahead to plunge into or remain in an abusive relationship that leaves me wondering. It's painful to think that there are people going through this. It would be unrealistic and foolish to assume that a guy has certain good character traits simply because he looks a certain way or because he displays only one major character trait that he uses to capture your heart all the time. It would be foolish to let one captivating action blind you from seeing the horns on his head and the three-pronged fork in his hand. I think that this is a case of misleading oneself and completely basing one's decision on assumption and lies.

I have also never believed in, promoted or bought into the idea that God picks a spouse for you without your opinion. My question would be; what does it make God look like when some people say that He forced them to marry someone they weren't in love with? He is not a killjoy. No way! Not the God that I know. Our Father God wants your happiness more than you want it for yourself. To see you happy and fulfilled in life is His reward for being a good Father, just like any earthly parent, only a million times greater, I would say.

"You fathers- if your children ask for a fish, will you give them a snake instead? Or if they ask for an egg, do you give them a scorpion? Of course not! So if you sinful people know how to give good gifts to your children, how much more will your heavenly Father give the Holy Spirit to those who ask Him" Luke 11:11-13, NLT

So when men come saying 'Thus sayeth the Lord, you are my wife', that is truly unfair to the lady. It is highly manipulative and can be likened to a bully's approach to conformity, knowing fully well that everybody wants to obey when they hear 'God said'. We ought to be careful to say 'God said' when He hasn't, we will be held accountable for every idle word we speak. God is your manufacturer, He knows how He knitted you together in your mother's womb according to Psalm 139 and He specifically designed you to fulfill a certain purpose and marry a certain person. When you discover that you are passionate about a certain profession, business, lifestyle, hobby or a type of man in your heart, know that He is the One that wired you that way so you can become what He created you to be.

Delight yourself in the LORD and he shall give you the desires of your heart. Psalm 37:4, NKJV

He also created a perfect match for you and has hidden the love for that person in your heart. When you meet that person, that part of your heart begins to awaken and glow with the glory of victory. Everything about your love life will suddenly begin to take shape and make sense. In all this, He gives you room to enjoy the process of waiting for that person, meeting the person, knowing and falling in love with that person and choosing to spend the rest of your life with them. If He could risk giving us the free will to love or not love Him, even when He knows that He is the only God for us and we are His beloved children, why would He force us to love someone else?

When I got that witness in my spirit that I had met my husband, I was bubbling with joy within and I was also physically attracted to him. Please note that we weren't strangers, I had been in touch with him and we had had a number of conversations together on the phone before then that had given me an insight into his personality to a good extent. The attraction I also felt that day in the library made me wonder where my eyes had been all along. It wasn't mystical. The friendship built up to a certain point before I began to see him in a new light. After John and Mama Ossai left, that night, I remember sharing the unusual experience I had excitedly with one of my sisters and dear friend in the Lord. I pondered on my response to his request and I felt I had done the right thing by telling him that I would give it a thought. I was only being careful, not wanting to make such a crucial decision while feeling emotionally high. I wanted to be sure that what I was feeling was real.

Discern Your Friends

Unfortunately, the time gap I gave was just enough for the enemy to want to destroy what God had ordained for me. Within this time frame, a lot had happened. I had written my exams and was preparing to start writing my final year dissertation. I had to travel to Abuja and was meant to return to Cotonou after a month to pick up details on the dissertation project from my professor which would require my immediate return again to Abuja to commence a research towards it. I was constantly on the road and was going to be spending more time at home working since my project supervisor was also based in Abuja. The easiest strategy for the enemy to apply at this point was for him to use my closest friend then as a tool of discouragement. My friend and I spent almost every single day together; she could almost read my thoughts, that was how close we were. She knew from the way I spoke that I was very interested in John but she seemed not to like the idea and attempted a few things within her capacity to stop me from making that final decision. One example would be the amount of effort she put into trying to get me reconnected to a previous relationship which I had completely moved on from. She spoke in derogatory terms about John that made it obvious that she was not on his team. Interestingly, her comments and thought were related to me as though she was receiving a word of knowledge concerning him. Being a spiritually minded person myself and one who was treading carefully, wanting to be sure that I was going to make the right decision if I ever decided to kick off a relationship with him, her opinion further threw me off balance launching me into a state of confusion.

I knew what I felt that day at the seminar when I looked at John and felt differently about him but fear and uncertainty had quietly crept into my soul from all the junk I was ingesting from my friend. Here I was, beginning to convince myself that I was being misled by my own emotions. I was trusting to a fault. I wasn't the type to rush into making friends but once I did, it was hard to convince me to think negatively about that person. My friend was very God-conscious, her love for Him and His work could be seen by everyone around her and she did everything humanly possible to draw closer to Him. I had always been a God-chaser all my growing up life as well and this attribute particularly drew me closer to her and made our friendship grow strong within a short space of time. I began to get uncomfortable with her style of hearing God and doing God's work when I began to observe that a number of spiritual guidance and instructions that came from her only plunged me or those around into some type of complicated mess. I also observed that her subtle disapproval and indirect discouragement were reflected in friendly persuasions for me to pick interest in other people I would naturally not consider my type. It was obvious, with time, that her emotions were being communicated as revelations from God. I am making reference to this to particularly help someone who always depends on third parties to either hear from God for them or help them make very important life's decisions. My personal sensitivity and ability to tell myself the truth was what I used in weighing the accuracy of the revelations she gave and that was what delivered me from losing out on God's agenda for me. The worst position anybody can ever find themselves in is to have a friend who seizes the closeness you share to manipulate your decisions against your will because of their personal interest or because they feel they can and I've also seen where people followed such manipulative counsel that eventually ended them up in a marital disaster and nightmare, because their decision was influenced by a third party. The harsh reality that you cannot deny to yourself is that you and only you are responsible for taking the final decision, for choosing to follow a certain counsel or choosing to follow your heart. No matter how much anyone influences you, they can only push you to the brink or edge of decision making, the final responsibility still lies on you to make the move or not. When you make choices with this at the back of your mind, there's a greater chance that you will be more cautious and determined to make the right choice.

John and I had been in touch on phone all along. I knew that with every call, he looked forward to when I would give him a reply to his dating proposal. His calls were always like a ray of sunlight into my day. His voice was always cheerful, he was fun to chat with and his optimism was contagious. He would always throw in a word of encouragement, it made me always wonder if he could see through me when he would say things that I just needed to hear to calm a worry or fear I was feeling within. I had grown attached to those calls that I looked forward to them, to hear the loving way he would ask to make sure that everything and everyone around me was okay. At some point, I had to wake myself up and ask, "Who was I fooling?" I couldn't keep enjoying those wonderful qualities when I was letting myself believe it wasn't meant to be. What I thought I felt for him had been corrupted by bad advice. I felt it was time to speak with him, it was time to let him off the hook, to free his mind from thinking that there was a future between us. I didn't want to raise his hopes with all those happy phone chats while I knew that it was only going to be short lived. The question on my mind was how I was going to say it for it to be convincing enough to get a dogged goal-getter like him to back off. His determined and passionately driven nature would not allow him throw it all away. I had to figure how to knock it in to him that it wasn't going to work.

On the day I decided to voice out, I received his call as usual but I had it all planned out. I was going to tell him that I had prayed about it and I didn't feel it was meant to be – "that alone should be good enough to discourage a Christian brother", I thought to myself. Of course, around that period, I had been praying about this decision too but I wasn't sure about what I was hearing anymore, because my mind had become divided between what I had been sensing personally versus what someone else was sensing for me. But just to seal it all up and close up any chances of this topic arising again, I was going to also add that he didn't fit into the picture of what I wanted in a man. By the time I was done, from the tone of his voice, I knew I had succeeded. I hung up the phone that day with a very deep cold breath. I told myself that I did it for his own good, I didn't want to waste his time on a merry-go-round type of friendship, besides, I was led to believe that there was gloom and doom lurking at the corner if I bothered to still go ahead. I was being ruled by the fear of the unknown and my friend succeeded in helping me make that fear my own.

When I told her what I had done, she expressed how happy she was for me and was satisfied that I listened to her. I didn't know if I was happy or sad. I felt like someone had pulled a plug in my heart, like something had withered suddenly within me. I couldn't explain it but I had lost something and I didn't know what it was. Weeks went by without any communication from him. I began to tell myself that this was how it was meant to be, I convinced myself that the earlier I allowed my heart let him go, the less painful it would be. I decided to keep an indifferent outlook and to carry on with my activities as if nothing ever happened. It was a deep sense of denial; denial of what I truly felt, denial of what I thought I had found, denial of what had just happened and denial that I was shaken or moved by it.

Dealing with Breakups and Heartbreaks

In life, it is quite easy to know when God is speaking to you because what God has spoken to you will always come with an atmosphere of peace around it. In my case, where John and I were concerned, the relationship that was about to kick off had been truncated by the enemy and produced emotions associated to a breakup. This is because, through spiritual sensitivity, I had a witness in my spirit that the relationship was meant to be and having to push myself to make a contrary decision not to go into it turned my life upside down. I thank God that much later, my willingness to be flexible and to flow with the Spirit of God became my saving grace! However, there's a thing or two every lady who has been in my shoes or experienced a breakup or heartbreak that was as a result of a failed relationship must know. A break up is one of the most dreaded parts of any relationship that nobody wants to experience. Sadly, it is something almost everyone that has ever dated or gotten married has been through simply because the world of relationships come with such experiences attached to it. I believe it is possible for breakups to happen without leaving a woman heartbroken. The decision between two individuals in a relationship to discontinue dating, (getting to know eachother stage), or courting, (the stage where both parties have agreed to get married and are working towards it), and go their separate ways is what I define as a breakup, meanwhile, the intensity of the emotional hurt caused by the dissolution of that relationship is what can be termed a heartbreak. They say if you don't stand for something, you will fall for anything. I will like to apply this adage here like this; if you are not well informed and guided by well prioritized qualities you want in a man that are aligned with God's expectations from the man as a 'worthy head of the home', every guy that presents himself will look like a potential husband. The lack of prayerful and careful attention in this decsion making period is what leads to several break ups that leave the woman feeling scarred and eventually, heart broken. I have also come to discover over time that the relationships that result in these heartbreaks for women are those where strong emotional attachment and bond to the individual has been created through premarital sexual activities between both parties. It requires prayers to break such bonds. There is a page at the end of this book with prayers specifically dealing with soul ties if you feel there is a relationship in the past you never really recovered from. Breakups can be minimized if you channel your priorities through the right order of what you should be looking out for in a man even before you meet him and heartbreaks can be reduced to the barest minimum or nearly eliminated if you keep your dating and courting life free of sexual bonds with the person.

Another way it can be reduced is when you learn not to jump into another relationship right after a breakup. It is emotionally unhealthy and has led many into the same mess as the first or worse. Every heart needs time to recover and heal, especially in a case where the relationship was already on the way to the altar. In this case, the tie has grown stronger as the relationship has also grown, with both parties also bonding with eachother's family members. However, I want to offer a piece of advice that could be a lifesaver to someone out there; it is by far better to have to confront a relationship that is not working and experience a temporary heartbreak than to ignore it, get married and live daily with a broken heart. After a break up, it is advisable that you give yourself some time to intentionally and thoroughly clear up the space in your heart, cleaning out the old to make room for a fresh start. So just like a computer gets reprogrammed, the brain will have to dissociate all further activities, plans and everything that seemed to revolve around that person before then and move on. Some women literally run back to their exes, not because they feel once again that there is a future between them but because they have not been able to readjust and move on. As I said earlier, this usually occurs when there has been sexual intimacy. They would rather go back, even if it is every now and then, just to find temporary comfort, not knowing that they are doing themselves psychological and spiritual damage.

This is what is responsible for a lot of baggage that ladies carry from broken pieces of past relationships that they couldn't discard permanently and completely. One of the best ways to let go is to allow enough recovery time before jumping into another relationship. In that period of recovery, fill your spirit and renew your mind with the Word of God. Don't go on a self-renewal journey by only having several dates with best friends and pouring out your heart to them. It's not the right time either to accumulate excessive credit card debt with unending shopping sprees. Use the opportunity to retrace your steps back to God if you've missed it at any point, get even more deeply rooted in His Word and in what it says concerning you and your future. Above all, view yourself through God's eyes and let that form the foundation of what you believe about yourself. Then and only then can you really begin to analyze the past relationship correctly – what went wrong, why it didn't work, what changes you need to make in your character that will enable you have a better experience in the future. You know, even if the guy was wrong in anyway, you still have to make changes somewhere so you don't end up in the same situation again. If you can see what he did wrong, you should be able to ask yourself; what is my area of weakness that opens me up to falling for a guy with those faults?

In my peculiar situation, I had to ask God "What is going on, Lord? I don't understand anymore, help me!"

(How To Know It's Her)

CHAPTER 6
Heaven on Earth

How do you know when God speaks to you? When what He tells you through His Holy Spirit lines up with the Scriptures and when what He tells you or speaks through you to someone else comes to pass. Look at this beautiful scripture below;

God is not a man, so he does not lie. He is not human, so he does not change his mind. Has he ever spoken and failed to act? Has he ever promised and not carried it through? Numbers 23:19, NLT

He sees everything. He is all knowing. Nothing is hidden from Him in the heart of every man. If I had not simply listened and obeyed the voice of the Holy Spirit that afternoon which was in line with the Scriptures according to 1 Corinthians 13:7 and Philippians 1:6, I wouldn't be here today experiencing Heaven on Earth in my marriage and writing this book on how we got here.

We spoke again and again and again. Elliana's response to me over the phone every single time made me want to testify because it was like a miracle. The sudden change and difference in her approach was like night and day. During one of those conversations, I couldn't believe my ears when she told me that she would be traveling back to school from Abuja and was requesting that I pick her up from the bus station. She also mentioned that she had something very important to discuss with me and would like us to find time to discuss at length. I wondered what it would be that needed a serious meeting. Somewhere deep inside I felt it was something I had been longing to hear but I didn't want to move ahead of myself. I had been through enough hurt the first time to allow myself assume anything that would spoil the joy and happiness I was already experiencing. When we met at the Bus station, I didn't hesitate in asking her out to lunch, which she gladly obliged. It was one of the happiest days of my life as I spiraled the car into a different direction heading off straight to the Silverbird Galleria in Victoria Island.

What dazzled me the most on that date was that as much as I was prepared to lavish all the money I had on me in entertaining her, even though it wasn't like I had so much on me that day anyway, she was so modest with her order in a way that I could tell she was more interested in hanging out with me rather than whatever I wanted to offer her which to me was a total far cry from virtually all the ladies I had dated before her. The simplicity of her modest personality was radiantly glowing all over her like the bright morning sunshine that breaks through the clouds after an all-night down pour of heavy rainfall. I remember how she behaved when we ran out of fuel just a few kilometers away from Silverbird galleria and I had to get a motor bike rider to buy us fuel in an empty plastic engine oil container from a nearby filling station. Interestingly and to my utmost surprise, rather than allowing me feel bad for such an occurrence on our first lunch date, she made so light of what would have ordinarily registered as an embarrassing situation on my part. I can't forget the sweet smile she wore on her face when she asked me if I trusted the bike rider to buy the fuel and not run away with the money. I replied her that I only acted by faith. How we both giggled hilariously like two love birds that had no single care in the world. It was our first lunch date together alone with each other and yet I felt so relaxed around her like she was my blood sister, for lack of a better word to describe how I felt. It felt like I was hanging out with my better half, my female version, my clone and without a doubt, deep within my soul, I knew what Adam felt in the Bible when he said 'this is the bone of my bones and the flesh of my flesh'.

Here is my take on this. If a man or woman is yours, you will certainly, beyond every doubt, have peace and joy within with him or her. Proverbs 10:22 says

The blessing of the LORD makes one rich, and He adds no sorrow with it. Proverbs 10:22, NKJV

We were having the time of our lives. It was such a spiritual moment together, there was so much going on around and within us that went beyond what we were saying or physically expressing to each other that I wished time could stop and allow us savor. I didn't want the beautiful time we were having together to end but she had to run, she needed to start her trip across Seme border early enough so she wouldn't be met by nightfall on her way. I dropped her off at the famous *Mile 2 Motor Park* where she boarded a cab that would take her across the border and back to school. It was one memorable lunch date I will always hold dear to my heart, even though it was just an intro to the sweetest days of my life that was about to start.

Back in my church, we got very busy preparing for our ministry's senior pastor's investiture to the office of a Bishop. It was billed to be a very large and laudable occasion in the Lagos metropolis, especially with the involvement of the Nigerian college of Bishops and top churches in Lagos Nigeria, as well as the team of Bishops and ministers coming from the United States. And while I was very busy with my father in faith going about the Lord's business, my bond with Elliana too was waxing stronger. At this point, we could spend hours unending with each other on phone, especially when I retire from the day's work while she too was through with her school lectures. I could feel our friendship morphing and building up stronger and faster into a more concrete relationship and I knew it was only a matter of very little time and we would officially start dating. Meanwhile Bishop Ossai, then Pastor, never forgot to keep reminding me of the lady he had in mind for me coming from the United States and of course, I wouldn't blame him because he also wanted to secure a good wife for me, knowing that I was searching at that point and he wanted to make his input by guiding me towards someone he felt he could vouch for, more so, I had not informed him about the recent progress made with Elliana. However, I couldn't be defocused as well from making my dreams come true with Elliana, not even when our friendship now seemed to have picked up on new and totally different dimension.

About three months after I had the first lunch date with Elliana, on one of our late night phone conversations, she chipped in her plans to have a two-day stopover in Lagos to spend time with me before continuing her journey to Abuja for her semester break. I couldn't believe my ears, it felt like I had just won a million dollar lottery. I remember stepping out of my house that night, not knowing if I should scream or jump for joy. All I could do was step outside to draw in a deep, very deep breath of the night's fresh air while staring up into the most beautiful dark blue star-filled night sky I had ever seen, with a heart filled with an overwhelming sense of victory and gratitude to God. The Bible, in the book of Proverbs talks about hope deferred making the heart sick but a longing fulfilled is a tree of life.

Hope deferred makes the heart sick, but a dream fulfilled is a tree of life. Proverbs 13:12, NLT

When you find your right woman and she begins to draw home close to you, everything inside and around you begin to come alive, even things you have always taken for granted. They all begin to blossom with a boisterous zeal for life. The world becomes a rich and colorful four dimensional environment around you.

The D-day I had been looking forward to sleeplessly eventually came, as Elliana called to let me know they had arrived at the motor park. I hurriedly hired a cab to go pick her and her friend up – not the other friend that had my spirit rioting the other time. This was a much more pleasant friend of hers I had earlier met at her campus fellowship the first time I travelled to minister there. It was already dark by the time I took them to the hotel I had booked for them along the same street where I lived. They had had to break their trip to visit her friend's mom in Lagos and the evening hours had caught up with them by the time they drew close to where I picked them up. I could feel Elliana's eyes all over me that night as I went about enthusiasthically trying to settle them in at the hotel. I won't forget stealing a glance at her a few times and catching her with radiant looks of admiration coupled with appreciation of the way I channeled every inch of energy to make them comfortable. They were my V.I.Ps that I owed the responsibility of taking care of, and I treated them so. We eventually parted for the night at about 10pm after we had spent a little more time together chatting in their room, which for me felt like it should continue forever as my joy of having her around to spend the night as my guest in Lagos knew no limit that night. At my residence, it was even worse. The excitement and planning towards the next day's outings with her left me sleepless till almost the break of day.

The following day was blissful. I tried to resist calling very early so as to afford them time to sleep in, get dressed and have breakfast in their room. The wait felt like forever. At about ten a.m, I called to know if it was okay to come over. She invited me over cheerfully and I walked so briskly from my house to the hotel yet it didn't feel fast enough. By the time I got there, they were having breakfast. I kept them entertained with stories about Lagos, we laughed, took pictures and later on, grabbed some lunch. I received a call and had to rush out to attend to something but before leaving, I asked her to get ready early enough so I could take her out and show her around and then eventually take her to dinner. By the time I knocked on the door, I was completely lovestruck when my stunning damsel opened the door to let me in. She took my breath away with her radiant beauty and her captivating smile that bathed me in the warmth of the love coming from her heart. Her fair skin tone complimented her outfit and beautiful body figure that made me bless God for such a complete package He preserved for me. Her friend decided to stay back at the hotel, she knew that her friend had an important decision to make and I know she wanted to give us that moment alone.

We began my little tourism trip around one or two interesting places in Lagos. I took her to an African cuisine spot where we had dinner and we ended up in a cozy lounge later in the evening where we had some finger food and a virgin cocktail. We climbed upstairs and sat closely together that evening on a two-seater couch in a dimly lit beautifully furnished ambience with lovely artistry, garnished with a soft music seeping out gently from the hidden speakers in the background and a window view that gave a picturesque image of the wide expanse of night lights in Lagos. I was still trying to ingest the reality of what was happening to me, until, while in the middle of our closely knitted soft spoken on-going chats, amidst so much charm and beauty exuding from our hearts and through our facial expressions towards each other, Elliana whispered something that did not just put the icing on the cake for the day but made me feel like the final piece of the jigsaw puzzle that gave me a sense of readiness to take on the world for Jesus in His purpose for me had just been fitted in perfectly. I could relate with Adam's feelings, once again, when he first sighted Eve in the garden and the only words that he could spill out were 'this is the bone of my bones and the flesh of my flesh!' The best scripture that could describe that day says;

...When the LORD turned again the captivity of Zion, we were like them that dream" Psalm 126:1, KJV

"John, you know... I've been thinking a lot on your proposal lately", she said. At that point my heart skipped and I felt it begin race faster. I sat more upright on the chair as I replied "...okay..." and in a sweet soft tone that blended in completely with the soft background music coming from the romantic ambience of the lounge. She told me that she was afraid initially to date me because she wasn't sure whether it would work, especially because of foreseen opposition from her parents and as much as every part of her wanted to go ahead, she kept holding back until she thought to herself that why not just give it a try, why not just let go rather than bottle up what she feels and later regret not having tried. With a few more said, she concluded "...and so my answer is Yes!" "Like for real? You mean you will go into a relationship with me?" I asked as an almost uncontrollable joyful intoxication wanted to make me scream out like I was out of my mind that night. "Yes I really do, even unto marriage" she replied.

While staring fixedly at her sweet innocent eyeballs, almost lost for words to express how I felt, I reached out to hold her hands and said "sweetie, can I call you that now?" "Of course, you can call me anything you want now" she chuckled. "Sweetheart" I said to her, "I will love you till my last breath like no woman has ever been loved on earth before". Surprisingly, we didn't kiss. With all the emotions bubbling within me, there was still a restriction that made me not want to overstep any boundaries that may trigger off a reaction that could affect her mood. The journey had come too far to a point of breakthrough for me to be bothered if we sealed it with a kiss or not.

I keep teaching my church members that Matthew 6:33 is the gateway to anything good you want in life. My wife is a product of Matthew 6:33. God knows where best to find your life partner and soul mate and the Kingdom principle that activates getting what you desire from Him is to get working on His own business first. Let me paint a small picture of how Matthew 6:33 works. In the course of seeking God's kingdom first, which started from when I gave my life to Christ, and according to the dictionary, to seek means to go in search or quest of, to seek the truth or to discover, I have come to realize in my faith walk that Matthew 6:33 is not a God-centered verse, it is not a verse given by God to corner us into working for Him but rather, it is a verse beneficial to man. It was given out of love, for man's own benefit. Let me explain. Everything was created by God through Christ Jesus as expressed in this scripture;

In the beginning was the Word, and the Word was with God, and the Word was God. He was in the beginning with God. All things were made through Him, and without Him nothing was made that was made. In Him was life, and the life was the light of men. And the light shines in the darkness, and the darkness did not comprehend it. John 1:1-5, NKJV

And whatever we need, want or desire on Earth must be routed through Him to get us the best results. I used the word 'best' here because a lot of times, we actually think we are operating on optimal potential and not realizing that what we're looking at as our best is actually average. Let me break it down in vivid pictures. I realized that it was in the course of seeking God's kingdom first that I became a better man, fit to be a woman's covering, as a lover and as a husband. The process of the journey of knowing God took off the old me; the wrong philosophies of relationships and concept of marriage, the self-centered and egocentric nature, the warped ideas and attitudes piled up over time through wrong and ungodly associations with secular friends and replaced them with a new selfless me, regenerated into Christ's nature, filled with the fruit of the Spirit and ready to shower selfless and unending love on a woman just like the Scripture says in Ephesians 5:25-33 rather than being the attention-seeking man.

When you seek God's Kingdom and righteousness first above all other things, you are not only preparing yourself for eternal reign with Christ, you are also on a journey of self-discovery and preparation to become a good and excellent steward of God's blessings and resources. You can only become the best 'You' that you can ever imagine being when you route your life and pursuits through Him who made you. When you have been trained to view everything you want to be and have through His eyes by making sure that everything about you exalts Him before men and brings Him glory, then and only then can He confidently commit the best and choicest of whatever it is you want in life into your hands. That is when He can trust you to be a good and faithful custodian and steward. Looking at my past now, I know I would have made a horrible husband to my wife if not that I allowed myself to be schooled and polished in God's Kingdom 'college of pruning', through making a conscious decision to seek His Kingdom first. And guess what? Little did I know at this time that my wife too was a Kingdom seeker before we met. I'm sure you will get to read that in her own account of her testimony in this book.

My question to you is; that young man or woman you are dating, is he or she a Kingdom seeker? If your answer is yes, then, you have just landed yourself a gem. And if your answer is no, you sure have a lot of work and praying to do. But first things first; are you, the reader, a Kingdom seeker? If you are not, then it's time to get it right in order to get the right person. If you want the best from God, then, you owe yourself the responsibility and duty of first becoming a Matthew 6:33 man or woman.

The Beauty of True Love

My relationship with Elliana took a totally different turn from that dinner date into a blissful journey of the most romantic relationship I can describe as 'Heaven on Earth'. We were so in love with each other and even now, after over a decade in marriage and after being blessed with four children, we are still all over each other on a daily basis.

Even distance was not a barrier to the extra-ordinary bond of love between us. I can't be exact right now but I think we were always checking up on each other via phone calls and text messaging almost every hour. We would wake up first to each other's phone calls and we stayed up very late into the night still talking on the phone. We were both very open and expressive on how much love we felt for each other. Every conversation was one to look forward to and it always ended affectionately. Sometimes, a new day came with a new pet name as an exciting addition to our conversations. I was and I'm still so overwhelmed with love for her that I live as though no other female exists on earth. My description of how much we love each other is simply to provoke a godly desire to make you cherish and protect dearly the person you will be getting married to and for you to desire to make the best out of your marriage too. It is possible for everyone to experience this and even more in their relationships, all they need is to find their clone. The Holy Spirit, the best counselor and guide is more than willing to lead you to him or her if you will choose to let Him sit on the driver's seat of your life's vehicle.

I remember that not long from then, my pastor's day of investiture crept in on us in City of Refuge Ministries, my local assembly. There stood, right in the midst of the team of ministers from the U.S.A, the lady my pastor wanted to pair me up with and to his dismay, I didn't fail to express my disinterestedness through my body language in as little as commencing friendship with her. I had finally begun my long desired relationship journey with Elliana that her presence was of no consequence to me. Hear me guys, the Bible says in the book of Proverbs;

Look straight ahead, and fix your eyes on what lies before you. Proverbs 4:25, NLT

When you meet the bone of your bones and the flesh of your flesh, you can never be double minded. Take it from me to the bank. I am saying it with all assertiveness. I hear guys say things like 'Let me just check out this other sister, just to be sure'. Listen bro, when you meet your clone, all other sisters cease to exist in your world. When you allow God to guide you in finding your clone, your true love, the person meant for you, you will not only understand the true meaning of love in all its manifestations, you will also come to the realization of what I call *just the two of us*. I refer to it as a place in your soul where all that matters where human relations is concerned to you is the two of you. It is where the only people existing in the garden of your world is just the two of you.

Adam did not make any remarkable personal comment that is recorded in the Bible concerning any animal in the Garden of Eden, despite the pleasure and power given to him by God to name all the animals. But on sighting Eve, something in him changed suddenly! There was a sudden shift of attention that came from deep within his soul. It gave him a sudden realization of having found the most important thing in his life that was going to get his primary attention over other things thenceforth in the garden, such that every other thing would become either secondary or almost non-existent. And then, he couldn't help at that point but to speak out the deepest and most emotional statement he had ever said to any creature in that garden before then. He didn't say "wow, she's beautiful" or "oh my, who is this damsel?" His comment "now this is the bone of my bones and the flesh of my flesh" speaks volumes. Firstly, he recognized she was his. He recognized without being told that this woman is a part of him. In other words, just looking at her, he knew that they shared the same DNA and she was his clone. He was in the center of God's Will for him at that time so it was easy for him to see that this woman was made for him. God didn't have to come explaining who she was and what her purpose was, he knew because his spirit was very much in tune with the Spirit of God. There's no way you can miss your clone if you keep yourself in close fellowship with the Father. I am sure even all the animals that were his friends and companions would have felt very jealous. I will expatiate more on this in a subsequent chapter where I will be expounding more on *the clone concept.*

I will not forget a very funny but beautiful incident during one of Elliana's trips to Lagos when we had started dating. She had completed her university degree program in school and was on her way back to Abuja en route Lagos as usual. This time, to spend time with me as well, especially as every opportunity to be around each other was always a paradise experience. Besides the distance we had apart from each other, I have come to realize that even after over a decade in marriage, we still nearly almost go everywhere together and do everything together; even the children have been built into our inseparable habit of always being together. I can recount that the only time that we have had to spend apart from each other in these years of marriage was twice and both were very rough road trips I made in the course of my work that made it impossible to carry my entire family along with me. On that her trip that I was talking about, we had booked her flight for 2pm from Lagos to Abuja and we arrived at the airport in good time, as early as two hours before her departure. While at the airport, we got so engrossed with ourselves that we never heard when her flight was announced for boarding. The only way I can describe that special moment was as if time had stood still. All I could hear were faint sounds and dissolved movements coming from the clamoring usually associated with the human activity around the airport.

My questions to you would be; Do you enjoy her company while you are dating her right now or do you always feel like helping her hasten whatever she has to do around you so you can move on to your next plan for the day? If you found yourself in a situation where you were locked up in the same room with your fiancée for a week, will you find it a haven set up for you or would you feel like you have just been sentenced to prison? I am not setting up this examplary questions from the angle of fleshly lust, which I am still going to talk about in Kingdom dating, but from the angle of communication. This is because the truth is, right there before you is a woman you are going to be spending the rest of your life with and you must naturally be able to enjoy each other's company, not endure it or tolerate it. Enjoying each other's company in communication, I believe, should not even be scored on an average scale where a healthy relationship needed for marriage is concerned; it should score an A plus because it should be one of the topmost things on your list. Good communication should be the strongest bond you both have. You see, some people think marriage is all about the opportunity to have sex in the morning, afternoon and night. Sorry to burst your bubble. When you get married, you will certainly eat your fill and then you will learn to balance it out with your daily activities. In reality, challenges pop up in life every now and then, be it financial, health or as simple as balancing running a career, a home with children and other responsibilities. In such moments, verbal communication and your ability to be open with each other becomes a gold mine. A close friend once asked me what exactly we talk about that keeps us hours unending on the phone and so inseparably and excitedly glued to each other whenever she was around me. And the only answer that came to mind to give him was a question I asked back. "Is there anything you hide from yourself?" and he went like "No, why?" I said "that's it, you just answered the question you asked because you see, Elliana is my other half and I can't hide anything from her, even my most deepest thoughts". We talk and discuss everything with each other from our future dreams, visions, desires, plans, family, finance, ministry, Bible scriptures, ministers, the Kingdom, personal immediate challenges, how our days went, things that made our day and things that got us upset...the list is unending. We would laugh, we were not afraid to cry in each other's presence when something hurts, we entertained ourselves with our own jokes or songs, we were not ashamed to act silly in our conversations. We were and still are soul mates paired from Heaven.

So back to my story at the airport, we were so enveloped in the atmosphere of love that she missed her flight. I remember clearly on that day that I was trying to teach her how to play chess on her phone when we realized that she was almost an hour behind boarding. As a matter of fact, the aircraft was already airborne. It was after we felt the flight was delaying that we went to make enquiries and discovered we were the ones who missed the boarding announcement. We had to spend a little extra to reschedule her for the next one. We had such a good laugh and were too happy to have more time to spend together while waiting for the next flight. It was while we had this long wait that she told me of her parents' plans to send her to the U.K for a Master's Degree program and wanted to know if I would be able to afford to wait through that process for her. When she heard how resolved and unshaken I was about wanting to spend my life with her and my plans to wait, if life was going to take her in that direction, that settled it for her.

Love Amidst Challenges

Sometime around August 2007, my elder sister gave me a very disturbing call. We were both residing in Lagos. She told me that our dad's health, which had been a bit unstable for a while, had deteriorated and he needed to be moved urgently, from Kogi State where we had our family house, to Lagos University Teaching

Hospital for a more thorough medical examination and treatment. That implied that I would be driving all the way from Lagos to Okene in Kogi State to bring him back to Lagos. I had to start the journey that same day and amidst the emotions of having my father in such a sickly state, I left Lagos by 5pm on a journey of eight hours, plowing and navigating my way through the night on a terrain of very bad roads filled with susceptible trappings of armed robbers and night marauders. I still remember vividly that what kept me strong through that burdensome journey was the Presence of God and the soft sweet voice of my love, Elliana, who kept checking on me almost every thirty minutes to whisper the sweetest words of love and encouragement ever spoken to any man on this planet. I remember at the same point when I had to tear through the thickness of the night and she knew how lonely and dark it was going to be, she wouldn't stop talking until she ran out of mobile airtime just so I don't feel lonely or doze off in the stillness of the night, till I arrived at my destination at about 2am.

When you've met or finally meet your soul mate or better put in my concept, when you've finally found your clone, you've gotten more than a good bargain of true friendship; a friend through thick and thin, one who can stay with you through the Nebuchadnezzar's fiery furnace of life and still make you feel like you were in Buckingham Palace. Elliana did not only stand by me through such trying moments while we were not yet married, but she was like a comforting companion sent by God to give me strength and keep me in a calm and joyous mood while I walked through the valley phase of my life.

Listen bro, when you're searching for your clone, make sure you're looking out for the qualities of friendship in her. Search for true friendship that can stand the test of challenging moments of life because truth is, challenges will come to you in life's journey and sometimes they just happen, not necessarily because of your choices, but as an attack from the kingdom of darkness. **Your wife must be your best friend and true friend** for you to be able to scale through that phase in victory. Proverbs 18:24 talks about a friend that sticks closer than a brother. When the woman of your marital choice is not your friend, ruin will be lurking somewhere around the corner. Elliana stuck close to me all through my return journey back to Lagos with my dad in the vehicle under the care of one of my brothers seated with him at the back seat of the vehicle while my protégé, with whom I went to Okene, sat on the passenger's side beside me. The love communication between us in the house that spanned through this journey was to later inspire Innocent Okafi, my protégé in ministry and business, to go in search of his own clone and to God be the glory he is a married man today. I remember that on the night I was to take Elliana to the altar, he said to me with so much admiration, "Rex, I have only seen this kind of romantic relationship between you and Elliana on T.V soaps and I have never believed in the reality of its existence until now... God please give me a true love relationship like that of Rex and Elliana" he prayed so desirously. I got wind that he found the love of his life and had gotten married using the practical guide of my relationship with Elliana as a template. I am sure my dad, where he was seated behind the car, but for the experience of slipping in and out of a delirious state as a result of the toll the illness had taken on his body, would have been wondering who was on the other end of the phone engaging me in long unending conversations at every interval of one hour. If he probably knew he was not going to pull through the illness, I guess he would have mustered a little energy to ask me if I had finally found her.

I had thought and dreamt that my dad would be alive to see me get married to the woman of my dreams. I had desired that he would get to spend time with his grandchildren, but as the Lord would have it, he passed on and went to be with the Lord a few days after I brought him to Lagos for better hospital treatment. As he aged, he had come to realize some of his past mistakes and had tried to draw closer to me, to build a father-son relationship and do the much of the little catching up that was possible. On a few of my trips to visit home, from our discussions, one of his major desires was to see me get married and have my own family, and I had always told him that I hadn't found the right person yet and when I did, I would surely fulfill his desire of settling down soon. My greatest joy however, that took away the sadness of not having him on earth as at the time I got married was the fact that I led him to Christ on his sick bed. He had always been a devout Catholic but had never really understood or come to bear with the concept of being born again. He always saw it as a Pentecostal concept and strategy meant to draw Catholics away from their faith and belief. But that morning, before we headed back to Lagos together, he accepted and confessed the Lord Jesus as his personal Lord and Savior as I led him through a short prayer of salvation. That for me was the best gift that could ever be given to any man on earth, the gift of salvation given to us by Christ Jesus. And I was happy, not just because of the privilege of being used by God as a vessel to achieve this, but also because I found my true love at the verge of his passing on. Though he didn't get to meet her, it gave me a sense of having fulfilled my words to him to settle down in marriage as soon as I find my other half – especially as his passing brought about Elliana's first major contact of being officially introduced to every other member of my family – both nuclear and extended. She risked a journey of four hours on a very bad road from Abuja to my home town, Okene in Kogi State, to be at his burial and that major unprecedented step opened up a totally new chapter in our relationship's journey to the altar. How she managed to pull it off, to travel away from her home to attend a burial ceremony of the late dad of someone not yet known, seen or even heard of by her family, especially her mother who would have been the hardest to convince, even to my astonishment, took a lot of guts and as a matter of fact, undaunted and unstoppable love from a naïve, angelic natured, sweet looking girl who had just graduated out of University. I have never met or seen such a strong and determined sweet angel like my wife Elliana and I don't think there is another replica of her on this side of the universe.

It was much later that she shared with me how she had to use my sister, Yvonne, as her get away card. Even after hearing the story, I could not help basking in the joy of such a great blessing that God had packaged for me in the embodiment of a lady I was about to take to the altar. There were still hurdles and obstacles ahead that would only take this kind of true love and courage to surmount. Our meeting point in Okene my hometown, where we were to lay my father's body to rest, was the starting point of another phase of our journey and battle to the altar.

(How To Know It's Him)

CHAPTER 6
Sensitivity Within

It is not usually the case that the first guy you meet will end up sweeping you off your feet and carrying you to the altar. Chances are that you might have to meet a few more. Some will not go beyond one or two dates because you know what you are looking for and some you won't date at all. Some will nearly seem right, you might even start courting and think he could just be the one but somewhere along the line, you will begin to give closer attention to some character issues that will make you question your ability to endure this for the rest of your life. In some cases, you might find that you both can't seem to agree on very key matters like finances, spiritual beliefs, sexual orientations and demands, or third party and extended family interference in your home. These are weighty subjects that if you both can't agree on, there will be no point investing time and energy in the relationship with the hope that someday things will fall in place, you have to be sensitive enough to know when it's time to let go and move on. You have to be sensitive and willing to tell yourself the truth; that this is a disaster waiting to happen.

I am of the opinion that every woman is gifted with deep inner sensitivity that raises red flags in her head, that sounds an alarm in her heart when she begins to feel hesitant about a guy even though he seems perfect and gentle enough not to hurt a fly. It is that sensitivity that makes her feel that something is not right. God wants to counsel and guide you till you meet His perfect will for you. It is the same way He stirs up restlessness, when you are attentive enough to Him, toward falling into sin with your fiancé that sometimes you'll literally sense it not to visit on a specific day because you can feel a set up in the realm of the spirit for sin to crawl in. He is always working in us, giving us the desire and power to do what pleases Him.

Well, that sensitivity is what a lot of women ignore and find themselves falling into the trap of questionable and dangerous men. The most ludicrous of all is when a lady refuses to let go of a relationship that she knows didn't feel right only to wake up months or sometimes years later in marriage to say that the man has changed because she knows he's cheating, engaging in other negative habits or not just acting in love with her. No! She ignored the signs, the nudging she felt, the bells and alarms that were going off when he did something that puzzled her but she knocked it off and focused on a certain quality that impressed her.

I have also come to realize that a guy that is pretending cannot do so for very long. Yes, I have heard of stories of men who appear to have been trained in the University of satan. They lie, deceive and pretend with so much skill that they have the ability to sustain an angelic appearance for a few years into marriage. The one thing we must admit and attest to is the fact that during the dating and courtship period, no matter how short, there was an air, an aura, an attitude, some apprehension that the lady did not settle down to discern or question. She felt it. 90% of the time, we feel it deep in our stomach but we refuse to listen to our spirit. Some women who have in-law problems were never well received from the start but they told themselves that 'everybody can't have perfect in-laws. It's all about me and my husband, once I get married, I'll maintain my distance from them'. I'm not talking about the resistance that plays out when in-laws-to-be are being extra careful, I'm talking about in-law issues where they have shown that they don't want you close to their son and it has graduated to name calling and insults. Well, guess what, when you marry a him, you cannot detach from his entire family so if they're already giving you hell before marriage, think again and know what you're getting into.

In reality, if you, the lady, are faking in anyway, you may not be able to discern that he is faking because you are both playing the same game. **The only way you can identify a negative spirit is if you maintain a pure one yourself.**

There was a time I met someone just before meeting my husband. He looked gentle and easy-going. He also indicated interest for a relationship almost immediately. I was in no way attracted to him but because he kept requesting to take me out on a date, I decided to push the pressure back on him by telling him that the only date I would go for was a church service date, at my church. He agreed. At the service, I observed how uneasy he felt. He kept a straight face and never turned to look around till it was over. It wasn't because he was in a new environment, it was more of a discomfort that I could read in his body language, an itchy feeling to want to leave that place. Even though he mentioned that he enjoyed the message, I picked up the incongruity between his behavior and his remarks. The few times we got to discuss, I discovered that his Christian values were warped, he had a very traditional and indigenous approach to marriage and running a family, he always argued unapologetically in favour of issues which I had an opposing opinion on. For example, he was a huge supporter of divorce, another big red flag out of the several I had seen. The bluntness and inconsideration with which he spoke about these sensitive issues was appalling. I even tried to pass my opinion across; that a couple should never go into marriage with a mindset of leaving a backdoor open even though this may not apply in an extreme case of domestic violence and extreme marital unfaithfulness, rather, they should go into marriage telling themselves that they're stuck with each other forever. I believe that going into marriage with this mindset will force both parties to do their best to sort out any issue and move forward because when there is no other way out and no backdoor, each individual will work on himself or herself to make sure they do not become the weak link. Well, he would not listen. He was intransigent.

The worst was yet to come. I was to return to school and he offered to take me to the airport. My bestie was with me so we all went together. When I returned a few months later, it was obvious that he had struck up a wonderful relationship with her. She told me how they had gone out severally to have fun, how he took her nieces to the park, how he drove them all to his house and almost made advances at her. When I heard this, I couldn't help but give both of them two big fail marks for their actions. Secondly, I thought to myself that if I actually had had feelings for this guy, this was how he was going start his cheating venture. I began to pity any woman who was going to have feelings for him that would not be sensitive enough to figure these things out before he eventually traps her with marriage.

Another incident where I had to apply sensitivity was the case of a pastor friend who began to pick interest in me. I really respected him and never thought he could even consider a love relationship between us. Well, I told him out rightly that it wasn't going to work but his strategies to win me over were manipulative and deceptive. He began to use the Scriptures to convince me that we met for a reason and he believed we had a lot to accomplish for the Kingdom together. He tried to openly display his affection for me at some point by kneeling down in the middle of a highway to beg me to date him, I was so embarrassed and scared for his life at the same time, I asked him to please leave the highway before a car crushes him because risking his life was not going to change my mind. Unfortunately for him, on a particular day, he was at the gate talking with me when my dad walked past into the house for his lunch break. By the time I got into the house, my dad asked in English, with his usual strong Italian accent "who was that man? He is really ugly eh!" I laughed about it but didn't just waive it away. I had come to respect my dad's opinion about people at first glance. He was never the type to judge people's character by their looks but knowing him very well, his tone indicated something more than just the look; it was a playful way of telling me not to consider having anything to do with him. Had I not been sure of what I wanted and sensitive enough to see that this guy was trying to use the same Bible we both professed to manipulate me into dating him and some emotional gimmicks to buy my love, I would have become one of the numerous cases of women who were manipulated into an unhappy marriage.

Here is another story to buttress my point on the need for sensitivity, with a lesson I have used severally to teach others. I was in a relationship that I felt could have ended up as a blunder in marriage. I dated this guy for a while. Everything seemed right; he was God-fearing and had a number of good qualities. I can't say that I was very in love with him but I felt he was a good guy and was worth dating. Long before I got into the higher institution, I lost my peace over the relationship. There was nothing wrong, he never offended me but I was very restless and couldn't stop the feeling. I began to pray and ask the Lord what this feeling was all about. Well, I was praying one afternoon in my room and fell asleep in the process and I had a dream. In my dream, I saw the Lord Jesus. We were in a train and I knelt before Him with tears in my eyes and began to tell him about every restless feeling I was having concerning the relationship. When I was done, while He kept smiling at me, I got an idea and spoke it out to Him. I said, "I know what I'm going to do, I will draw a table and write out the advantages and disadvantages of being in this relationship". He smiled at me again and nodded in affirmation. I sprang up from that bed, found a paper and did exactly that. To my surprise, I saw that I was hanging unto the relationship majorly out of pity, not because I was in love. So my prayers changed. I had realized that we needed to part ways but I needed the Lord to break it up Himself because I didn't know how to, after all, like I said, he hadn't offended me.

A semester after I had gained admission, I was in my hostel when I was told that I had a visitor. I was shocked to see him. He said he was in Lagos for an event and thought to drop by. He continued that he didn't know how I would take this but he'd been having a feeling of giving our relationship a break. He said it was a pressing feeling of needing to let me be free. I can't even begin to describe what I felt at that moment. I was in awe at the Lord's ability to even orchestrate a peaceful breakup. You will not believe that we walked back together to the nearest point where he was to board a cab back to Seme border and we waved at each other as the car drove away. The sensitivity within was what made me give attention to the restlessness I felt and it made me pray about it till I got an answer from God. Can I shock you a little? A few years ago, I saw it on a friend's Facebook message that he had passed on. I searched to make sure and yes it was true, condolence messages were flooding his younger brother's timeline. God was not only trying to protect me from a mistake, He had also orchestrated my steps to Cotonou where I was destined to meet the love of my life, my other half as ordained in heaven. If I had stubbornly continued in that relationship, I probably would have ended up marrying him, still out of pity, and my case would have been a miserable one. Be sensitive to detect feelings like restlessness and uneasiness. Be sensitive to also sense the Lord leading you away from a relationship, it is always for your good.

Finally, while I was courting my husband-to-be, there was a pastor from one of the leading churches in Nigeria with whom I had to correspond for my office. This was when I was already preparing to get married. After our first meeting, he told me point blank that he wanted to marry me. It is not strange for situations like this to arise in the middle of a courtship or wedding plans, I've also seen women struggle with feeling confused in such a situation but honestly it's a very simple thing to overcome. Your responsibility is to overlook it and carry on. You cannot expect to know someone you just met better than someone you've known and grown to understand for months or years. Every individual has weaknesses and flaws and guess what, nobody comes flaunting their weaknesses or flaws when trying to make a first impression. So, don't be deceived; the grass is not as green and plush as you think on the other lawn. If you dare leave your lawn and draw closer to the other, you'll find out this truth and it might just be too late to go back.

In the next chapter, I will be unrolling my secret scroll of the qualities I sought after that led me to this beautiful love story that I have. I hope you find it useful too.

(How To Know It's Her)

CHAPTER 7
Keeping Up With Her Family

After my dad's body had been laid to rest and she got to familiarize with my family, Elliana and I were on our way to Abuja. Our decision to travel together to Abuja was for two reasons. The first was to avoid having her travel back home alone and the second, based on our analysis and conclusion, was to use it as a good opportunity to subtly get me to meet her parents, and the latter for me was as important as the former as I was going to establish a major step in bringing my dreams of spending the rest of my life with Elliana closer home.

Our journey towards the country's federal capital was one romantic abstract memorabilia that will forever remain imprinted on my mind. Despite all the fears and anxieties, especially the recent one raised through some unfriendly sarcasm by my elder sibling and her friend on the evening of the day after the funeral service, when we all decided to hang out together in an open air garden restaurant just to temper a little of the sorrow in the atmosphere with some family togetherness, they analyzed my soon-to-be in-laws' ethnicity and nationality from a malicious, presumptuous and provocative angle. They made slashing comments that were only geared towards dampening my morale to see my relationship move to the next phase and forward into marriage. I chose to remain calm on this remarkable journey to her family home and savor the beauty of the countryside scenery with my fiancé snuggled close to me with her head resting on my shoulder and our fingers locked tightly together as we sent vibes of unspoken reassurance to ourselves while the driver of the saloon car drove calmly with obvious expertise and familiarity with the pot-hole ridden highway as if trying to intentionally add more comfort to the air of romance for the 'love birds' at the back seat of his vehicle. "One step at a time" I told myself as I shut my eyes to join Elliana's meditative solitude which spoke volumes about how we both anxiously anticipated what awaited us ahead in her family home, with no knowledge or desire to predict how things would go. We could only put our trust in God.

We arrived in Abuja before midday. We were welcomed by her beautiful looking German shepherd first as we stepped in through the gate to the family residence. I almost got carried away with the way it wagged its tail and came around me that I felt it was a good welcoming sign to me into the family until Elliana told me it had been spoilt silly by her dad. "Okay…" I thought, now I had to find another sign that things would work in my favor. The next person we met as we opened the front door was a very friendly, gentlemanly and pleasant looking steward called Emmanuel. He popped out of the kitchen with such glee and a good-to-have-you-back-home cheerfulness. He gave me a very warm welcoming hand shake and ushered me into the warm and tastefully furnished living room that exuded an air of foreign touch. I decided to hijack his response to me as the sign that I sought. I wasn't sure if he was trained to welcome everyone like that but his niceness felt genuine and from the heart. It didn't take him long to decipher who I was and he seemed pleased about it. We were later to become very good friends till date.

I felt a sense of relief when we noticed the absence of her parents and Emmanuel mentioned that they weren't both back home yet. Apparently, her dad was meant to make his routine stop for lunch which was supposed to be soon and her mom didn't go very far. It felt like judgment day and I began to feel like postponing the encounter as so much tension was building up in my belly. I had barely settled in to take a sip of the soda served me by Elliana when her mom busted in through the front door with a very strong air of authority. You could tell from a glance that she was the alpha head. I ran a quick profiling glance at her as I stood up to politely greet her while at the same time switching into the best of my disarming charming look that depicts the type of sweet gentleman any mother would like to have for a son-in-law. She fitted perfectly into Elliana's description of her even as she too was doing her best to put up a beautiful good girl act to create a casual and playful ambience in introducing me as Yvonne's brother who thought it was nice to escort her and ensure her safe return back home. I could tell that her mom was not the type to get fooled that easily. More so, judging by the very quick plastic looking smile she wore to welcome me and her deliberate avoidance of eye contact with me, I didn't need a prophet to tell me that from this point onwards, I would have to pray my way through to make it successfully to the end of this marital journey. And true to my thoughts, not long after I got introduced to her, barely after she had settled in from dropping off the things she brought in on the dining table, she turned and climbed upstairs into the master bedroom of their duplex home. Elliana's dad came in around this point looking a bit exhausted from work. I stood up to greet him like I did her mom. The encounter I just had with my mother-in-law-to-be made me expect to see him pull out a shot gun at me. I couldn't believe it; I had to sit down to absorb the utter shock I felt at his unexpected gentle and warm response to me. I call him the man with the golden heart, Angiolino Barzasi, the wonderful man that I owe a large part of the gratitude for making it easier for me to marry my wife. He came in and gave me a warm smile when Elliana introduced us, and for me, that went a long way to strengthen my hope of the chances of having him on my side. He went to be with the Lord in December 2019 and praise God, just like with my dad, I was able to lead him to Christ when his health began to deteriorate rapidly. All through the first years of my marriage, before he departed earth, I always called him 'Daddy'. He was a very unassuming, non-materialistic, kind-hearted and generous man to a fault. He was my best friend for many years. My relationship with him grew beyond a father to a son-in-law; he actually filled the void of a father that was left empty by my biological father.

After Elliana and I sat down to continue talking, a few minutes later, we heard a loud call from upstairs. It was Elliana's mom calling out her name. I knew instantly that she was about to face a debriefing from her mother. It was much later that she told me that her mother accused her of travelling under the guise of Yvonne's father's burial and lying to her instead of telling her she was going to see her boyfriend. I know she would have done a number of these stories some justice on her side of this book, please take out time to read that also. Women are better storytellers, especially when it comes to relationship matters. What impressed me the most about this one-in-a-billion God's gift to me was her unperturbed and resolute determination to go ahead with pursuing our goal to the finish line regardless of how her mother felt or what she wanted for her. I have had a situation in the past where I liked a lady and she liked me as well but her mother was to later act as a deterrent to our friendship which I had hoped would grow into a relationship. This was not the case with Elliana. She was totally different, one of a kind. And guys, hear me, if she is sincerely in love with you and she loves you real enough, she will stand her ground against anyone and defy all odds, no matter how challenging, to be able to spend the rest of her life with you.

I have had cause to counsel people in relationships where the excuse from one of the couple to be for not being able to continue has to do with parental consent. It is even more annoying when it is the man having to give such an excuse. And then my question to them would be; have you ever wanted something so badly that you are willing to pay any price or do anything within the confines of what is scripturally right to get it? They would usually respond in the affirmative. So, my follow up question would then be; what makes you think you should back out on this one that has to do with the person you will be spending the rest of your life with? If you allow your parents to choose a life partner for you, you are making a terrible mistake because you are the one that will be in that marriage to deal with any problem you uncover by yourself. Your parents can choose for you but they won't marry the person, you will. And they won't handle the responsibilities or challenges in that marriage; you will face the consequences all by yourself. Guess what, if anything goes wrong, they will still turn around and blame you. They will tell you things like "If you were that sure of your personal choice, why didn't you go for it?" Or you'll hear something like "We only introduced you to the person. We didn't force you into it. If you really didn't feel right about it, you should have voiced out, after all, it's your life not anyone else's". It is at this point that everybody withdraws quietly and realizes that it's your life. Please don't let it get here. The only person's opinion you need to be concerned about is God's and if He has given you the go ahead, then what are you waiting for.

I didn't have the opportunity to meet the remaining members of the family such as two of my wife's cousins and two other adopted little girls living with them as I had to make a return journey that same day back to Okene so as to prepare for my trip back to Lagos the next day. One thing was certain with that trip, I had registered my presence and it had established a major step into the next phase of our relationship. In Romans 8:28, the Bible says;

"And we know that all things work together for good to them that love God and to them who are the called according to His purpose". Romans 8:28, NKJV

My biological father's passing on was not for nothing. Laying his body to rest created an opportunity for us to get to meet each other's family members, something that would have required strenuous effort especially on my part.

Leaving Elliana behind in Abuja that day felt like leaving a part of me, but it also felt like I could still feel her right beside me as the dusk fell into the night to usher me back into my family house in Okene, Kogi State.

(How To Know It's Him)

CHAPTER 7
The List

A lot of times, our experiences in life and who we allow to influence us can determine the type of men we end up with as husbands. It is when we try to deal with the damages done by our upbringing in isolation that we end up finding a carbon copy of the very character we are running from, because we cannot uproot the spiritual seed sown in us on our own. My dad, for example, was not the very affectionate type when he was younger. He never put restrictions on me, which is not a good thing as a parent. He left most of the parenting to my mom and believed that a child would turn out good if they wanted to. I also made many conscious decisions and choices myself based on what I knew was right or wrong before God. I don't think he understood the importance and impact of a father's role in the life a daughter. To be honest I don't blame him at all because when he grew much older he had become a transformed person, he did everything he could to spend quality time with me and his grandchildren until he eventually got saved on his sick bed and went home to be with the Lord. His parenting style made me decide that I would find a man that would be very involved in the upbringing of our children, as a father and a guide to them.

For a very long time, my dad couldn't understand why a young girl like me was so immersed in church. Within this period, I saw how my mom struggled with being committed in church because her going to church was always a source of conflict between the both of them. I couldn't imagine making the mistake of marrying a man who was not a God-seeking and church attending believer, it would wreck me to think that I would have to fight over going to church or praying too loud in my home or fight spiritual battles alone. I vowed that these things would not repeat themselves in my home.

The first step toward making a wise decision and avoiding a spouse with negative character traits just like that of one of your parents or guardians is to have a relationship with the Lord Jesus. Make Him Lord over every area of your life, including your love life. It takes away the chances of ending up with someone you'll regret being with because, as the Master of your life, He'll lead you by His Holy Spirit into His perfect will for you. The Holy Spirit will give you discernment, fill you with wisdom and good judgment and let you know when you're missing it or getting it right. If the Lord Jesus says that He is the vine and we are the branches, then we cannot live at our optimum capacity if we are detached from Him. We cannot fulfill purpose or walk according to His plans for our lives if we're not connected to Him. It all starts with asking Him to come and live inside your heart and take the lead; that is when your life can begin to follow the original plan that was written about you before you were born. But, you must be willing to let Him lead you.

So I can boldly say that my journey to finding true love started when I got saved. It positioned me in the right place where angels could be activated to work things out for me and my husband's paths to cross. I can assure you that it's never too late for God to reorder and readjust situations in your life, He is a Master at restoring lost time, let Him know you trust Him to do so and don't stop trusting.

You have heard me say this frequently because I really want it to sink in; that your values in life will determine what you look out for before making any choice. Let's take, for example, people who love to live around very busy environments. They enjoy being close to the heart of commercial activities where everything they need is just a walk away. This preference can make them forego comfort or yard space if houses around such areas are small or cramped up into high rise buildings. Someone who values serenity or nature, on the other hand, will find themselves gravitating towards options a little away from the busy city center. This same principle works in relationships. If, for example, what you value most is financial security, then you'll find that your decision of a man will be based on the size of his bank account, his material success and your ability to find comfort in them, pushing other qualities you seek down the list. You will find yourself tossing out guys without a strong financial base. The unemployed guy who is filled with visions and a drive to succeed does not even stand a chance with you; you won't care to find out his other good qualities before you jump into conclusions. Say you, however, put love and compatibility at the top of your list, it will determine how you see a man and what you see in him. Interestingly, we are spirit beings and we are wired to attract what dominates our minds, our words and actions. **What we most desire and seek begin to move our lives in the direction of where we can find it.**

My love for God made me place, as number one on my list, the desire to find a man after God's heart – a genuinely born again man. It was later on as I grew in my understanding of what makes relationships stand the test of time that I discovered it was actually correct of me to do. A man who has accepted Jesus into His heart as His Lord and Saviour is the first and most important thing a woman should look out for in a man. It is the unique factor that will tie every other thing together, the very thing that can turn an ordinary relationship and marriage into an extraordinary one. My environment contributed to my early maturity, it made me able to see the flaws of certain parenting styles and some adjustments I had concluded in my heart to make in my own home. I told my spirit, soul and body, with all sense of conviction, that I would not make a mistake in finding my husband. I had resolved that even if everyone else was having marital issues, my case would be different. An idea came to me to write out everything I wanted in a man in the order of preference and priority. I also concluded that once I found the first four most important things to me and God, I wouldn't let the rest stop me.

So here is the order of priority I will like to recommend to you based on my personal experience and how it led me to finding my divinely ordained husband. If you can adopt it and let it influence how you create your list, if you can get sold out to the reasons you have come up with in this list, it will become a mental list that your brain locks in and says 'it's the list or nothing'.

1. He must be genuinely born-again

Your chance of making a mistake in marriage becomes nearly impossible when you make this number one on your list. You literally have the devil's hands tied because you have narrowed down your options in a way that he'll find it really hard trying to push the wrong guy your way. Your desire should be to find a man that is stronger in faith than you; if you are hot spiritually, he should be hotter. A husband is meant to be the spiritual leader and priest over his home, not the woman. He is supposed to lead you with wisdom and guide you through God's word.

But I want you to know that the head of every man is Christ, the head of woman is man, and the head of Christ is God. 1Corinthians 11:3NKJV

God (comes first)

Christ (secondly)

Man (is right under the Lord)

Woman (is under the man, her husband)

This order of hierarchy described here in 1Corinthians 11:3 is where this generation is missing it. If this order is rearranged in anyway, it will create problems in a relationship or marriage. A man under Christ simply means a regular every day man who is submitted to the leadership of the Lord Jesus. I am not talking about wanting to marry a pastor or thinking that the man under this hierarchy must mean someone with a pastoral calling. A man does not have to be a pastor to be deeply rooted in God, we are all supposed to know God and live a life of intimacy with Him, no matter our profession, vocation or calling. There's another very important twist to finding a Christian brother that I want to help straighten out. When we truly understand how weak the flesh and human mind can be, we will be able to weigh our weaknesses or the flakiness of our decisions better. When trying to find your God-ordained spouse and after learning that a brother in church is who you should be looking for, you are expected to still allow the Holy Spirit guide you and lead you into the perfect relationship for you. Please listen closely; human beings are imperfect everywhere, the people in church did not drop down from Heaven as saints. They were sinners who got washed by the Blood of Jesus. It takes a continuous transforming process for an individual in Church to become more like Jesus and bear the fruits of the Spirit. The process starts in the first place, by the individual's willingness to be broken and remoulded into the image of Christ by obeying the Word of God. Therefore, even in the Church, you can meet a pretentious, double-standard-life type of person; after all, even among the twelve disciples who walked closely with the Lord, there was a Judas Iscariot. This is what the Lord says;

Jesus answered and said to them, "those who are well have no need of a physician, but those who are sick. I have not come to call the righteous, but sinners, to repentance". Luke 5:31-32, NKJV

The Church is made up of ordinary, everyday individuals with weaknesses and imperfections living in a fallen world, who have consciously decided to have a relationship with God, be transformed by Him to become what He created them to be. Among these people, you will still find the ones who have refused to allow the Spirit of God work in them to change them, but because they have hung around the Church environment for a long time, they have understood Church culture, Church language and have a form of godliness that is simply superficial without a visible sign that the power of God and the resurrection power of the Holy Spirit is at work in them. Some of them work in departments in Church and are more political about their service in God's house than spiritual. So, the fact that it is advised that you find a Christian brother does not mean you should throw caution to the wind and say yes to any brother that shows up at your doorstep because he belongs to a Church. Sometimes, our laziness to grow makes us prefer to make mistakes and push the blame on someone else. You cannot blame the Pastor for the lifestyle of a member. The teachings of your Pastor are meant to help you get understanding over a matter and motivate you to play your own part in following God's leading and digging deeper to grow your personal relationship with Him. In the extreme case of some people who prefer enquiring about everything from "prophets", even about whom they should marry and going ahead to do so without any confirmation in their hearts about it being the right thing is still a result of laziness; laziness to know God for yourself! The point here is that some ladies out there think that it's okay to marry just any Christian brother. **You cannot measure a man's intimacy with God by the fact that he goes to Church every Sunday**. It's a good thing to have a man that goes to Church, a very good thing, but it is not all it takes to grow spiritually and is not what should be used to measure spiritual maturity either. It's the person's conduct outside the Church environment and their lifestyle when no one is watching, in their closet, that is the real them.

I've also seen where some women who believe that when a man is God-fearing, even if he is of another faith, it is okay to marry him. They feel it's all about being 'generally' God-fearing. That is a big No! Jesus is the ONLY Way, the Truth and the Life; no one comes to the Father except through Him. That is what the Bible says in John 14:6. Going against this Scripture is tantamount to stepping out of the order given in the diagram or hierarchy shown earlier. It is the greatest error any woman can make because she is about to be unequally yoked as the Bible warns against in 2 Corinthians 6:14. Such women, before long, end up converting to the man's religion because in the first place, they were not grounded in theirs. Christianity was simply a religious background they were born into, nothing more; no relationship with Jesus, no understanding of the things of the Kingdom and their purpose on earth. Women that make this mistake obviously don't know that they are first followers of Jesus and the name 'Christian' is supposed to mean that they live a lifestyle of walking with the Lord in a beautiful relationship. Money, comfort and financial security are usually top most on the list of priorities of the women that fall for this cheap trap.

Another situation that presents more than the aforementioned is, where the woman is more spiritually mature than the man and she becomes the man's motivator, eventually having to take the lead on spiritual matters in the relationship or marriage. From Scriptural viewpoint which is our basis for establishing the truth about anything, it is the wrong order. He should lead spiritually. He should be able to give you a clear blueprint of where you are both headed in the relationship and how you plan to get there under the leadership of Christ. When I say clear blueprint, I don't mean that the man will have to draw up a physical plan and lay it like a war strategy on the table for you to approve. Injected into the several conversations that you will both have over the course of time, he should at one point or the other have mentioned or expressed how much he loves God and how God has influenced key decisions he has made in life. You shouldn't have to ask him if he is born again or have a personal relationship with the Lord, his words, his actions, his associations make it glaring. What you may want to ask, if you want to test his ability to make godly and wise decisions, is for counsel over a pressing matter in your life or workplace at that point. His response will tell you how much the Word of God influences his decision making style. Ultimately, his relationship with the Lord should challenge you or be a motivation to you to walk more closely with the Lord.

2. Character

Character, as defined by Oxford dictionary, is all the qualities and features that make a person, groups of people, and places. Another dictionary defines it as the mental and moral qualities distinctive to an individual. A person's character is often intertwined with their personality or temperament. One's personality or temperament is their180ehaveioural style that is often biological, that means they are born with it and it forms the emotional core of their personality. It is also visible at first contact. For example, a person that is an introvert will most certainly appear quiet, less sociable and reserved while an extrovert is the direct opposite. There are great resources out there you can look up that further explain this topic extensively. Character, on the other hand, is learned behavioural traits formed based on a person's values, beliefs or goals. They are built by repetition and can be changed by volition if a person decides to focus on a new self-concept and new values. All a person needs to do is practice a new action like self-control, respect or gratitude consistently and it becomes part of a new character trait formed. As easy as it may sound, these changes require commitment, self-discipline and consistent practice for them to form one's new identity, and one way to know a person is committed to changing a negative character trait is by committing it to God and having a respected person or mentor be part of the change process so as to hold them accountable. That said, when seeking the love of your life, you must first tell yourself that **there is no perfect person out there. You are not perfect yourself; we are all work in progress**. It is how much you are willing to admit that you need work in certain areas of your life and how much you are willing to work towards making that change that differentiates those who will soar to greatness in their purpose from those who will wallow in mediocrity.

Having understood the difference between a person's personality from their character, you cannot expect an introverted man to become an extrovert for you, you cannot change the emotional core of any human being to suit your preferences. That action in itself is witchcraft. If you know that you don't fancy guys that are loud and bursting with energy, don't date one hoping to 'tame' him. Please don't kill him psychologically by trying to make him the cool, calm collected MI5 agent character you have been dreaming of. Someone else wants him just the way he is! Like I always say, if there's something you know you can't stand, please take a bow and leave. There's another way to put it; imagine that he will never change, that he is going to remain the way he is forever, can you live with It? If your answer is no, then you know what to do, if not, you will be the one who ends up dissatisfied, giving the devil a foothold to either creep in with unfaithfulness or depression. Please, kindly understand, I said it earlier that we are all work in progress, nobody can have it all. You were not created to change people to who you think they should be, you're not God. If there's anybody you should constantly work on changing and perfecting, it's YOU.

So, this is about your ability to define what you want, what you can endure or deal with and what is unacceptable, basically, teaching you to know where to draw the line. We all have excesses here and there and with correction or advice from our loved ones, we constantly make adjustments. But when someone is unwilling to become a more refined version of themselves, you must learn to hands off and move on. The reason I am putting all these issues into perspective is because character traits, which research has proven changeable over time can be quite hard to change. In reality, it takes God to change something negative in a man's character, especially addictions. It takes only God. Please don't settle for a man with issues because you feel he can change with time. Go for a man who fears God and makes decisions with a desire to please Him. Go for a man who exhibits the fruits of the Spirit; some might be more refined and visible in him than others but over all, you can see them in him, particularly love and self-control. That's how you identify a good man.

Now, it takes an interesting turn from here. We've established that a man with good character traits is the very next thing you should seek, after making sure he is saved. No matter his personality, you should be able to see the fruits of a good person in him. Good character cannot be hidden; it makes it all worth it. When it's all said and done and you are both married, the character of your spouse will largely determine how much you both connect, how much you both enjoy each other's companionship and how much you will sacrifice to make your marriage work. Therefore, the best approach will be to watch and analyze the way he handles different situations by being friends with him for a while. To know a man's character, you need patience and time. You need some time to be able to observe his approach to different situations. You must listen with utmost alertness and care to be able to read between the lines. Listen to how he talks and what he says to his mom, his sisters, his friends, his colleagues, his pastor, artisans, the poor and needy, strangers, listen quietly to what they also say about him on their own accord. Is he capable of criticizing himself or always defensive and egotistical? When someone offends him, how forgiving is he? Is he too hard on everybody around him expecting perfection or is he a joy to be around? Do people enjoy having him around? What emotion does he pull out of people? How does he display his relationship with God, is he proud of it? Do people identify him as God-fearing? Is he happy to introduce you to everyone around him as his fiancé or does he shy away and keep pushing it off? Does he take a stand for and defend his beliefs and interests when around his immediate family? Are there people or areas of his personal life he refuses to talk about or prefers that you steer clear? Can you see that it will take some time of purposeful dating and courtship to be sure of your responses to these questions? On a more hopeful and relieving note, just like detectives and intelligence officers depend on facial profiling to identify criminals, when you see a good hearted person, it will reflect on their face. Habits and character traits have a mysterious and yet scientifically proven way of transforming an individual's countenance no matter how much he tries to pretend.

I strongly believe that there is one way you can calmly but surely confirm if you are headed in the right direction, if there's one additional thing that should seal the entire decision making process for you, it is your ability to be relaxed and silly around the person. When the relationship is picture perfect and uptight, something is very wrong. If both of you cannot be best friends first and relate from a place of simplicity, playfulness, excitement and laughter, you haven't started yet. If both of you cannot express your hurts and dislikes to each other as your way of being open and honest to each other, there's a problem. Your approach towards expressing displeasure or hurt and how quickly you both long to fix the problem so that you can get back to enjoying the love and joy of being around each other can be used as a measuring scale to know the kind of person you are dealing with. I have seen a couple in a counseling session who were not married yet and were finding it hard to own up to a certain mistake let alone apologize; they kept pushing the blame back and forth as we spoke. They did this playfully but wouldn't change their stance on the matter as it dragged and dragged. You already have an idea what kind of marriage they were working towards. They were both proud and unable to connect in one of the most crucial levels necessary to make any marriage work.

You must find someone you can be yourself with, someone you can feel vulnerable with and someone whose loving emotions and responses to you, you can trust to be sincere and real. If for any reason his reactions to you for being yourself or having imperfections make you feel ashamed or less confident, you've got the wrong guy because **flaws are the imperfections that make two God-ordained soul mates feel specially carved out for each other**. All of this must come naturally for it to be real. It can't be forced out of anybody.

3. Vision - He must be a vision carrier and You must share one Vision

There is no vision carrier who is a lazy person. When you meet a man that is full of ideas of wealth and greatness, you don't need anybody to point out that this man is driven and passionate about where he going and there's no doubt that someday he will get there. This is where I beg to differ when it comes to how some clergy and parents have defined a successful man, a man capable of taking care of their daughter or a man ready for marriage. I am in support of a man having a source of income, in fact, if he has a vision, it should have motivated him to have what I can qualify as a 'means to an end'. It might not be all that, it might not be a white collar job, it doesn't even matter what type of job he is doing as long as it is within the confines of what is considered clean before God, his effort to make ends meet alone shows that he is not lazy and that with time, whatever his dreams are, they will begin to take shape and manifest. It also shows that he will do everything in his power to put food on the table.

When you have a man who is a vision carrier, who can paint a mental image of the future he envisions for the both of you with action plans on the side, it's just a matter of time, I can boldly say that he will bring the world to your feet. There are way too many success stories of men that started out as "nobodies" who ended up becoming the envy of many. I personally know a lot of these dumbfounding testimonies first hand. There may be women out there who are looking for already-made success stories because they feel they are a success story themselves, that is, they already have a status that may not permit them to go below a certain level, that's fine. I mean, all love stories don't have to follow the same pattern, but the man should have the first two points enumerated above for the relationship to be built on a lasting foundation. As long as the success was birthed by hard work and he still has a drive and burning desire to become all that God created him to be, as long as they both find a common ground to pursue something greater together and are not basing their love on the other person's achievements, then it's fine. The woman must also be able to submit to his authority and he should be able to take on his role as her spiritual leader who is submitted to the Lord Jesus.

If a woman discovers that the man she's in love with is financially comfortable, earns a good salary, praise God! That is also okay. But here, I'm talking to the woman who believes she has found everything she could ever ask for in her man but the only challenge is that his income is not there yet. As a woman, you can see that he is a good man full of ambitions but right now he seems to be struggling. This is directed at you. Don't let him go because of something as inconsequential as money. Money is just one of the things included in the list of wealth. Wealth includes health, visions and dreams in the incubator of a man's heart, soundness of mind, a personal relationship with Jesus, a winsome personality and character, these are all part of wealth. Moreover, there is such beauty and power in two people coming together, believing in each other and loving each other beyond their material status at that point in time, sometimes, with nothing to their names and yet, they stick to each other, working hard, praying together and encouraging each other until, little by little, they begin to climb higher, till they finally step into that glorious testimony together. I lack words to describe how captivating it is but I can talk about it passionately because that was how my husband and I began and all I can say is that the bond between a couple that toiled together and never gave up on each other till God came through for them is indescribable and unshakeable, far beyond that of those who never went through any challenges at all.

When I met my husband, the security outfit he jumpstarted with a friend, plus his Nigerian movie productions were some of the things he was doing to earn an income before we met. The movie productions were capital intensive and having experienced a set back with a production that was ruined by a compromised camera, he ran a loss, ran into debt, which he had paid off long before we met. However, it affected his capital base and ability to finance his next production. The security outfit business he was running was brought to a standstill by the several weekly trips to Abuja from Lagos for our pre-marital counseling classes in my former church. The rules were so strict that if you missed a class, you were not going to be allowed to fix a wedding date until you attended a makeup class with the next set. We weren't even sure when the next session would be and we weren't ready to delay our wedding for any reason. These weekly visits for eight weeks gave his assistant ample room to desensitize their clients in order to gain favor for himself. This made his income drop right after we had gotten engaged. It was such a struggle to do a lot of things. We didn't even know how we were going to scale through the introduction which has financial requirements in the Nigerian context, let alone the wedding preparations. I wasn't moved by it one bit because I knew that financial success is one of the easiest things to achieve when you have discovered your purpose and vision. There is provision attached to every vision. Once you're on track, the provision will be the one pursuing after you. How much more when you find the man God has ordained for you and you both begin to run with a unified vision; the money has no choice but to come.

The second part of this point is as crucial as the first; sharing the same vision means knowing that you are both headed in the same direction, that you are both in agreement with the future plans your husband-to-be has for your home. The Bible says;

Can two people walk together without agreeing on the direction? Amos 3:3, NLT

He cannot tell you that he is a pastor and you think it will work when you feel you have a political calling. Once there is a conflict of interest and both of you have to work separately to fulfill your different goals and dreams, you have conjured a recipe for a break-up. Even if your professions are directly opposite, there has to be a unifying vision that gives both of you a sense of oneness and compatibility. Your job is different from your life's purpose. Discovering your purpose will help you know if you share the same vision with your man. For example, a conservationist will be most compatible with someone who loves animals and nature. You can't pair someone like that with someone whose dream is to be a real estate investor and live in a condo in the center of New York. When you begin to observe such extreme differences in your likes and dislikes, just know that the friction cannot allow for a smooth flow between the two of you. I had always loved the media and television production. There is no doubt that I also have a ministry calling. It couldn't have been any more perfect than when we both discovered we loved and were both involved in television productions. He was also a pastor and I was an assistant pastor in my campus fellowship. We are both big dreamers, we are both workaholics, we know how to work together as a team, we are each other's greatest fan, we are best friends and share several other seemingly inconsequential similarities. As much as they say opposites attract, and this applies where temperaments are concerned, where vision and purpose are concerned, you must find things you share in common.

The next point I will be talking about, which is 'physique', was not the number four item on my list, in reality, it was somewhere between number five and six. What I had as number four was personal; it was linked to number two but was more specific, like, one of the character traits I would really be looking out for that needed to be more visible than other traits, if I were asked to choose. I chose to talk about physique as the fourth point, however, because I have seen ladies prioritize it unnecessarily. I have seen those that missed the chance of having a beautiful marriage because they were looking at the man's outward appearance when those first three points were perfectly in place. I have also seen the enemy deceive people into marriages that they were never drawn to physically, all because they were given a misconception about what to seek in a life partner. The beautiful thing about seeking the first three qualities is that they have a way of making a man look attractive. If you don't believe me, try having a conversation with someone you could even refer to as 'ugly', who is extremely nice and loving, very God-loving and fully driven to fulfill purpose. Even if he is crippled or blind, you will be drawn to his persona so much that your focus will be on those attractive inner qualities way over and above his physical attributes; because goodness has a glow and radiance that accompanies it.

I knew what I wanted the man of my dreams to look like, I wrote them down but I didn't sit on it forcefully as though any man that doesn't come looking like that will be trashed no matter what other good qualities he may have. I made decision making easy for myself by placing it way down 'The List', because I considered getting the most important first three qualities first; all I wanted, if it got right down to it, was to find him attractive to a certain measure – he didn't have to have all the features I had listed out. That's how much I valued the first three points I was looking for. Surprisingly enough but true, money was almost not on my list as well. Don't get me wrong, everybody likes comfort but this list was a drawn up to remind myself that money or looks were not going to stop me from picking a man I felt had the major things I wanted. You know the amazing thing, just like Solomon who asked for wisdom from God and was given much more than he asked for, because I sought a man after God's heart and my priorities were in the right order, all other things were added; God gave me exactly what I wanted my husband to look like physically and every other thing I wrote down.

***Physique**

I have heard different angles to this point of finding a good-looking man. Some are of the school of thought that looks don't matter, some believe that God will choose the man for you and even if you don't like how he looks, don't question it, you have to live with the Will of God. I believe that marriage is as superficial as can be, it is as physical as it is spiritual. How in the world are you expected to fall in love with someone you are not physically attracted to? Please understand what I am saying, the way the movies and fictional novels describe 'attractive' does not truly define it. Do not make the mistake of building your taste or opinion of what a prince-charming should look like by the tall, well built, sex appeal superhero appearance given to this figure by Hollywood. You will end up in a pit if you get carried away because there are a million and one visionless guys out there with extra six packs to give away. They themselves are so attracted to their own bodies that they have become their own idols. You will have your head buried between your thighs every day in tears when you discover that they were not going to let their good looks go to waste as one woman is not enough to fully appreciate the work of art they feel they are.

Is it every good looking guy that thinks this way? Absolutely not, but it is very easy to know a guy that has struck a balance between keeping fit and every other important thing in life from one who is obsessed with looking good. I am strongly of the opinion that any man obsessed with how he looks, who will spend time in front of a mirror is not ready to for the important things of life. A real man is purpose driven and vision consumed, he doesn't care if its shampoo or dishwashing liquid he has to wash his hair with. If he keeps a beard, he is not treating it like an idol. Sometimes, the beard is still there because hasn't found time to shave, not because of making any fashion statements. Sometimes, he keeps a clean shave because he can't afford to waste time trying to carve some look that will grow out in the next few days. Don't get me wrong, keeping a beard is not a bad thing and there are men and women who like it, however, when life cannot move on because a man has not been able to carve his beard at a barber's shop, then it has become a point of concern. Some men are not necessarily good-looking but the confidence and charisma they exude is what makes the difference. The first thing I always do when ladies ask me what a serious minded guy should look like is to give this analogy; "what inspires presidents, people holding sensitive positions and offices in nations of the world, doctors, soldiers, the most successful entrepreneurs and business moguls we know around the world to look the way they look?" They're not out to follow or set any fashion trends, they don't keep any outrageous hairdos, over ninety percent do not keep a beard, they don't care about tattoos or piercings. Why is this so? Because they are too busy making life changing decisions! They understand the seriousness of the office they occupy and are too preoccupied handling their resposibilities, which sometimes, can hang between the borders of life and death. They sleep, eat and wake up to the vision and burning passion to fulfill purpose, provide solutions, make the world a better place using their various fields of specialization as the lives and wellbeing of many is dependent on their success. Even if they work out, they do so to stay healthy and relevant, not to have a body worthy of a 'Selfie'. If you meet your future husband having six packs and looking like his shirt is about to be ripped off his chest, that's awesome. Don't be carried away though because after five to ten years in marriage, it might become a thing of blessed memory. When responsibilities set in and make him not have time for the gym anymore and you keep churning out delicious meals that make him go for a second helping, don't push the blame on the "he has changed" theory.

Having established that finding Mr. Universe is not the standard for good looks, simply go for the basic things that you love. It is wise to choose someone that has some of the basic things you get attracted to in the opposite sex because those qualities will always be attractive to you even in old age and those are the features that help you keep your eyes fixed on your man, leaving no room for loopholes that can open doors to temptations in the future. There is nothing more satisfying to a man than loving him just the way he is and so also a woman; we all want someone that will love us just the way we are. If you find yourself wishing you could change this or that in someone, that is your warning sign indicating that you need to pause and reevaluate. Do not proceed until you make up your mind to accept him the way he is, or until you are sure that the love you feel goes beyond his physical appearance and you can't find yourself living your life with someone else.

I have arranged the first three points on the list according to how I prioritized them when I was searching and I can assure you that to keep them arranged in this order of importance will reduce anybody's chances of making a mistake to zero. Like I said earlier, physique is subject to change depending on how convinced you are about the man and the level of peace you sense within, associated with the compatibility you feel. I know of a very good man who had a birth defect on one of his legs. He was actually successful in terms of living above the average income in Nigeria, he was on fire for God, well loved and respected by everyone around and dedicated to his passion. With all the disappointments he faced from women who judged him based on his defect, he still got married and was blessed with children. The woman who married him, most likely never imagined her future husband was going to have a bad leg, but, some things about a man's physique become of little or no relevance when you become sure that the man has those three points listed above and the depth of love and connection you feel makes you love him just the way he is, his physical flaws become part of the reasons you love him. They are still very happily married.

(How To Know It's Her)

CHAPTER 8
Climb Every Mountain

Sometime in October 2007, Elliana went off to camp for her National Youth Service, a one year mandatory program by the government in Nigeria for all graduate students from the Universities and other equivalent tertiary institutions. Somehow, she had been able to get her mother's consent to be in a relationship at this period and for us, it was one giant mountain climbed in our dream path towards our marital plans. By the end of her third week, she was out of camp and had secured herself a place in Christian Broadcasting Network, Africa's regional office in Abuja. It was the same place where at some point earlier, she had been a TV presenter. This time, she was absorbed to work in their marketing department and as fate would have it, CBN had rolled out part of its marketing strategy to sensitize people about their outreach activities around the world through an avenue called *Shiloh*, a yearly global program organized by Living Faith Church, one of the largest Pentecostal churches headquartered in Nigeria. Elliana was part of the team going to Lagos for this event, which for me was another type of the lovely opportunities we always sought, as we always looked forward to any activity that could close the seven hundred and fifty two kilometers distance between us, and give us a reason to always be together.

I had gone the following morning after their arrival to Shiloh campground and located their marketing stand. I was so excited to see the love of my life again after a long stretch of almost three months that I didn't know when I picked her up and threw her sky high, not minding the conservative stare coming from the beehive of worshippers clustered around the different array of stands with their displays of different Kingdom products brought to the campground for sale. She didn't hesitate to gladly introduce me to her cheerful and welcoming head of department, Mrs. Humphrey whom she had already told so much about me. Even Jerry, the pleasant bus driver was also not left, His disposition toward me showed me he was pleased to meet the much talked about John Rex. Without delay, I joined in on sorting out all the products they came with unto their stand as we engrossed ourselves with catching up and expressing how much we missed each other. Mrs. Humphrey, a boisterous, high energy, hilarious and self-driven business woman with a slight edge of mischief to her attitude threw one of their branded T-shirts at me to join in on the day's marketing without caring to find out how long I had to stay. It was quite some fun as I joined to help get many people registered as partners of the *700 Club*. I will always live to remember the love struck stares, the glances at each other in the midst of work, expressing our innermost feelings towards one another, and the contagious smiles that we shared every time our eyes met. It flowed so freely from the depth of our souls like unending ocean waves moved by currents that were beyond human comprehension. Our spirits were completely immersed in each other in the midst of the noisy ambience that characterized the exhibition stands and tents. The joy of being around each other produced so much energy that our boosted morale positively and directly attracted customers to us and several partnership registrations, in spite of the team's late arrival to the program.

Usually, at the end of the six-day power packed program, after Bishop David Oyedepo has pronounced the final blessings on the crowd, people would go to the altar of the over fifty thousand seater auditorium to pour out their hearts and raise their petitions unto God. I remember holding my love's hand and leading her toward the altar to go and raise up our heart's cry and desire towards our wedding preparation before our Heavenly Father. At this point, we had identified clearly the obstacles we needed to surmount to gain victory. And did God answer our prayers? He answered every bit of it; from the biggest to the least on our list that we dropped at His feet on the altar at Shiloh.

Elliana was so ready, willing and totally submissive to my spiritual leadership. Despite her spiritual maturity, she still humbled herself to yield to my spiritual guidance and direction as the man she had chosen to place over her life. It is very important for you as a man to have your woman show signs of submissiveness to your leadership, especially in spiritual matters even before taking her to the altar. I have discovered from my little experience that when a woman loves you, she yields herself totally to you. And so, if she is not open to your guidance and accepting of your position as the spiritual authority God has placed over her, then something is wrong somewhere. It's either she has a big issue where submission is concerned generally or she doesn't love you enough to allow you lead her. On the other hand, maybe your spiritual maturity and wisdom where it comes to your relationship and knowledge of God through Christ is not matching up to hers or her expectation. She probably may just be feeling she knows more than you and that is enough to make a woman uncomfortable, which brings me to my counsel to you brothers; that you need to develop yourselves spiritually in Christ Jesus and in your purpose in His Kingdom before you start thinking of searching for your clone. You are designed by God to lead her to purpose and destiny fulfillment by God, and not the other way round. Think about it for a second, a beautiful young lady is about to commit her whole life and destiny into your hands and you don't know God enough to lead her into God's purpose for your lives according to His blueprint for you in Heaven? You cannot lead someone into a path you have not discovered yourself neither can you give what you don't have. That is why I have repeated it over and over again, you must discover your purpose; you must be able to say where you plan to be five, ten, twenty, thirty years from now. In the course of your conversations with her, you must be able to communicate to her clearly where you were headed before you met her and how you plan to achieve this better with her in your life. For example, here are some topics you might want to find a way to communicate; the direction you are going, your vision, the vision you have for both of you, the vision you have for your home and family and the impact you believe God wants you both to make for His kingdom to the glory of His name.

Now, sisters this is for you; do you know your man well enough? I mean the man you want to get married to. Does he have the capacity to lead you to Heaven or to hell? I mean literally. No matter how holy you are before you met that man, if you don't make sure he is your clone and he has what it takes to lead you spiritually, he can crash your destiny and end both of you down in hellfire. Brothers please develop yourselves. Build yourself up in the most holy faith says Jude 1:20 and sisters, please learn to start practicing sensitivity and obedience to the

HolySpirit so that your choice of a man does not truncate your destiny.

My First Formal Visit

In January 2008, after the New Year's festivities, I took a trip to Abuja and this time, it was to go and give an official and formal introduction of myself as the young man in Elliana's life. My first appearance was when I escorted my wife to Abuja from Okene, after my dad's burial had given me an opportunity to meet her parents. While her dad was okay with what he saw, especially knowing that his daughter had a preference for a black guy than a white man or even a bi-racial person like her, her mom was not going to be a walk over. This was not necessarily because she didn't like my look or appearance but because I discovered that her close affiliation to her extended family background makes her filter every of her major decisions through the eyes and perceptions of her siblings, relations and her closest friends. I guess the approval she gets from those around her acts as a proof that she is headed in the right direction. For example, one of her main concerns about me, especially where she felt her elder brother would raise an eyebrow, was the tribe I come from. She was stereotyped about the Ebira tribe in Kogi state as a violent, diabolical people who exhibited infidelity in marriage, as biasedly broken down to her by her brother in the course of her fact-finding mission and enquiry about the tribe. Besides, according to the direct and indirect comments that were made in between a long interrogative conversation she had with me, her dream of wanting to see her only child get married to a Caucasian man seemed to have been completely thwarted by my presence and the feature motion picture shoot of her proposed daughter's life's script was thrown away.

I remember how she had earlier almost dashed our hopes when she vehemently and blatantly turned down Elliana's request to get married to me. Elliana had called me on the phone on that heavy rainy day where I was over at a friend's house and broke the news to me. Amidst the instant disappointment and sadness it created, all I could think of in the flesh was eloping with her, in fact, we both concluded at that time that it was going to be our next point of action if her mom continued in that insistent way. But, as we spent more time brooding over it while allowing the Spirit of God to step in and take control of the situation, we realized our best action was to pray and trust in God totally; if God got us this far, He'll get us through the rest of the way. And as God would have it, she filtered her decision through two of her closest friends who gave her good counsel to allow her daughter choose a man for herself. The reason, as she later explained to Elliana, was so that she would not be held responsible for any undesirable future outcome. That was how God changed her mind, to give Elliana her consent. He made a way out for us to continue our journey into marriage.

My first official trip to Abuja to get myself acquainted with Elliana's family turned out to be quite a successful and receptive one, especially where her dad was concerned. We got along almost immediately I arrived at their home. It was almost as if we had known each other long before we even met. He was a good-hearted person with an outspoken personality and he always had a witty way of expressing himself with lots of jokes. We could spend long hours talking with each other and never run out of what to say. We just had a great connection from the very onset. I spent about a week in Abuja and it afforded me the opportunity to meet Elliana's extended family members as well. Some, receptive and some others were not very receptive. But one thing was certain, from the way Elliana introduced me to them with a very strong sense of assertiveness, they knew I had come to stay.

When you meet the right woman, I'm talking about a woman who truly loves you or better still in my concept once again, your clone, she doesn't go about introducing you to her family and friends in an apologetic tone or manner. She puts you up on her wall of display as the best thing that has ever happened to her. And sisters, please hear me, the way you portray, display and stand up for your husband-to-be before others, especially your family members, will go a long way in determining how they will treat him. If you make it look like you are not very sure or confident about him, they will soon convince you against your will and help you kick him out of your life. But, if you put him up as irreplaceable, they will have no choice but to submit to your will and choice. **Assertiveness and confidence is a sign of faith** and confidence in God's ability to finish what He started. It actually requires the Holy Spirit giving you boldness to speak when you find yourself in a humbling situation. In Ephesians 6:19-20, Paul asks his friends to pray that he might speak boldly as he ought to speak. It is my prayer that God will give you the wisdom and boldness to surmount any such resistance.

(How To Know It's Him)

CHAPTER 8
Moment of Truth

About two months after I battled with making the right decision based on the misleading counsel I had taken from my friend, precisely on a Sunday, something happened that would change the course of history in my life. It was the second sign I got from the Holy Spirit, which could not be ignored. It was His way of saying I am with you and no man can alter My perfect plans and the hopeful future I have for you; to bring you to an expected and glorious end.

For I know the plans that I think toward you, says the LORD, thoughts of peace and not of evil, to give you a future and a hope. Jeremiah 29:11 NKJV

You saw me before I was born. Every day of my life was recorded in your book. Every moment was laid out before a single day passed. Psalm 139:16 NLT

Services in my family church were split into three separate services for the convenience of attendees. Being that every time I returned from school, I would naturally align myself back to my duty post as the choir leader in the youth department, it was normal for me to attend all three services just to ensure that delegated roles and choir ministrations were delivered on schedule. We had just rounded up one of the three services and I decided to take a walk to the main entrance where some refreshment kiosks were stationed. I was with my best friend and on our way back from having a snack, we stopped at the car park to talk with a few friends who were on their way home. In that instant, for no particular reason, the same rushing feeling of joy and happiness that I felt when I saw John in our campus fellowship library flooded my entire being all over again. For a split second, it felt as though everything happening around me came to a standstill and my thoughts became louder than the conversation we were having. Thoughts of John flooded my heart afresh and it brought such peace and hope to my heart that translated into smiles on my face, the type that made me beam from ear to ear. I am sure that the people I was talking to would have thought I was responding to them, they had no idea that I had been transported to a new realm of revelation. I had a new and exciting realization of the path that I should follow. I could almost hear the Holy Spirit say to my heart "this is the path ...walk in it". I mean, this time around, the joy that bubbled in my heart felt as if I had hit a jackpot. It felt like a river of hope, as if there was still hope for the both of us to get together again and make it work. I could perceive something great and fulfilling in a future with him, and in that same instant, I began to feel a strong and passionate desire to see John and to start a relationship with him. It was as though a blindfold had been taken off my eyes and I wondered why exactly I let John go. I longed to jump into his arms and give him a resounding Yes! Yes! I want to be your wife! Whatever it was that had a hold on my mind had been lifted and all the fears and confusion

I felt fizzled away, leaving the same certainty and deep conviction I felt in Cotonou, that this was meant to be.

As we walked back to the church building, my friend could not help but notice the radiance on my face and she knew that the smile was not triggered by anything external. We stopped for a moment somewhere on the walkway as she asked what was going on with me. Without hesitation, I told her about every single emotion I just felt and the very strong leading I had to say yes to John. I further mentioned to her that I planned to do so quickly. We both knew that I was meant to travel to Benin Republic soon and now, we knew that what I meant was that my stopover in Lagos this time would be a defining one. She was calm and collected but I captured the split second shock that reflected in her expression when I mentioned my decision. I couldn't care less at this point, the joy and excitement I experienced in my new decision generated so much zeal and passion that when I spoke about it, she looked at me, appalled and speechless. I knew that it was because she had never seen me so resolved about anything like this before. With a smile on her face, she wished me well.

As God would orchestrate things, for some reason John decided to call me. What a set-up from Heaven, there was no way I would call that a coincidence. He told me he just called to say hello after such a long time and to check up on me. Well, that was the icebreaker I needed. I was planning to strike up a conversation but because of how bad I felt, being the one that brought it all to a halt, I had been wondering how to do so. As far as I was concerned, his call was a confirmation to me that it was God that spoke to me and He was at work to restore what the enemy almost destroyed. I can bet that he didn't expect my response to be so welcoming. I was certain that he called back to surf my countenance and mind, to know if there was an atom of hope for anything to be resuscitated between us before totally letting go and moving on. My response to him must have also been a testimony and confirmation to him.

Our conversations became very consistent and seasoned with a lot of love. At about this period, I was preparing for one of my trips to school but this one was 'The Trip'. I looked forward to it with everything in me; I couldn't wait to tell him. I couldn't help but let him know ahead of my trip that I had something very important to tell him when I arrived Lagos. He could hear the excitement in my voice but he seemed to be careful not to have his hopes raised and dashed by making any assumptions. I knew that he maintained a happy yet gentle response to my statement to keep his heart safe.

I was on my way to Lagos when news reached me that one of my Dean of International Studies was planning to leave the school for Nigeria the next day. I needed him to sign an important document and couldn't afford not to achieve that in this trip. I joyfully asked John to pick me up at the bus station, which he gladly did. He requested if he could take me to lunch which I gladly accepted too. We had such a beautiful time together that I wished it wouldn't end. It was the first time we were together on a date alone and the first time I was completely free to be myself without putting up a mental wall that was meant to hide if I was in love or not. I was ready to show my love for him. I didn't mind letting him see that I wanted to date him, after all, I was planning to scream it out from the roof top for the world to hear. Making this announcement to him was so special to me that I didn't just want to say it in passing, it mattered to me to make that moment a special and memorable one so I decided to hold it back because of my need to hurriedly get to school. Right after lunch, we drove to the motor park where he dropped me off like someone who was longing to travel with me. If he could leave all his business engagements to follow me, he would have given anything to be able to do so; I could see it written all over him. We parted ways with a promise to see again on my way back. I had to spend the rest of the semester in school and because of the work I was doing on my project, the workload was heavy.

Whenever time came to travel back home from school, it was not uncommon for students to travel in groups of twos, threes and fours for companionship and safety. Certain unplanned journeys, however, did not give room for such arrangements to be made. I have had cause to travel alone severally because of this and I would just make sure that my trips never ran into the night. This time around though, I deliberately sought someone with whom I could pair up and travel because this was no ordinary trip. John and I had been in touch all along while I was in school and when it was time to travel back to Abuja, I told him that I was going to stay in Lagos for two days so we could have enough time to spend with each other and have the long awaited talk I wanted to have with him. My plan was to spend as much time as I could in the day with him and then take my friend along to spend the night in my aunt's place. My friend knew what this specific meeting with John was about and she was willing to sacrifice her time to help me achieve my heart's desire. If there was anything I wasn't going to do, it was to lie to myself. I knew how passionately in love he had always been and I knew how astronomically my love for him was growing and overwhelming me. I knew that making this announcement and declaration of love to him was going to launch us into the next level in our relationship and make us fall totally in love with each other without reservations. It was going to be an intense and euphoric moment and I knew I needed someone close by that I could be accountable to, someone whose presence I would be conscious of, that would keep me in check and stop us from crossing the line. It was my responsibility to set up an environment where my flesh would not be permitted to act freely.

I would highly recommend this for even scenarios that don't have anything to do with giving your consent to a proposal. You would have to make conscious decisions and efforts that would help you keep sexual sin at bay, even while dating or courting. A mistake of intimacy that happens in a relationship has never really been an accident. Whether we get caught off guard or we see it coming, we have a responsibility to create personal restrictions and boundaries to be able to resist and escape the traps of sexual sin. An example would be visiting your fiancé in their home, alone, and not expecting a measure of intimacy between the two of you that can lead to sex if not guarded. Some even deceive themselves that they can sleep over and nothing will happen. My dear friend, if the goal is abstinence before marriage, then some rules cannot be broken or else your goal is out the window. A father in faith once said "there is no such thing as a strong Christian, only a wise one". You must flee all appearances of evil. Fleeing is a display of wisdom in this case.

With this in mind, I applied wisdom by travelling with my friend and co- campus fellowship leader, Faith. John convinced me to stay in a hotel nearby where the unending traffic in the constantly busy Lagos metropolis would not get the best of our stay together, which made a lot of sense. It was already running into the evening hours when we got to where John was. He was aware that I was on my way with a friend and had booked a hotel room for us. We all went somewhere nice to eat and went back to the hotel for more chit chatting until late. I was still holding back my announcement for the next day's date because I wanted it to be a moment between just the two of us. I wanted to be able to take my time to express my feelings and I wanted to be able to see him respond with all his heart unhindered by the presence of a third party. That response was worth the wait because I knew how he longed and prayed for this day to come.

Soon enough, the next day was here. We all hung out together in our hotel room in the morning. John eventually had to attend to business but promised to be back later that afternoon to take me out. Faith joined in to get me styled and prepped up for the date and the process alone shot my excitement level over the roof! I had played out our conversation at this date in my head countless times. I tried out different approaches to saying yes to him, the dramatic, the calm or the excited. It was such a remarkable and joyous moment for me, to know that this was it, the day when our journey to the altar together was going to commence, when I could say officially that I was courting the man I plan to marry.

Let's revisit the difference between dating and courtship. Dating is a situation where a man and a woman initiate a relationship with the intention of knowing each better with or without marriage as a goal. It is the start-off point for any relationship that plans to grow. But, courtship always has marriage as a goal. In courtship, the two parties involved have crossed the dating phase and are resolved that they have found the person they want to spend the rest of their lives with. For me and John, dating happened subtly when we were getting to know each other. I had studied him to a very large extent. At this point of accepting his proposal, with the level to which I had become so sure that he was my God-ordained husband, we moved straight into courtship.

John arrived at the door step of our hotel room with a rose in his hand. He looked more handsome than ever in a crisp white shirt tucked into a pair of jeans with his sleeves rolled up to just below his elbows, as usual. I felt as though my knight in shining armor had appeared. My appetite was gone. I didn't care if we ate or took a stroll, I just wanted to be with him and keep looking into his eyes. I was so certain in my heart of hearts that I was doing the right thing, there was no doubt in my heart that I had met my missing half, my clone, my life partner, my priest, my best friend, my twin, my soul mate, my husband and dream come true.

We went around town a little and then visited the first location which was a Nigerian-style food and barbecue place with an indoor eating lounge. He was giving me all he could afford at that time and I was more than content with it. I didn't even care if we ate or not, I was over saturated with love and having his presence around me, that was all that mattered to me. I had studied him for a while and knew without a doubt that if he had the whole world, he would relinquish its entire goodness to me. I can speak about him like this at that early stage of our friendship because generosity was one of the things I looked out for in a man I would marry and I spotted it in John. It mattered to me to find a caring and generous man because God had planted a seed of compassion in my heart from a very young age that I could not imagine being with someone who was tight-fisted with money. I have had to give out countless one-and-only precious personal belongings without batting an eyelid, including last meals; it wasn't going to be easy living with someone who was a direct opposite.

I don't think there is any woman who ever wants to end up with a miserly man. Some women have their way around such men but in my case though, it is completely off the list of things I want to tolerate. It is not a bad thing to have a man who is financially prudent, who has a plan for a comfortable future that he is saving toward, in fact, it is a very good thing. However, it goes overboard and becomes a source of concern when he cannot make room for a little pleasure without calculating expenses to the very last penny. When a man is generous, it will show and he doesn't have to only give to you for you to conclude that he is. One sure way to know if he has the seed of generosity in him is if he can give God first place over his income. He should be able give to God, give his tithe, his offerings and be open to promptings of compassion to help someone in need. Unfortunately, he might give to you just to impress you, especially if you start announcing how generosity in a prospective husband is a big deal to you. Don't set him up for pretense. Just be yourself and allow him to be himself. It's the best thing you can do for yourself in the process of discovering each other's personalities, orientations, belief systems, strengths and weaknesses.

So, it's his general outlook on money and what it should be spent on that you want to find out. Generosity is not measured by how much a person can give at a time but by how much others are blessed through that person when he has just enough to meet his needs. People say it's not the amount that matters, it the thought that counts. Giving is scripturally never about the quantity, it's about what it costs you.

So, we ordered for drinks and something to eat. We talked about everything we could think of that centered on us; individual visions, goals, visions of the kind of home we individually desired to have, friends, family and more. At this stage, he was certain that I was interested in him but I had not given him a yes and we had not officially kicked off our relationship. That was what he was praying and hoping for, to be able to say that I was officially his. When we were done eating, we drove to another interesting point, a more posh location. He had gotten a particular car hire service driver he always called on whenever he needed car hire services who drove us round the city, it was his way of giving me a little tour around the nightlife in Lagos; a beautiful and vibrant city with round-the-clock activities which makes people refer to it as the city that never sleeps. It was fun driving and enjoying the scenery, but while in love and with the person you're in love with beside you, it's one of the most liberating and breath-taking feelings you can ever have. We got to the lounge and climbed upstairs to find a more serene, comfortable and beautiful spot that overlooked the city. In the midst of several other topics that got us enveloped in our own world, I asked him to pause for a second and told him I needed to tell him the very important thing I had wanted to say. He looked at me very expectantly with a gentle grin on his face. I told him that my reason for refusing his proposal the first time was that I was not sure if I was ready because there were external influences that tried to dissuade me. I explained to him how these external influences gave me a negative perspective of the outcome of a relationship with him and how, unfortunately, it generated uncertainty in me. I explained how I had an underlying fear of an opposition that could arise from my home front based on my parents' expectations and my decision earlier not to go into a relationship was to protect us both from any eventual heart breaks and pains. However, having had a lot of time to think about it, now I'm certain that this is what I want and I would rather give the relationship a chance and see where it goes from here than live in regret that I never tried to see if it could work. I told him that I had decided to say yes to him because it would make me the happiest person to know that I chose him and did what I wanted. I added that even if it eventually didn't work out as planned, I would be more satisfied knowing that I gave it a try rather than not trying at all. And so I gave him a Yes! "Yes,

I would love to date you! I decided long before now that the next relationship I will be going into will be with the man I want to marry, so, I am going into this relationship with plans to marry you".

The joy and excitement I saw on his face was tangible, he was ecstatic. If he could scream without creating a scene, he probably would have done so. He held my hands so firmly and yet softly for a few seconds and told me how this was the best thing that was happening to him after salvation. He professed his love for me with such overwhelming words. We were both over the moon as he kept asking me every now and then jokingly but excitedly "do you mean we're officially dating now?"

We came back to the hotel where my friend and I were staying, in the taxi hire that had taken us round town that evening. I called Faith to let her know that I was downstairs. We stood within the hotel premises and chatted for an extra hour. It seemed as though we had so much we wanted to say to each other that had been bottled up inside and now we had been given the chance. There was so much laughter, oneness in understanding each other's point of view that it felt as if we had known each other for much longer than we had. There was an openness with which we communicated, a quality I value so much which we still enjoy in our marriage that made our relationship one without pretense, fakeness and lies. He didn't try to be someone he wasn't to impress me. He told me exactly where he was in life, how he struggled to get there, the bright future he knew was ahead of him and the different ideas and visions he was working on to get there. I also accepted him the way he was. I didn't have it in my plan to pressure him into becoming anything. I just wanted to be with him. I was also sure that we were destined for the top. Two hard working believers backed up by grace in the Lord can only keep climbing higher until they reach the peak of thier calling in Christ. Our openness was made possible because we were not afraid to feel vulnerable to each other.

Because of the circumstances surrounding my childhood and my decision to show my husband and family the type of love that I had always desired, I promised myself that when I am sure the man I'm dating is the man I want to marry, that I would open my heart to him without reservation, after all, I wasn't saving a part of it for someone else, neither was there anything to lose. The only thing I was going to reserve was the intimacy from sexual intercourse, which I felt, was not only scriptural but also would give us something to look forward to and a reason to hurriedly get our wedding plans rolling. I had taken my time to make this decision, I had almost lost him the first time but somehow God worked things out divinely and now, I am a hundred percent sure that I want to spend my life with this man so why show love with caution. I wanted to know what it felt like to give your all without fears, doubts, anxieties, 'plan B's, no backdoors left open to jump out through, in fact, no backdoors at all. We parted ways that night just because it was too late to stand out there and keep talking. We couldn't wait for the next day, and the next and the next.

(How To Know It's Her)

CHAPTER 9
Intimacy in Christian Dating

Two months after I had gone on a courtesy and familiarity visit to Elliana's family home in Abuja, we found ourselves back in her school, Houdegbe North American University in Benin Republic again where it all started. It's just that this time, it was more of a casual trip we undertook together with one of her friends and fellow campus fellowship leader, Francisca. They had both decided to take a trip from Abuja to their former school in Cotonou, on a mission to retrieve the hard copy of their bachelor's degree certificate, and the trip was routed through Lagos, as was necessary for me to also join in on the trip. We had barely settled in when Pastor Niyi, their campus fellowship pastor cashed in on our divinely ordained trip, according to him, to get me roped into preaching at the fellowship that evening. I remember him introducing me and Elliana to the entire fellowship as an about to be wedded couple, at the point when he welcomed me to take over the pulpit. There was such a large roar of cheering and screaming and clapping ovation from the excited congregation of students that made me know how much her fellowship members loved her and how much impact she had made within her four years of being through that school. After my first ministration in their school with a message titled "What Do You See?" centered on the subject of vision, I sensed that they felt their assistant pastor, Elliana, had seen well and made the right choice. We were a perfect match and I believe a symbol of a perfect role model to them.

That night, after a wonderful ministration at the fellowship and after we had had dinner, we retired to the roof top of the fellowship house and laid side by side each other to gaze into the beautiful and brightly lit up night sky. The sparkling stars and the cool whispering sea breeze that brushes against our skin lured our bodies into a tempting close contact towards each other. It was a night of struggle between the lustful desires of the flesh and what was morally and scripturally right, which brings me to the subject of sex during dating and courtship.

Sexual intimacy during courtship or dating cannot be fully treated as a topic or sub-topic in this book, as a matter of fact, it is a subject that deserves a whole book dedicated to it. However, for the purpose of this write up on our journey into marriage, it is important I throw a little bit of light on it, especially considering the weight of some statements made in passing which could be misinterpreted by readers; for example, in certain instances where I wrote that we 'were all over each other' or when I said 'I picked her up and threw her sky high' or statements that involved the use of the word 'romantic'. I would like to put up a disclaimer at this point that these were not words, sentences or statements meant to construe an approval for sexual intimacy in premarital dating or courtship relationship. As a matter of fact, I am in total agreement with the Bible and scriptural stand point and view where this matter is concerned, that any form of sexual intimacy outside of marriage is totally an unholy and sinful affair. The Bible makes this very clear in several scriptures such as 1Thessalonians

4:3-5, 1 Corinthians 7:2, Hebrews 13:4, Galatians 5:19-21, Genesis 2:24-25.

God's will is for you to be holy, so stay away from all sexual sin. Then each of you will control his own body and live in holiness and honor – not in lustful passion like the pagans who do not know God and His ways. 1 Thessalonians 4:3-5, NLT

But because there is so much sexual immorality, each man should have his own wife, and each woman should have her own husband 1 Corinthians 7:2, NLT

Give honor to marriage, and remain faithful to one another in marriage. God will surely judge people who are immoral and those who commit adultery. Hebrews 13:4, NLT

When you follow the desires of your sinful nature, the results are very clear: sexual immorality, impurity, lustful pleasures, idolatry, sorcery, hostility, quarreling, jealousy, outbursts of anger, selfish ambition, dissension, division, envy, drunkenness, wild parties, and other sins like these. Let me tell you again, as I have before, that anyone living that sort of life will not inherit the \kingdom of God. Galatians 5:19-2, NLT

This explains why a man leaves his father and mother and is joined to his wife, and the two are untied into one. Genesis 2:24-25, NLT

Besides, this book is written from a totally unapologetic Kingdom point of view, in other words, it is a Christian guide to dating and courtship, based on a true life story. Fornication and adultery in my own school of thought can't really be counted a mistake because occasion is given to it in the true sense of the matter. But, if for any reason a couple intending genuinely to get married and on their journey to the altar, find themselves in such a fallen state, they should genuinely repent before God and hasten their wedding plans as a solution to constantly falling and living in sin. In other words, it is best for intending couples on their way to the altar not to delay in getting married, in order to avoid premarital sexual intimacy. This is why Paul made it clear in 1 Corinthians 7:8-9 that;

So I say to those who aren't married and to widows – it's better to stay unmarried, just as I am. But if they can't control themselves, they should go ahead and marry. It's better to marry than to burn with lust. 1 Corinthians 7:8-9, NLT

And so, based on our desire for us to freely express our love to each other in sexual intimacy within the confines of what is right before God, according to Scripture, Elliana and I concluded to hasten our journey to the altar by every means necessary through Christ Jesus. I know that one other effective strategy we applied so we could be ahead of our flesh was to arrange our meetings in public places or have a friend go with us to a private date or location. I can't even begin to tell you how effective this simple but wise strategy is. No virtuous lady or man of honor will mount sexual pressure on you during dating or courtship. When you have your partner begin to subtly or overtly make sexual demands on you, then, there is a need to question his or her character in relation to his or her spiritual maturity and scriptural conformity. Moral purity should be a collective drive and responsibility of both partners during dating and courtship.

The consequence of sexual intimacy during courtship can be devastating physically, spiritually, psychologically and emotionally. And so, when God gives a Biblical instruction to abstain or refrain from it till you are joined together with your partner in marriage, it is strictly for the purpose of a mutually beneficial partnership relationship with you. Sexual sin is the only sin the Bible describes as sin against the body. When our bodies therefore have become the legal property of God through His Holy Spirit, to execute His Kingdom agenda on earth, you have no right to abuse it on your own selfish terms or interest anymore. Your body belongs to you and God when you become a Kingdom citizen.

Don't you realize that your body is the temple of the Holy Spirit, who lives in you and was given to you by God? You do not belong to yourself, for God bought you with a high price. So you must honor God with your body. 1 Corinthians 6:19-20, NLT

(How To Know It's Him)

CHAPTER 9
A Decision of a Lifetime

Early in 2007, I had graduated from the University. I was expected by my family, like any well behaved and obedient daughter, to wait for her parents' plans for her. I knew I was expected to move on to my NYSC and enter the job market but there was also an underlying plan to send me to the United Kingdom for a Master's Degree. The next phase of my life was being planned out for me but unbeknownst to them, I had been planning simultaneously and I dare say that God was working contrary to their plans too by empowering my plans. The challenge before me was how I was going to pitch my plans and visions to a family that believed things should be done a certain way.

This next phase was so critical and yet, looked almost difficult to surmount. I knew it would have to take God to come through for me. I was hoping to announce my relationship plans to a family that had subtly knocked into me, over the years, with stories, with indirect statements and direct counsel that I was expected to bring a man with a bank account fat enough to accommodate the entire family. You couldn't be from the Eastern part of Nigeria and not understand that money is of utmost importance in choosing a spouse. You had to get a man who could withstand the initial financial tests from the woman's family by financing all the requirements listed out for him to provide to the kinsmen and giving a handsome amount as bride price before they can consider him worthy to take their daughter as his wife. To get a man who would make your wedding day a showstopper and be able to meet subsequent demands or pressure from her family without interfering with the comfort he is expected to give their daughter in her matrimonial home was considered the perfect guy. It was a thing of pride to have such monetary displays, for family members to be able to raise their shoulders high around their friends and brag with flamboyance. When it comes to fulfilling these financial responsibilities, the people from the Eastern part of Nigeria will not acknowledge love as an excuse for a man not to play this role. Love is a stranger where money matters are concerned; only money has a voice here.

The issue was not John's ability to meet all their requirements financially, it was the fact that I am bi-racial so the 'price' on me was higher. Not only that, my extended family from my Nigerian side was supposed to be able to boast that my husband and I literally stuffed money down the throat of anyone that was in need around us or demanded for it, as our duty. There was a general, yet silent expectation that a girl like me would bring home a man from a prominent family, the cream of society, an aristocrat. At least, I confirmed this further when a few of my cousins were telling John during our introduction that 'this sister of theirs whom he is about to marry was reserved for the nobles of society'. I thought to myself that these people don't mind if one ends up in a mess of a marriage, they wouldn't care if one ended up in the hands of an unfaithful husband or becoming a victim of domestic violence, after all, in their eyes, all men are the same and there are women out there who have learnt to absorb some of these unexpected marital mishaps just so they can continue to enjoy comfort and be a source of financial assistance to their relations.

Unfortunately for them, I disappointed them. I was expected to wipe all their tears away and erase poverty from my mother's lineage. Instead I found a lowly and respectable young man, full of dreams, visions and aspirations, garnished with the fear of the Lord. What were they supposed to do with a man just being God-fearing? Besides, if I wanted 'God-fearing', there's no way there wouldn't have been one out there who was also very financially established. So why John? Visions and aspirations that had not materialized made no sense and were of no benefit to them.

Knowing that I had deviated from expectations, I had to summon the courage to introduce John to my family. I had been used to approaching my mom on important matters through my older cousin who grew up in the same house with me. She seemed to understand my mom better and the right time to speak with her, depending on the issue on ground. I had grown comfortable hiding under her shadow for fear of pushing the wrong buttons and triggering a response I would regret. As much as I wanted to, I was afraid that passing this decision through my cousin who was very conversant with the Eastern tradition would put an end to the mission because she would most likely give me a hundred and one reasons why I needed to reconsider my choice based on her knowledge of what stood a chance in the family. The last thing I needed at this point was any extra form of discouragement.

I came to realize that this conversation could not be routed through anyone. It was a mature decision, a decision of a lifetime. It would help her see me in a new light, in the light of a grown up young lady who had grown to a marriageable age rather than the little girl identity I had in her eyes that seemed difficult to change. My future was hinged on this decision and I knew I had to be bold to discuss with her woman to woman. The question was how in the world I was going to bring up the topic. I could only ask God in prayer to give me a strategy and an opening to break the news to her, and the boldness to do so.

At this period, John's father was terribly ill. His health seemed to be deteriorating rapidly and we were all worried about his condition. I was in touch with Yvonne and my mother in-law-to-be on the phone just encouraging them and hoping to hear a positive progress report. In my heart, she was already my mother in-law because John and I started this relationship with the end in mind. We were not together to play hide and seek, we were resolved to get married.

The Strategy

On one fateful day, John called me to break the news that what we were all afraid of had happened. His father had passed on. It was devastating to think that all this happened not too long after we started our relationship. I was saddened by the fact that I never got to meet my future father-in-law. His death did not only affect my fiancé, whose pain was my pain too, but it was also the passing of Yvonne's father, my protégé and friend. As hard as this incident hit me, I never knew that it would afford me the opportunity to approach my mom concerning my relationship with John.

My graduation had barely come and gone when I informed my mom about the passing on of my school daughter's father. That was the strategy! My mom had great value and respect for the relationship of a school mother to a school daughter. It was an informal practice in schools in this part of the world where a senior student would unofficially and informally adopt a junior and younger student within the same institution voluntarily as a result of a special bond built by both parties. The senior takes on the role of a guardian or an elder sibling to the younger, guiding, counseling, protecting and supporting them and seeing to their welfare if they ever had a need. She always told me about her school mother and bragged about the wonderful relationship they shared. She told me how she sustained this relationship for a very long time, long after she graduated from school, traveling to spend a number of holidays with her school mother in their family house.

This divine idea that I got couldn't have been more precise. I had two birds to kill with this one stone and it was guaranteed to do so. The first was to facilitate a permit from my mom to travel for the upcoming funeral; there was no way I would have been able to leave Abuja for Kogi State without a good enough reason that would appeal to her conscience. If Yvonne were not in the picture, the question would have been "whose father's burial?"

I was obligated to be there for Yvonne and John. She wasn't just a friend; she literally took over a number of responsibilities from me at the campus fellowship when I rounded up school. She had to be my daughter in ministry, in other words, I had to endorse her for my lead pastor to entrust her with the roles that he did. I needed to go as her pastor and a representative of the fellowship. I also had to go as her friend and sister in-law to be. Therefore it wasn't out of place to say that she was my school daughter. This wasn't an event I was permitted to miss either. It would be callous of me not to make an appearance at such a sensitive and important event to the entire family as a fiancée.

The family was hoping to meet me even though it was not the most relaxed and sociable atmosphere to get to know each other. I had met a number of them almost a year earlier before I started dating John. He offered to pick me and my best friend up from the bus station one of the times I had to travel to school by road. He also needed to pick Yvonne up so we drove together to his elder sister's house where I also met his mom for the first time. We weren't anywhere close to dating then but when we eventually began our relationship, it was easy for them to connect the dots.

Like a round peg going through a round hole, my request slid through smoothly with a positive response. It was not given any further interrogations when she heard the details of my travel plans, which ensured my safety and that the trip was all expense paid.

The second bird to be knocked down was introducing John to my family. Getting him to visit before this trip would be like thwarting my own plans with my own hands. His presence from the beginning would raise suspicions that could compromise the entire mission. So, I concluded that I would travel to Okene, Kogi State alone and then he would make his first 'silent' appearance as my school daughter's brother who travelled with me to ensure my safe return.

Meeting John's Family

The game plan had been drawn and here I was on my way to Okene in a Lagos bound Marco Polo luxury bus. John did not want me travelling alone in one of those smaller unnamed vehicles for security reasons and I had also been given the name of the filling station where I was told to alight and wait for Yvonne to pick me up.

I was in touch with John and Yvonne from that morning, all through the journey. John was in one of the vehicles driving behind the ambulance bringing his father's body to Okene. He and his brothers were already on the road while he kept track of my movement. While on that bus, I was caught in between feeling nervous and not knowing what to expect. I was about to meet John's entire family both nuclear and extended. I had John's mom and Yvonne on my side. I had built a wonderful rapport with his mom and we had been in touch over the phone, she was very easy going, loving, sweet and without a care in the world but there were four more siblings to meet and get along with and several aunts and uncles. Yvonne and John had encouraged me respectively on the phone during the preparation for this trip and said everything they could to help me relax and believe that everybody would love me and were excited to meet me. Even though I knew his mom had a gentle and loving personality, the thought of meeting her once again, this time as her son's fiancée, and probably having a longer and deeper chat with her gave me butterflies in my stomach. I wasn't sure what she would expect her first son's fiancée to do to show she was 'wife material'. I wasn't sure what anybody would expect me to do to prove myself. I didn't even have a clue what their culture was like and how wives-to-be were expected to comport themselves based on that. John had assured me that his family was not the culturally minded type but I knew that there was no way there wouldn't be individual expectations. To further complicate things for me, I am mixed race. I've always been seen as 'Oyibo', which is a word in Nigeria referring to a person of European descent, a foreigner or a westernised person. I was going to be on the spotlight and everyone, from the least to the greatest member of the extended family, was going to attempt to weigh me to see if I could fit into an African family or maybe I was one of those lazy, over-pampered 'oyibo' girls that would starve their son by feeding him salads and finger foods. My thoughts ran across imagining what the ones I hadn't met would look like and their personalities. I felt that there certainly had to be the inquisitive ones, the critical ones, the cultural ones, the educators, the prejudiced and the carefree ones amongst them. When meeting a crowd of extended and very extended family, they typically fall into various groups of philosophies and mindsets. I had no intentions of winning everyone over, that would be an unrealistic mission. The best thing I could do for myself was to be myself. The battle of winning people over would usually be centered on the mother in-law and the sisters, especially the youngest, who would screen her older brother's fiancée to ensure she was cool enough. Well, incidentally, I was so blessed to have both John's mom and his youngest sister, Yvonne, on my side.

By the time I alighted at the designated filling station, Yvonne and John's immediate younger brother were there to pick me up. That was my first meeting with another sibling. He had a warm and welcoming countenance that not only allayed my anxieties but made me wonder if I was overthinking things. Yvonne and I maximized the brief ride to Federal College of Education (F.C.E) guesthouse catching up on things from where we last stopped.

I had arrived pretty early. John was still on the way from Lagos. His mom was at the family house a few kilometers away from us, where many relations and friends were visiting to commiserate with her. The guesthouse, however, was where everybody else was. It was where all the preparation toward the funeral and funeral reception was taking place. When we arrived, Yvonne did the most precious thing ever. She didn't just give a tour to get me acquainted with the people there and the environment, she also took me aside and described the personality of everyone in the family and that of those who were very close to the family. She further encouraged me to relax and know that she's got my back. She said it like a mafia boss, with so much love, certainty and sternness at the same time, giving me the confidence that nobody could oppose me even if they tried. She assured me that any opposition was a failed venture because I was already a part of the family and there was nothing anybody could do about it.

I didn't struggle one bit with believing her because her older brother, Peter, and the other siblings that I met later, gave me a rather surprisingly warm welcome. I knew at that moment that I was in the midst of very easygoing people. The only person I had a hard time flowing with at first was Yvonne's older sister, Franca, who was really hit by the passing of her dad. It reflected in her countenance and attitude. She was also overseeing and coordinating several preparatory activities toward the upcoming funeral. One of such activities was the food preparation. I believe the weight of the entire thing took a toll on her and placed her on the edge. I knew and respected my boundaries and didn't try to push it, I felt she would come around later when it was all over but for now, my confidence was on the fact that every other sibling had given me a reason not to fret and I was satisfied with that.

From the bags of ingredients I saw and the way everyone was deeply engrossed with their share of work, I thought we were about to feed the entire village. There was peeling here and washing there, cutting, local stoves and giant utensils being prepped and lots of instructions being hurled out in the native Ebira tongue. Franca had asked me to make myself comfortable and join in on any task I preferred. The somberness in the atmosphere did not call for any other thing beyond work. I looked odd moving around while everyone else was busy and I couldn't wait to find a company to hide myself in. I swiftly looked around and made a decision to sit with the English-speaking group who had been introduced to me by Yvonne as friends of the family from Lagos. Yvonne had left me earlier after receiving a call that her attention was needed at the family house. She expressed her desire to protect me from extended family members who had choked every inch of space around her mom with their presence and downheartedness. Some could not be vouched for spiritually so I was required to stay at the guesthouse and not bother trying to see my mother in-law-to-be until the day of the funeral. She assured me that a phone call was good enough and her mom had put this into consideration before I arrived. This was undoubtedly true from her mom's response to me on the phone.

It had been a long while since I set my eyes on the love of my life. In the midst of the funeral cloud that hung over the setting, I longed so badly to see him. I desired so much to console him and help him find hope in our new found love. I hoped he wouldn't be too shaken up by his father's passing and wondered if he would greet me with a smile or with tears. I prayed for the fortitude to bear the weight of his heart and mine together knowing that he had been traveling for almost nine hours straight with the burden of the loss of a parent. My inability to connect with him before arriving to Okene did not come as a surprise because we were both aware of the poor telecommunication infrastructure in the several rural communities along the route of this journey, which presented with poor network signal or even none at all if trying to keep in touch with a traveller. I could only wait and anticipate their arrival by my estimation of the length of the journey and how much time was left for them to arrive.

I engaged myself with the vegetables I was cleaning and the activity going on in my group. A particular lady whom I later got to know as a very close family friend kept everyone interacting on a lighter mood with her bold, unapologetic and overtly blunt personality and humor. I felt a little uneasy with her style of communication for the fear of some offensive or discourteous joke being thrown at me. I would have found a way to distance myself from her type of temperament on a normal day if not that this situation was different. Little did I know that I would have more reasons to be around her to experience that very thing I was running away from.

John eventually arrived in the evening. He came to meet me at the spot where the cooking was going on. I was overwhelmed to see him and was relieved to see that he was poised and unshaken physically. He had to be strong for a lot of people but there was grief in his heart, I could sense it. I gave him a big hug and a mild peck on the lip as I enquired about his trip. It was already getting dark, everyone's goal was to tidy up everything necessary that night so as to facilitate cooking for the chattered caterers who were expected to start cooking very early the next day. John went into his room to freshen up while I joined in to transfer all the cut vegetables into a storage room.

The next day was the funeral. I knew there was so much ahead and so I prepared my mind for unforeseen encounters. Much to my surprise, things rolled very smoothly. The Reverend Sisters who were associated to John's family, by virtue of his aunt being a Mother Superior, had fallen in love with me and we practically worked together at the reception to serve the hundreds of people in attendance. Franca, who initially seemed unwelcoming had begun to warm up to me, everything seemed to be sailing smoothly without hitches until the next evening when John and his siblings had planned a sit-together at a nearby bar/restaurant along with their friends.

We all went to the family house the morning after the funeral, where mummy, as I fondly called my mother-in-law-to-be, was. By evening, we decided to visit the local restaurant all together as a family. There was only one vehicle that all of us were supposed to drive in. Somehow, we were able to fit into it, even though it was tight. John was driving and I sat on the passenger's side next to him. The very blunt lady I had to clean vegetables with the other day was much closer to the family than I imagined. She was a very close friend of Franca's who had become like one of John's mom's several adopted children. She was with us on that ride. Her tongue was razor sharp and her opinions always caught everyone's attention because it was very dramatic, loud, extreme and unfiltered. She had not been mean to me but she had a domineering edge to her that sent the message across that she was not going to hold back if she had any reason to unleash venom on anybody, including me. She had, however, been observing and making hilarious and sarcastic comments about how John and I were so in love. Even when we got to our destination, there were quite a number of loose and aggravating comments that were made but I chose not to give attention to them. I had an idea of her personality after we had spent hours working at the cooking station together. It wasn't the comments she made that was the issue in this scenario, even though they were too forward for my liking, it was because those comments initiated a talk that put our relationship on the centerstage before everyone, putting us on the spotlight and analyzing our immediate future with sarcasm and ridicule in a very uncivil and jealous manner. When a few others began to inject their opinions as well and laugh at those demeaning comments, we decided it was time to go. At this point, John was already fuming. When we got to the car, the same lady brought it to everyone's notice that I was way slimmer than everybody else and that it would be better off if I sat at the back with everyone else while someone bigger took my seat. It wasn't welcomed at all from John as a suggestion because it was obvious that she wasn't doing it for the general comfort of everyone, she had just found it an opportunity to hit at us again and make it look like their discomfort at the back was because we wanted to play 'lovebirds'. John was already upset that she stirred the conversation in a direction that gave a bad first impression of his family to his fiancée who had never had close contact with them before and the mood she made us all leave the restaurant with did not allow her suggestion find a landing spot. John rebuffed it at the same speed with which it came. As if he was expecting her to speak, he sternly and unhesitatingly replied "No! That is not going to happen!"

Unfortunately, people with such attitudes carry a spirit that poison the minds of others with an intention to divide and rule. As you can guess, everyone agreed with her point as they all, all of a sudden, began to reason with her. At this point, it was all in John's hands. However he chose to handle the situation would not only determine the value he placed on me, it would also give me an idea of how much his family could influence his decisions, especially concerning me. It would show me a side of his character I had never seen before. I knew how strong-willed he could be but I had never seen it in action in a dicey situation like this.

I was frozen by the car door where I stood, not knowing if a fight was going to break out because the debate got louder and was evolving sharply into an altercation. John wouldn't budge. He insisted that it was a short ride home and there was nothing that would make him send me to the back sit and have someone else in front with him. He felt deep inside, as he told me later, that it was not just about the comfort but a game of control. He also mentioned how he had had to deal with her attitude in the past and how she had stepped in severally to contest final decisions made on crucial matters in the family. That statement reminded me of how it took a bit of a drag, weeks before the funeral, for her to agree that I could wear the fabric she procured for the immediate family to wear at the funeral, because she felt I wasn't family yet. What an irony.

There's no doubt that the way he handled the situation made my respect for him go over the roof. After we got home, John and I drove out alone almost immediately to deliver large quantities of food packed for a number of mummy's family friends at their residence. I fell in love with his firmness of character as he seized the opportunity in the car to reaffirm his love for me with a very resolute tone. He was very hurt that his family put on the display they did around me with that squabble that ensued earlier. He kept emphasizing on the fact that nobody could displace me or intimidate me and he further reassured me that he would love and protect me, with his life.

In every relationship and situation with extended family or third party interference, nothing gives a woman more security and confidence than having a man who is bold enough to confront issues with his immediate family concerning her in a protective manner. Third party interference, be it by family members or outsiders, is inevitable. It should be expected and guarded against by both parties. I learnt from a well respected spiritually minded senior colleague at my workplace while I was preparing for my wedding that the best way to shield off such interference is to adopt the "we" word when communicating anything to these external parties. Once their suggestion or advice on a matter is contrary to what you know will maintain peace in your relationship or marriage, you have to respond by saying "we agreed as a couple that..." or "we have decided that..." It is your duty to help all third parties know from the start that you are a team and that there are boundaries they are not permitted to cross. Your resolve must say to them that you're not confused or contemplating the choice of the man you made, they should know that your relationship has come to stay and they should accept it. Of course, this counsel will be most beneficial to a relationship established under God, with the person that, without a doubt, you know is your God-ordained husband.

You have to cut your fiancé a little slack if he does not approach his family yelling and fighting over you, all men will not approach situations the same way because their temperaments are not the same, neither are the circumstances identical. Notwithstanding, even if a man is gentle and soft-spoken, all men who feel a threat toward something they love and value will instinctively protect and defend it fearlessly. Men are designed to rule over and defend their territories. They are seekers and hunters by design and will work hard to get what they want. There's no man who does not have a desire to protect his territory and all within it, so, if you say your man loves you, then watch his actions. His ability to stand up for you, protect you and treat any matter concerning you as important enough to drop anything else for, will tell you what direction you guys are headed. A relationship where a woman cannot boast of feeling protected under her 'husband-to-be' is trouble brewing for the future.

John's First Meeting With My Parents

Day one, I arrived Okene. Day two was the funeral. Day three, I spent a lot more time with the family at the family house. I got to talk at length with my mother in-law-to-be, we all forgot about the issue that occurred at the restaurant the night before and tried to get to know each other better. We cooked together, cleared the house together, cheerfully conversed the afternoon away in the living room and Franca, John's older sister, made efforts to connect with me one-on-one and welcomed me to the family. By the morning of day four, I was set to travel back to Abuja. John and I had been planning and praying toward this day. We hired a cab that would drive us to my doorstep. Along the way, we stopped to buy an indigenous hand woven fabric popular with the Ebira tribe, hoping it could serve as an icebreaker with my mom. We were both excited and anxious at the same time, having an idea of what to expect and yet hoping that someone will greet us with a smile and a warm welcome. As much as I wished that John wouldn't have to go through some of the things I knew he would face, we needed to cross this phase and the next and the next if we ever wanted to get to our final destination. This road to the altar required strength and perseverance and we had understood that some pursuits in life require that you dive in headlong to get the result you want and on this matter, there was no turning back.

We arrived a little before midday. My dad was going to be home any minute. The house was quiet because my mom wasn't home as well, except for Emmanuel, the help, who welcomed us with a radiant smile. He started working with our family from when I was a teenager. He was an adolescent too at that time but operated the maturity of someone twice his age. He practically watched me grow up and could predict me by my actions. He is still like a brother to me to this day. He had seen me turn several guys down, including the ones that he later confessed during some of our usual chatters in the kitchen that he had ripped off some change with false promises that he would speak with me in their favour and persuade me to have a rethink about them and consider dating them. Emmanuel saw me have only one relationship in the past but this time around, I could read it in his countenance that he knew that I had brought a man home to meet my family. He greeted John enthusiastically and at my request, told me how long ago my mom had stepped out. We proceeded to sit in the living room hoping that someone, my dad or mom, would walk in and make this visit worthy of its purpose. If we failed in using this first visit to make John's first silent introduction to the family, it would require restrategizing. He would have to come on a later date, most likely by himself. I wasn't ready to stretch the anxiety of facing my family over introducing John to them.

I had thought this through extensively and chose this strategy because I felt it would merely pass him across as Yvonne's older brother who wanted to ensure that I returned home safely. Somewhere deep within, I knew I wasn't going to fool anyone with that story, but, even if at the back of their minds they suspected that he was interested in me, the last thing I wanted was for him to come with visible dating intentions from the first visit or else, knowing my mom's approach to such matters, she would have simply connected the dots and concluded that the relationship had started before the funeral came up, linking my main purpose of traveling to him rather than to Yvonne. I, on the other hand, wanted to give an impression that we had just met and it was a completely platonic friendship. I feared for anything that would provoke them to anger or make them prejudiced from the start, reducing the chances of having them view him as an individual first before labeling him a threat to their plans for me. Ultimately, I wanted his initial introduction to my family to be free of tensions, for all parties involved

To our greatest relief and dismay all at once, my mom came through the front door. We both sprang up as if we had both been tasered by the sound of the door. She glanced at John, as he bowed to greet her, with so much reservation in her smile and a look that spelt suspicion as she made her way to the dining table, which wasn't far from the front door. Her answer "Ehen, you are welcome" was a typical Nigerian style of response to a greeting from a stranger or someone with whom one had no emotional attachment. I introduced him as Yvonne's brother who volunteered to bring me back home, which she smiled at before returning to the serious look she wore initially. I also presented the Native fabric that we bought with a little explanation as to how it came about. She thanked him for the gift and told me to leave it by the cupboard beside the couch. John sat down again as she proceeded to untie a black bag containing somethings she came back home with. She fiddled with it as though she was crosschecking to see if the items in the bag were intact and still wearing the same seriousness on her face, without looking in our direction, she made her way upstairs to her bedroom. I had a goal here and I had achieved it, that was all that mattered. There is no approach on the face of the earth that I could have used to introduce John that would have earned him a welcoming embrace, so, I could as well just jump into the furnace of her fury early enough and move on faster to hit my target.

We had not finished taking a deep breath and swallowing the effect of her indifferent and cold disposition when my dad walked in for his lunch break dressed in his usual short sleeved shirt, a pair of Khaki shorts, black socks that stopped a little below his calves and black work shoes. As a mechanical engineer, his clothes were always smeared with grease, giving them a perpetual stain pattern and smell that no amount of wash ever completely removed. His fingernails always had a contour of dirt from handling automobile parts; it was never his thing to receive visitors during working hours because of his appearance, he preferred to see people after he had been able to freshen up. But, I was left with no better option; I couldn't bring John to visit late in the evening after work hours because he had plans to return to Okene that same day and then travel back to Lagos the next, so this was the only chance we had, even if it didn't seem perfect. In spite of my dad's preferences, I was surprised that he was more receptive and welcoming than I expected. John stood up to greet him as he did my mom. The relaxed and pleasant tone coming through his Italian accent put us more at ease. "How are you? You're welcome" he said warmly with a smile as he dashed upstairs for his normal ritual of washing his hands, using the loo and checking on his wife. Whatever comments or questions that were raised in the few minutes up there could not have gone beyond finding out who John was and why he was here. Before long, he was back downstairs to eat and almost immediately, my mom yelled out for me from upstairs. As if my heart stopped beating for a split second, I knew that tone, it was always associated with an interrogation or displeasure from her.

I took a deep breath and climbed to her room. Without delay, she blurted out "You didn't tell me it's your boyfriend you went to visit in Okene". My mom believes in confrontation and does it without remorse. The last thing I wanted to do was pretend I didn't understand her, I would only be asking for that session to be prolonged beyond measure. I quickly explained once again that "He simply volunteered to bring me home because he felt it was the right thing to do, to ensure my safe arrival". "Yvonne couldn't travel with me, she had to stay with her mom" I added. "Well, what about the native clothes he brought?" she enquired with her eyeballs wanting to pierce through me to get to the truth. I explained once again that we bought it from some indigenous women selling it at a certain filling station on our way. I wasn't planning to pretend that Yvonne bought and sent it, neither was I going to say that I bought it. The earlier we find a way to reveal the truth, the better. Unfortunately, I should have also known that based on the Igbo culture, a gift from a man to a girl's mother is not just a gift. They don't take such actions casually because every man around their daughter is a potential suitor and every of his actions must be scrutinized. Bringing a gift is usually a non-verbal way of saying I'm interested in your daughter. It was an oversight on my part but the deed had been done; it was time to face the consequence. She made it clear that she wasn't going to receive the gift and told me that I could leave. John stared at me as I came downstairs hoping he could discern what ensued upstairs for the few minutes that I disappeared.

It was already time for him to leave, if he was going to make it back to Okene before sundown. He greeted my dad who was still eating as we both walked out the front door. John desperately wanted to know how our talk went as we strolled to the road to catch a taxi that would take him directly to the motor park but I only gave him a hint of how she was already suspicious. I did not want him worrying over it, there was a long journey ahead of him and he needed all the strength and positivity available for it.

(How To Know It's *Her*)

CHAPTER 10
The Proposal

August 2008, I was in Abuja, with one major objective and mission in mind; 'Operation Propose to Elliana'. In the cool of one of the evenings in Abuja, I had taken a cab to see her in a salsa dance studio where she was taking dance lessons. Meanwhile, prior to that time, I had arranged with her salsa dance teacher, Dan, to build my proposal script around the salsa class she enjoyed attending. We both rubbed minds together and perfected what the scenario was going to be like. Dan decided to prepare the dance class in a location around town where we wouldn't be interrupted or hastened by the official closing hour of the real dance studio. He invited a number of his friends to give the class a feel of an on-going full house session. At a certain point, as planned, the music would be interrupted to get everyone's attention and then I would propose. We had also set up a refreshment corner for us all to celebrate together after the proposal was done. Elliana was to be totally oblivious and taken unawares.

It went exactly the way Dan and I had planned. I knelt down and amidst the emotionally captivated dance students and instructors who were enthralled with the proposal speech and the three stone engagement ring I had bought with all my fortune from Lagos as I slid the ring on her finger. It was such an exhilarating moment for us as a couple that brought the whole class and proposal to an exciting end.

Two days after I had proposed to Elliana, I went over to her family house as usual to hang out with them, particularly my father-in-law-to-be who had gotten fond of me in a short while, especially as his talk partner. Elliana had also told me how she made an open and joyous display of her engagement ring to her parents as a subtle but sure way of driving it home to her mom and her other relations that our relationship had taken a giant leap forward, and that her intentions to get married soon was no joke. And so we planned that it would be best if I came around and we both expressed our desire to get married soonest and also get their blessings to swing into action on our wedding plans. I remember how all my father-in-law-to-be had to say to me was how beautiful the engagement ring I gave Elliana was and from there, he went on to talk about his own past relationships and how he met Elliana's mother. I can't remember him ever putting me on the edge, ever, not once. As far as he was concerned, I was already his son-in-law and a member of the family. The rest was just a matter of ceremony and formality. I won't forget when he needed to take a short trip to Italy during the course of running the pre-marital counseling classes in Elliana's family church then, he looked at me with a fatherly smile on his face and told me he was leaving me in charge to take care of the home till he got back. He gave me a father-son relationship I never even had with my own biological father while he was on earth. I will always live to miss and remember him.

On the other hand, on the part of Elliana's mom that evening, I was put on a slightly hot seat with loads of questions ranging from why we were in a hurry to hit the altar to how much I was earning, why her daughter was my choice and what happened to the relationships I had before meeting her daughter. The questions were unending and at the end of our session together, I barely scaled through with a pass mark, primarily because of my ethnic descent and my, then, meager income. Meager was calculated by her own conclusion of what the income of a potential suitor's for her daughter should have been, not necessarily because it was too low for a newlywed couple to start out life together with. The pass mark I got was because she saw that Elliana's mind was made up and unchangeable, and my then father-in-law-to-be was already on my team as well.

The Choice is Yours, Not Your Pastor's

In the month of September 2008, shortly after I had proposed to my fiancée, we enrolled into her family church's pre-marital counseling class. It was a mandatory eight-week weekend session for all intending church member couples looking forward to tying the knot. A good concept I initially lauded until the marriage counselor assigned to the group we were in almost made it a nightmare. Church leaders and ministers need to be very careful to walk in the Spirit in the execution of their God-given authority towards the body of Christ. It does not matter how perfect and flawless our leadership skills may be or our knowledge and administrative abilities are as ministers of God, if the 'love' factor is missing out, we would be nothing short of a sounding brass or clanging cymbal.

Though I speak with the tongues of men and angels, but have not love, I have become sounding brass or a clanging cymbal. And though I have the gift of prophecy, and understand all mysteries and knowledge, and though I have all faith, so that I could remove mountains, but have not love, I am nothing. And though I bestow all my goods to feed the poor, and though I give my body to be burned, but have not love, it profits me nothing.

Love suffers long and is kind; love does not envy, love does not parade itself, it is not puffed up; does not behave rudely, does not seek its own, is not provoked, thinks no evil; does not rejoice in iniquity, but rejoices in the truth; bears all things, believes all things, hopes all things, endures all things.

Love never fails. But whether there are prophecies, they will fail; whether there are tongues, they will cease; whether there is knowledge, it will vanish away. 1 Corinthians 13:1-8, NKJV

Until we start seeing the church of Christ as one body, unity of faith will keep eluding us and purpose will continue to be dissipated at the expense of the Kingdom's enlargement and readiness for Christ's second coming. In my years of walking with God as a minister, especially having been around a few church denominations, I have come to realize how much we need a lot of brokenness and repentance as a church, in the areas of love towards one another, not just within our different local assemblies but largely in our interdenominational relationships with one another. It hurts the most when I see this disunity stemming from lack of love being reflected in the bias of ministers of God in their preferential selections and manipulations of their protégés', mentees' and church members' decisions in something as sensitive as their choices of life partners in marriage, which usually and most times, ends up hitting the rock with a resultant effect of more mess being created in the Kingdom.

I have seen ministers and church leaders manipulating the choice of preference for their members, all because they don't want to lose certain members they consider resourceful to their ministries, as if the ministry is theirs and not Christ's. Their aim is to have their members marry from within their local assembly and so, when their members meet potential life partners who belong to different churches or ministries, they blantantly refuse to give their approval or, in some cases, make the procedure frustrating enough to discourage him or her from marrying their member. Several churches are making this mistake and need to discover that it is self-centered, it is wrong and it is a form of witchcraft.

According to Scripture, God only clearly commands against intermarriage between His children, Israel, and the heathen nations. In Genesis 24, Abraham made his servant swear to get Isaac, his son, a wife from among his kindred. This is because God was guarding against the heathen spouse corrupting the Israelite spouse with their beliefs in idolatry and everything that was contrary to the God of Israel. Now, Abraham here represents our common unifying Kingdom patriarch and his kindred represents the sphere of God's Kingdom manifested through the Church (His body). In other words, God does not permit us to marry outside His Kingdom, strictly because of soul pollution. It is called 'being unequally yoked'. Therefore, if we share in the commonwealth of Israel by adoption through Jesus Christ, that means we have the freedom of choice within the twelve tribes of Israel and because the Old Testament is a shadow and type of the new, then we can apply it today to mean that a Redeem Church member has the freedom of choice to marry a Deeper Life Church member or Living Faith Church member and so on, just as a member of the tribe of Judah has the right to marry from the tribe of Dan or Benjamin; because we are all from the family of father Abraham, bonded together by the love of God through Christ Jesus.

Back to my pre-marital counseling class in my fiancée's church, it was obvious and clear to me that I was not accepted in anyway because of several factors, one of which was because Elliana did not pick a man from within the assembly. I was told to my face by one of the lead pastors that they didn't like Elliana's choice of a partner and that they weren't in approval of her getting married to me. The reasons were made clear to me too; it was based on my financial and material status, the age gap of ten years between us and my desire to move with my wife, after getting married, to another church. One of the questions Elliana was asked in my presence was why she could not have found any other guy around the church there? They had absolutely nothing good to say to me. All these were besides the unwelcoming attitude of the counselor assigned to our group of four couples. For some reason, he wasn't favorably disposed towards me either. I remember in one of the sessions, he uttered a very sour and heart rending statement openly of how I could take my wife and live on a tree for all he cared - because he knew at that point that I had not secured an accommodation in Abuja yet.

After all said and done, God's purpose and Will can never be stopped by man's pursuit of self-aggrandizement and thirst for vainglory. In proverbs 19:21 and Psalm 33:11, the Scripture talks about the counsel of the Lord standing forever, and the plans of His heart, not man's, from generation to generation. The Church is established by God, through Christ and designed to encourage the marriage institution, not aid and abet the devil's plans and orchestrations to annihilate it, as visibly seen and noticed all over the world presently.

We were eventually cleared at the final screening table to go ahead and start our wedding plans by a few pastors who were kind enough not to give attention to a number of some of those 'faults' and draconian barriers raised along the way. I thank God for His unending faithfulness and love; He has never allowed us to be put to shame. Our marriage has only moved from glory to glory, to the glory of God Almighty, the Alpha and the Omega, the One whose Promises to us are 'Yes' and 'Amen'.

A Soothing Comfort

One thing is very certain, given my experience during our journey to the altar, God will never leave you without an evidence of Himself and His goodness, when you are careful to stay in the center of His perfect Will and choice for you. Just as the Bible makes us understand, He will never leave us without a Comforter, which is the person of the Holy Spirit, one of the ways the Holy Spirit gave me a soothing comfort at a moment like that was through my father-in-law-to-be, Elliana's dad.

After that day of the scourging scrutiny encounter I had with one of the lead pastors from Elliana's home church, I was left almost drained and discouraged. I mean, if someone of spiritual authority over your fiancée says blantantly to your face that they are not consenting to their daughter in the Lord going to the altar with you and you know that church is supposedly her family church, does that not give you a red warning alert of serious danger ahead from where parental misgivings and beclouded judgment will be fanned to flame? My concern rested especially on her mom. I wondered what my fate was. I hoped that my father-in-law-to-be could find a way to intervene in this matter even though a matter revolving around the Church was an unfamiliar terrain for him. To my utmost amazement, joy and relief, he was terribly infuriated to my favor against the comments we received from the Church leadership. He was so mad that he nearly concluded he wasn't going to allow us wed in that Church. I will never forget one of the infuriated remarks he made with his very strong Italian accent that enunciated every single word with a melodious tune to it in his sort of broken but refreshing English, he said "John don't worry eh, she will tell me if Elliana is her daughter or my own. I tell you John, that is why I no like this type of church system, they try to control your life as if you be their property eh." As much as I was happy to get such respite from my father-in-law-to-be, I could also tell that this was not a good testimony for the Church especially given the state of his faith, his understanding of God and the Church at that time. We need to know that our actions as ministers of God go a long way beyond us, in actual fact, they have eternal consequences and value and God will hold us accountable for everything we do as stewards of His mysteries one day.

(How To Know It's Him)

CHAPTER 10
My God Has Answered Me

John never faked his status to me, neither did he ever buy me gifts that were beyond his capacity at that moment, and I preferred that. I preferred getting a gift from him that he didn't have to break his neck getting; it made me feel that he was being himself around me and that I had not made myself seem hard to please. It made me see him in the true light of who he is and what he had at that time. That does not remove the fact that he, on several occasions, would go the extra mile to make an event extra special. Let me explain it this way, a picnic, taking a drive round town and stopping to grab ice cream, or a walk in the park together, for example, can have the same or even a better effect than some other 'expensive' activities that are perceived to be more special. I know there may be young ladies who can't wrap their minds around what I just said but just hold on, you'll understand me in a minute.

The word 'special' here, based on this discourse, can also be relative, depending on the values and lifestyle of the individual. There are people, for example, who would value hiking or mountain climbing far and above a luxurious dinner, and in this context, I'm referring to 'special' as something considered exceptional due to the monetary and popular value given to it. However, understand this, sisters, the love you feel when you experience a pleasant surprise, be it at a picnic or a five star restaurant with your beloved, is the same. Your love for someone you genuinely care about does not increase because he spent money on you. As a matter of fact, how expensive a gift or pleasure trip is does not take away or add to love; if truth be told, people usually mistake excitement for love. What happens is that perhaps the thrill of the experience will be different and it becomes a very memorable event that you won't forget in a hurry, but, for two people who are very much in love with each other and have chosen to accept one another without comparison to other people, every experience is a memorable one. They derive more pleasure in spending time together than even the activity done together, let alone measuring the monetary value of it. I can state categorically that **the quality of an experience, gift or event is not in how expensive or cheap it is; it is in the emotions shared by the two people who are involved**. Have you ever been given an expensive gift by someone you feel has hurt you? You'll practically throw it in the bin and wouldn't even care what it's worth. I've seen women return expensive engagement rings, perfumes, name it, to men whose presence 'turn their stomach', these are men who fall into the category of cheats, liars, fakes or abusers; the gift, or whatever it is, loses its monetary value at that point and is equivalent to something rotten in their sight.

I encourage you to enjoy whatever level you and your husband-to-be find yourselves on. Please make the best of it, it's only a phase. Nobody stays on the same spot forever. Things will get better and you will both look back at your past and give God all the glory for how far He has brought you. The beauty of life is in its simplicity, in what you can make of what you have and how much you can live your lives free of people pleasing and comparison. Sadly, people begin to miss the whole essence of life when everything they do has to be filtered through what someone else thinks, how certain friends will rate them, how they measure up to what's trending and what will be said of their public image. There is more to life than that. Life is worth much more than what we will eat, drink or wear, according to Matthew 6:25. Take life easy and enjoy every moment of your God-given relationship.

In this season, for another long stretch of time, John and I could only build our relationship over the phone. Those phone conversations were some of my own confirmations that he was indeed 'the one'. It was not just in the way we shared the same vision, the same philosophy about life, faith, family, work and wealth, it was also the sincerity that I appreciated. We kept it real. We communicated. We expressed the depth of our love for each other in words. It is very important that you learn to communicate your feelings with words! Those phone calls felt like a boost of life for me, they were the lifeline of our relationship. I don't have words to describe the depth of love that overflowed from within me every time we spoke. Our text messages were out of this world. My phone's ring tone and message tone became the best music I had ever heard, they made me feel like I was floating through space like a ballerina who danced without a sense of gravity. And right before I commenced a descent to planet earth, I would hear that tone that refreshed all the feelings in my heart for this wonderful man that would catapult me back into a place I call 'love beyond measure'. We would text jokes to each other, quizzes, sometimes compete on a challenge we would give ourselves to be executed before the end of the day. Our phone conversations were extraordinary. Some were simply heartfelt affirmation of our love for each other while some were words of wisdom coming from John over some challenge I would seek his counsel over. Sometimes we sang to eachother, other times, we discussed serious matters pertaining our future together and some other times, we prayed together. We just moved with the flow without a preplanned thought as to how a proper conversation should sound like; we naturally and informally balanced the details of every topic with simplicity. I preferred to lie on my back on the floor of my room to make those lengthy calls as it gave me an imagination of lying under the stars without a care in the world and just fixing my heart on the most beautiful feeling I ever felt. Most importantly, we loved to discuss our future together. We loved to picture it and we could paint and paint and paint every dream we wanted to fulfill together till we knew it was time to hang up the phone or else no one was going to get any sleep. We would have to say good night repeatedly in between new topics that would arise until we both decided to hang up the call simultaneously.

Seeing Eachother Again

I never planned to court my fiancé for too long so getting to see new events and plans unfold gave me a feeling of progress. Personally, I consider anything above two years as overstretching it. In a short distance relationship, I strongly suggest cutting the courtship time shorter if you want to successfully resist the temptation of falling into sexual sin, especially when you are sure that you have met your other half. It took us applying a lot of wisdom, whenever we were in close proximity, to resist temptations by doing everything in our power to have our dates in public places or with an extra person coming along whenever we were around each other. We derived strength from hurriedly planning our wedding; the short time frame reminded us that very soon, we would be wrapped in each other's arms day and night. We would have made it shorter if we could.

The announcement of my National Youth Service Corps program, set to take off in October 2007 for the next one year, pushed our chances of making things move faster further away. Based on the structure of my family and the time frame required to execute other necessary requirements that the Nigerian culture insisted on before talks that centered around the wedding itself could commence, John and I knew that our job, at that moment, was to maximize the youth service year by planning every other achievable thing at that level to facilitate our wedding plans after I was done with the program.

Back home, it was shocking but also not surprising at all that for weeks, the gift John and I brought along on the first day he came to visit remained by the cupboard, leaning against the wall beside the couch, the exact spot where it was dropped when it was first brought. I guess we all pretended it wasn't there. Emma never made any attempts to take it upstairs either; I'm sure he could sense the tension in the atmosphere from the day John visited and knew he would be doing himself a great favor to steer clear the matter. On the flip side, he possibly might have asked my mom at some point where he could move it to and didn't get a very pleasant response which made him ignore it, but for whatever reason, not even my dad gave attention to a stray looking polythene bag that laid conspicuously in a living room where everything had its place. That was an obvious statement to me and to the inhabitants of that house that whatever hidden intention that was behind that gift, which they could guess had to do with dating me, it was not accepted and welcomed. Well, I wasn't going to le that deter me. The next thing on my mind was finding a way to move to the next stage of revealing to my parents formally that this man, whom they feared was after their daughter's heart, was indeed after it and I was equally interested in him. I had calculated in, the reaction I was going to receive for pretending that their assumptions were false, it felt like it would be judgement day for me and I had braced up emotionally for it. If I could successfully pulled that off and pull through the anger and reaction, I wasn't going to wait too long before including that John had indicated interest in dating me with the intentions to marry me and I was equally interested. I was willing to take another major leap of faith; if I sensed that the discussion had created an opening for me to merge both informing her about dating John and also a desire to date towards marriage, I concluded that I would go for it without hesitating.

One of those evenings when everyone was at home, I felt a leading in my spirit to move, to meet my mom and have a heart-to-heart talk with her about it. I casually sat with her in her room and told her I had something very important to discuss with her. It was as if she sensed it and saw it coming, yet, it did not change the fact that she looked surprised and taken aback by my boldness and choice. I guess the Holy Spirit wanted to save me the trouble of confronting this situation twice but for whatever reason, I found myself informing her, in one seating, about my intentions to date John and to date him with marriage as my end goal. It did not also come as a surprise when she turned me down after listening to all I had to say, even though I had still hoped that by a slim margin she would lean towards a positive response. Her irritated and firm tone of rejection was what sucked strength out of me. I left her room that day broken and disoriented. I wasn't sure of what I was going to do next. I wondered what could be done to ever change her mind, if her mind could ever be changed at all. Every antidote that came to mind didn't create a single spark of optimism or excitement. I felt like I had hit a dead end, I knew at that point, as I tried to absorb the impact in my room, that it could only take God to perform a miracle. Another part of me wondered what would happen if she decided not to budge, even if I got to the point of finding some respected persons to speak with her in favor of this decision I had made.

I began to wonder if I would have to get married without my parents' consent. Growing up, I had pictured myself bringing home my dream man someday and watching my parents love and accept him, welcoming him with open arms. I always dreamed that when that day came, I would sit with my mom by her bed side, tell her how much my fiancé and I love each other and she would encourage me by giving me uplifting and wise marital tips as we discuss by her bed side. I imagined us picking out my wedding dress together and making all my wedding arrangements together with so much excitement. Parental consent mattered a lot to me for the mere fact that I did not want my marital life to include resentment and bitterness with my extended family. It was never a part of my plan but the conversation we just had made eloping with my fiancé feel quite appealing to me, all of a sudden, and I quietly began to accept the possibility that my family might not be a part of my wedding. The discussion I had with her woke me up to reality; I had taken my day dreaming overboard and taken too many Hollywood movies that I had seen too seriously. Notwithstanding, if there be a need to carry on with your marital plans because your family has refused to give their consent when every requirement in choosing the right spouse has been met before God, then take the next necessary steps with the guidance of your pastor or church leader.

John was devastated as I shared the outcome of the discussion with him. He was aware that I planned to discuss with her whenever I found the right opening but he didn't think that it would be an outright rejection. We both knew that surmounting this challenge was going to require a divine intervention. There was one thing he said to me though that I still use as an approach to relax myself in the face of challenges, he said "we will take it one step at a time". Every time I began to complain and worry, he would say the same thing. I became more and more convinced as I looked at our love story and saw the hand of God writing it carefully and lovingly, my faith became more unwavering that He who began this good work is able to complete it. I knew He did not bring us that far just to leave us in the middle of nowhere, so, John and I took out time to commit the situation into His Almighty hands. We prayed, fasted and trusted Him to be in control.

Less than a month later, the most incredible thing happened. My mom sent for me. She said she wanted to have a talk with me. I picked it up in my spirit that it had to do with the last conversation we had. I felt flutters in my stomach for fear of not knowing what to expect this time. I was afraid that she wanted to say something she forgot to mention about her disapproval of my relationship. I went to meet her in the guest bedroom downstairs with a mindset of someone who had been dealt the hardest blow already, "what more could she possibly say that will be worse than what I've heard so far?" I thought to myself. I sat on the bed and listened to her speak from the long red couch beside me. She told me that after much deliberation, especially with her close friends who pleaded with her to allow me marry a man of my choosing, that she had finally decided to let me go ahead and marry John. Was this a dream? I could not believe my ears! How did this happen? I was so ecstatic that I jumped up and spread myself over her as I hugged and thanked her. Without a single delay, I ran off to call John to inform him. I screamed with so much excitement as I told him over the phone what just happened. We were so happy it felt like we were physically there together with the way we gesticulated over the phone, we were bursting forth with joy, excitement and thanksgiving.

After this approval, we were set to fly. All we needed to do next was to fix a suitable wedding date, get planning and start putting money aside towards it. There were some basic requirements we had to put into consideration before choosing a wedding date. No matter how soon we wished the date could be, if those requirements were not met, it would be impossible in our situation to make progress in our plans. There was a need for me to round up my youth service program, go for the introduction, which my mom insisted as we spoke further, would be in her hometown in Abia State. We were to attend a pre-marital counseling class in my family church, which we were expected to attend if we expected them to officiate the wedding. All these and other unforeseen things that could pop up as we moved forward had to be put into consideration. The introduction, a traditional requirement in Nigeria, required a measure of financial preparedness and had to be fixed around a period when everyone, including my dad, could travel to the Eastern part of Nigeria. There wouldn't be a wedding date if this has not been done. As we progressed and discussed further, my mom made it clear that my dad could only come along during a long holiday when he wouldn't have to rush back to Abuja afterwards to meet up with work. Most likely, the Christmas holiday season was the best time to do this; it was long enough, it was also when everyone we were expected to deliberate with in the village would be available. The people from the Eastern part of Nigeria have a habit of travelling to their hometown for the yuletide celebrations so we were sure that everyone necessary would be present. However, it couldn't be the next Christmas holiday, which was just two months away; my dad never enjoyed traveling and he sure was not going to fix a trip hurriedly because of any one, neither were we financially ready to carry the weight of the bride price and other expenses, which were part of the tradition. As usual, the village elders had some bureaucracy that required patience to follow; decisions were made by the kinsmen and they had to be formally informed and given time to respond by issuing the listed necessary financial requirements. In every case, we needed time because a lot of preparation was meant to go into it and all fingers pointed to Christmas of the next year, 2008.

With that settled, we knew that the wedding was going to be in 2009. We also knew it would be very early in that year, after all, there was nothing stopping us anymore. As if everything else was happening at top speed before our eyes, before long, my youth service came. I got posted to Christian Broadcasting Network (CBN) an organization I already had a working relationship with when I hosted their youth music TV show called *One Cubed*. I was going to be there as a youth corps member for a full year under the marketing department. It was familiar territory and I was happy with that. In December of 2007, the entire marketing team traveled to Lagos for a Christian convention called Shiloh, hosted by one of the largest Pentecostal churches in Nigeria. John and I wouldn't miss such a precious opportunity to reunite again. As you can guess, CBN gained a voluntary staff for the three days we stayed there. He was given one of the staff t-shirt and we did all our marketing together joyfully. Marketing became one of the most enjoyable things I had ever done. During our lunch break, we would stroll to other kiosks and outlets to find something interesting to buy or something new to eat. After the convention was over, we decided to take a walk into the empty massive auditorium to pray over our plans. We went straight to the altar and knelt on one of the steps where we met other people also quietly crying out to God on their knees. We were aware of the cultural responsibilities ahead and we knew that the battle wasn't over because there were still a few other respected family members that could influence my mom negatively and make it a whole new ballgame. We also knew that all our savings put together had not scratched the surface of the pending needs. We held hands and asked the Lord to intervene, to keep His promise to us and complete what He had started.

The Second Visit

With the progress we had made with my parents, John could finally make his second visit to my house with a more relaxed disposition. This time, it was his first visit as the man I was interested in and the man who wanted to date their daughter. I was expecting reactions to him to be different and more positive and thankfully, it was. My dad who was a naturally chatty person warmed up to him and in no time, their voices could be heard from upstairs even if you weren't trying to listen. My dad liked him, I could tell. Till the day we got married, he never asked me a question about John, not even what he did for a living. He had the right to ask even if my mom was furnishing him with any information he needed. He was indeed a very easygoing person who never demanded too much of life except for some measure of comfort and good health. He was easy to study in one sitting; one conversation with him could give a full insight on his philosophy about life. He could breakdown his life experiences and history in five minutes and his carefree personality would keep the house lit with his high pitch explanations and humor as he linked one topic to another without giving his listener room to say a word except for exclamations. I knew without being told that he didn't want to appear to be putting John on a hot seat either whenever they spoke so he relied on his sensitivity which I had always likened to that of a prophet to help him discern John's personality while they talked. Severally in the past, he wouldn't have more than one conversation with someone before drawing his conclusions on them and discerning them. Once he was done with the process of studying an individual, there was nothing you could do to change his mind about the person, and interestingly, even if it took the rest of the family a few months to discover his conclusion over a person's character, he always ended up being correct. Well, in John's case, I got to know what my father thought about him at a dinner party with some Italian expatriate family friends. I was sitting next to him as he shifted focus on me in his conversation with another Italian friend sitting across the table from him. He talked about my desire to get married so early. He, however, made a very striking comment that amazed me. He repeated to his friend, about three times, that the young man I was about to marry is a very good guy. In his words, he said "...un bravo ragazzo". I couldn't find more peace and comfort hearing his opinion, it mattered to me a lot. My dad had done his personal assessment and had drawn up a conclusion that nobody could change.

John was planning to spend almost two weeks during this visit. We had never had a long stretch of time together in one city before so, he worked out some free time, got his assistant to supervise his business and came to Abuja. Most of our time spent together was over the phone but John felt it was important that we invested time to be together physically in the same location and get to see each other face-to-face. It was a superb idea because our long distance relationship was ready, at this stage, for close contact with family members. He stayed at his uncle's place, which was also in a central part of the city and so, it was easy for him to spend most of his day in my family house or with me outside the house and return there in the evening.

John had also gotten a new business idea that he was working on to increase his income now that we would have need for extra money to raise a family and so, sometimes, we would go to a park together with packed lunch, our books and folders, where we could quietly build the business idea and our wedding plans, together.

I could tell that my mom still had her reservations from the way she maintained a measure of formality, though she had certainly eased off, considering her reactions to his presence the first time. She did not fail to drill him in private and ask every single question that would bring her to terms with his decision to marry her daughter. It did not seem to matter to her that I was equally in love with him and that I was responsible for my own emotions. It is normal for mothers or parents to want to understand the intentions of their daughters' husbands-to-be by being interrogative but it goes a little beyond pleasant lines when the message coming through to the man is one that makes him feel that he isn't good enough for their child.

Parents also need to be careful not to frustrate their children simply because they find it hard to let go or are extremely picky. This possessive attitude they exhibit is a result of an insecurity within them that has its roots in a self-centered mindset which has consequently resulted in late marriage for a lot of people who find themselves in such families. It has to be discouraged vehemently and a conscious effort made to tame the excesses because it is witchcraft. If you find yourself in a situation where one or both of your parents constantly disapprove your relationships without considering your liberty to make a choice, neither do they present biblically founded reasons that are beneficial to your emotional and spiritual health, and they exhibit toxic behaviour that kill your self-esteem and make you feel less of an adult, then you must be strong because there's a battle ahead. Be prepared to stand firm before them for what you want that affects your destiny and never make the mistake of doing so without preparing prayerfully.

In a selfless and genuine circumstance where the parent is making observations of disturbing character traits in the future husband or wife, it is their responsibility to protect and inform you. They, however, should first pray for the light of God to expose the situation and for Him, God, to open their child's eyes to the truth. The timing and tone with which they uncover this discovery to their child is equally important. So, the key here for the parent is selflessness. **The more selfless people are, the more sound their decisions**. As for me, I drew my confidence from my dad's response. I knew my mom would have felt the same way if she could allow herself relax and look away from what people thought, but she was prejudiced because of her inner circle of influence and her personal philosophy on the things that can be considered inconsequential matters. Matters like owning a car, which was also one of my mom's concern, should not be used to rate your choice of a man. Cars will come, houses will come and money will come; they are only by-products of hardwork and God's favor. The hardwork and godliness traits should be on the rating chart instead. Our parents can do better if they know better but knowledge and wisdom is no automatic prerogative of old age, so, if you have been blessed to know better, kindly but firmly bring it to the table.

Believe me I have taken out time to study both successful and failed marriages. I didn't study something written in a book somewhere, I took out time to follow marriages of people whose weddings I attended, and I drew up a few conclusions from true life stories told by others. The conclusions will astound you but it's true. The marriages that were founded on love but very little comfort at the beginning always ended up thriving meanwhile the big, flamboyant weddings never made it far. I'm not generalizing and giving a word of finality that big lavish weddings equal failed marriages, no. I am saying that from my research, I found that **financial success is in no way a determinant that a marriage will be happy or successful**. If anything, it stands that chance of failing because comfort becomes part of the foundations for the union and any shaking experienced in that part of the foundation rocks the marriage. The question becomes; what are you choosing as the foundation of your marriage and home? I have friends and family members working with security agencies and I have heard gory stories of women who conceived and plotted their own deaths right in the center of the affluence and beautiful luxurious homes, stories that would have been unbelievable but for the surveillance camera footages gotten.

What you really need is the surety that you have found a good man that loves you genuinely and that you love with all your heart. You can go ahead and introduce him to important people in your life that will further help you confirm your thoughts. I did not mind introducing John to neutral individuals whom I knew could give me their unbiased thoughts so I could, in turn, weigh them against the view of some close family members who weren't encouraging. I always went with John to pay a visit to these reputable mentors in my life who would have also felt side tracked or offended if I had not let them into my plans on such a major and important decision as marriage. Interestingly, they always got into a conversation with John and at the end of the day, to my joy, I never received a mixed message or concerned response from any of them regarding my fiancé; rather, I got very direct, unwavering positive observations and responses from them, even in private. The Bible says that;

"By the mouth of two or three witnesses every word shall be established."
2Corinthians 13:1 NKJV

You shouldn't be afraid to hear what important and trusted people have to say about your relationship and if majority of them are leaning in a certain direction, then you owe it to yourself to listen to what they are saying. If you want to enjoy your marriage, you must be willing to receive counsel and tell yourself the truth. One way to do so is to introduce your fiancé to your pastor, spiritually minded and unbiased mentors and friends. You can save yourself the horror of waking up one day in marriage to discover you married a monster. Another thing you must know is that no matter how much a man pretends, he can't get past several mature and experienced people whose discernment have been sharpened over the years. You must also admit to yourself that not everyone will be wrong. If everyone is complaining or uncomfortable about something, never ignore them. That is the right time to go on a fast and pray fervently to God to expose any falsehood, lies and deception in your future life partner. That is also the time to keep your eyes open and to observe.

Based on my personal experience, when you meet the 'one', the Holy Spirit will be the first person to notify you in your spirit. He will send two, three or more people who will confirm His opinion to you and I can assure you that you will not have any reason to fear. Everything will fall in place so conveniently with such a flow of ease in your spirit that you will be able to put your heart to rest, for the first time, because of the peace that will flow through you.

(How To Know It's Her)

CHAPTER 11
The devil Struck at the Introduction

In December of that same year, 2008, for me, all roads led to Elliana's maternal hometown where I had to register my presence for a formal introduction according to the Ibo traditional rites and customs of making a valid request for a woman's hand in marriage from her parents and relations. Since her dad was not African, it was decided by her maternal extended family to still get it done through their side, which her dad never minded anyway, as long as it wouldn't hurt anybody and as long as the ultimate end of our getting married was achieved.

Two weeks to the date of departure from Lagos to Abia State in the Eastern part of Nigeria, my mother, who by tradition was to travel with me, fell seriously ill to the point where she had to be hospitalized. Once again the devil struck! A plan B was needed urgently else the introduction wouldn't hold and it was going to inadvertently affect our wedding plan which was slated for the 14th of February, 2009, the following year. Friends, the devil hates the marriage institution with a passion and that is why we must do everything within the confines of the Kingdom authority given to us to stop him. Do not take your desire and plans to get married for granted or as an issue meant to be handled with levity. **There is always a strong purpose of God in the marital union of His children** that's meant to be birthed, and so, we must begin to learn to see, not just the marriage itself, but even the journey to the altar, as a spiritual battleground where we must fight to win through Christ Jesus. 2 Corinthians 2:11 says that we are not ignorant of the devil's devices and here's how Ephesians further explains those we're up against and what lies in our battle arsenals to handle them.

For we do not wrestle against flesh and blood, but against principalities, against powers, against the rulers of the darkness of this age, against spiritual hosts of wickedness in the heavenly places. Therefore take up the whole armor of God, that you may be able to withstand in the evil day, and having done all, to stand.

Stand therefore, having girded your waist with truth, having put on the breastplate of righteousness, and having shod your feet with the preparation of the gospel of peace; above all, taking the shield of faith with which you will be able to quench all the fiery darts of the wicked one. And take the helmet of salvation, and the sword of the Spirit, which is the word of God; praying always with all prayer and supplication in the Spirit, being watchful to this end with all perseverance and supplication for all the saints Ephesians 6:12-18, NKJV

It baffles me when I see people who think that the journey to the altar should be an all 'romantic' fairy tale story that popped out of a Hollywood movie or from one of those secular fiction novels out there. Seriously, except you are not getting married in line with purpose, because, if you are, expect that old fallen angel who does not want anything good for the children of God to resist you.

Back to my planned trip to Elliana's maternal hometown. The big challenge here became finding who was going to fit in as a perfect plan B to represent a parental figure that would be readily available at such short notice to go with me to Abia State to ask for Elliana's hand in marriage according to their traditional rites, now that my mom wouldn't even be able to stand from her hospital bed, how much more travel. Strangely, no one could avail themselves within that timeframe. There were two distant relations my mom had in mind but they occupied very sensitive positions at their work place and based on that, taking a sudden leave of absence could only be on medical basis. Remember, we didn't inform anybody ahead of time because we never thought we would have need to involve anybody else, we never foresaw my mom's health suddenly going under attack. Thankfully, my mom remembered that her immediate younger sister was supposed to fly into the country around that period. She is a Catholic Reverend Sister and a neurosurgeon specialist who was expected to arrive from the United States on a medical assignment to their Convent at Ikot Ikpene in Akwa Ibom State, one of the southern states in Nigeria, approximately a two-hour journey away from Abia State, where the introduction ceremony was. She seemed to be our only glimpse of hope, but we weren't even sure if her trip to Nigeria would be postponed, because of the way she spoke about it on phone. At this point, I had to take a cue from our patriarch the Psalmist in his Psalm 121, especially verses 1-4,

I will lift up mine eyes unto the hills, from whence cometh my help. My help cometh from the Lord, which made heaven and earth. He will not suffer thy foot to be moved: he that keepeth thee will not slumber. Behold, he that keepeth Israel shall neither slumber nor sleep. Psalm 121:1-4, KJV

Two days to the slated date of the Introduction, I had to travel to join Elliana and her family at her mother's village in the Eastern part of Nigeria. My mom and I agreed that she would stay in touch with my aunt, whom we were prayerfully expecting, while I proceeded to Abia State. What a relief it would be, even though we couldn't rubber-stamp if she would be in the country before the Introduction. Her constantly tight itinerary has caused her to reschedule her flights severally in the past to attend to other pressing needs first before finally coming to Nigeria, as such, we chose to believe that God would do a miracle this time, and indeed a miracle happened. My mom eventually called to say that my aunt was finally in the country and was already on her way to the Convent. I had an indescribable surge of joy on that day, I felt truly loved by God.

The Introduction went successfully well, but of course, not without a number of upheavals and traditional hurdles to be crossed, and crossing them was indeed an experience especially given the Ibo custom where there was a dowry demand to be met and every elder in the extended family set up had to be paid a measure of homage and obeisance, not to mention the fact they all felt they had a say and opinion over whether the suitor should be accepted into the family or not. Needless to say that I fell short of their tribal and of course financial status expectation. If it hadn't been for Elliana's dad, I probably would have been skinned alive with different expectations and criticisms. For the elders, they felt Elliana should have brought in an already-made man, financially speaking, and preferably of an Ibo descent. As succinctly put by one of the elders, "my daughter, as beautiful as you are, you should have brought a minister from Abuja or at least somebody from the presidency". Her numerous cousins did not also fail to make it known that they had expected her to bring in a financial deliverer who will make all their dreams come true at the snap of his fingers. I won't forget how Elliana's dad could not hold back his disgust for the culture and tradition being displayed with an unhidden sense of greed and materialism. At a certain instance, he couldn't hold back his emotions anymore and had to resort to an argument with Elliana's mother over how I was being overtly and unnecessarily stressed, and I heard Elliana's mom tell him "...But that's the tradition", "What tradition" he replied "What stupid tradition will make them stress a young man this much because he wants to get married, after all I'm her father and all this is supposed to be done in my place anyway, so let's go to my hometown in Italy then, and let them come over there if they can". I remember how at certain points, when I had to go and visit and introduce myself to different village family heads, he would console me with very soothing words and tell me how it was going to be over soon for us to all get out of there. It was almost as if he was even feeling the stress more than I did. I keep telling people that God used him to ensure the union between Elliana and me. He loved me the way a father would love his own son.

Guys, the lesson here for you is that when that relationship is Heavenly ordained, you will certainly encounter resistance from the devil, who by old subtlety and skilled guile, works through human vessels that consciously or unconsciously yield themselves to him. And so, when the going gets tough, that's not the time to lose your focus and give up or start venting your frustrations on your clone, instead, that is the time for you take a good look at the devil and laugh at him, shove him to the side and move forward. Another important point is that in all the battles and obstacles, how do you recognize the fact that God is still strongly with you? He will always leave a way of escape for you, using 1 Corinthians 10:13 in this context as a double edged sword; God will not leave you without a comfort through His Holy Spirit. For example, through all that I had to go through in marrying my wife, the Holy Spirit gave me His comfort majorly through my father-in-law. Of course, it is common knowledge that the bride's father has the final say, well, God gave me so much favor with him that I could feel the thick venom of anger and envy in some of Elliana's extended family members who never wanted things to be, as ordained by God.

We went on to fulfill our dream of getting married on February 14th, 2009. That's how much we were swimming in the ocean of love; we chose a date that we felt was recognized by the world as a day of celebration of love. I have also chosen to leave the story telling about our wedding planning and the events that unfolded on our wedding day to my beautiful wife. One thing I can say in addition to her account of the whole thing is that for years, we could not even play the video recording of our wedding because of the sour memories of some events that we didn't want to recall; I believe this will give you a hint of how things went. Now we can look back and laugh at a lot of things that happened on that day and interestingly enough, time seems to have exposed the reason the enemy attacked on that special day. After all the enemy plotted to ruin our joy on the wedding day, here we are celebrating the victory we have in Jesus over all works of darkness, returning all the glory to God and acknowledging His goodness and faithfulness in keeping all that is entrusted into His Mighty and able Hands. It is our Father God's specialty and pleasure to make all things work together for good to those who love Him, to those who are called according to *His* purpose (Read Romans 8:28).

(How To Know It's Him)

CHAPTER 11
The Proposal; From My Diary

After John's first lengthy visit to Abuja to see me, he made some more trips to see me and I remember that around this time, we had cause to travel to Cotonou together. Before then, I met an old friend, Dan, from a Christian youth group we belonged to who told me he was the dance instructor of a new salsa class within a gym I knew. I took a few classes there and I had filled John's ears with how much I enjoyed it. One of the times when he came visiting, I took him there to have him try out salsa for the first time. Dancing was certainly not one of his strengths but he did his best to follow through with me and it was very endearing to watch him struggle through the steps just because he wanted to make me happy. When we were done, I knew better than to put him through one more class. I could not make out time to stay consistent myself so, it became one of those activities I engaged in whenever I found the time.

The next time John was to visit Abuja, unbenownst to me; he had decided to make this salsa class of mine work to his favor. Therefore, he came around one evening to take me out on a date to an unspecified location. It was a pleasant surprise to see him take the lead in deciding where we went that day since I was the one who always chose the location by virtue of my knowledge of the city, it was the city I lived in for about 14 years at that time. The only hint he gave me was that he had found a new salsa class somewhere in another part of town that he wanted to show me and he wanted to have both of us enrolled. Well, what a laugh I had and what an interesting development that was. I could not believe this idea was coming from him. We hailed a cab and off we were to this newfound location. As we approached the front door, I could hear the music and the sound of people dancing, laughing and having a good time. There were a number of couples in there and they continued dancing even after we got in. well, I was more surprised and left speechless when I saw Dan, my dance instructor, coordinating this class. I should have gotten suspicious and inquisitive then but I had known him from years back to associate himself with everything dance; from partaking in dance presentations to joining dance groups and performing dance dramas on stage. In a way, it did not feel strange to find Dan a part of a new dance school. It could have been a partnership between him and someone or his personal establishment, I thought to myself. I concluded that I would ask him after the class knowing that he was only working for an employer in the other dance school at the gym.

Dan created room for us and got us into the rhythm in a few minutes. As we danced and followed his instructions for a while, the music was stopped abruptly. He said there was something important he wanted John to do. "What exactly could John have learnt more than me that would deserve a solo performance?" I thought as I smiled and watched with intrigue. John turned to me, went down on one knee and brought out a ring. Oh my goodness! I should have seen it coming! I knew something was deserving of some answers when he decided that he wanted to enroll in a salsa class and all the dancers seemed to be advanced dancers from the way they moved. Everything made sense all at once. That entire dance class was set up just for the proposal and my dance instructor had gotten some of his dance colleagues to fill up the class and make it look as real and unsuspecting as possible. I never expected such a well thought out, romantic and captivating proposal, it took my breath away and made my resounding 'Yes' come out with so much excitement. I gave him a hug and a kiss as everyone cheered in excitement. I had said yes so many times in my heart, we only made it official with the proposal. Dan put the music back on as we all celebrated together. I was too blown away by the euphoria that I couldn't have more than one or two of the long stretch of finger food they had also prearranged.

As we got back to my house, John didn't want to go in so we stopped at the main gate of the building. He gave me a kiss and got back into the car to get back home to his uncle's place. We parted ways knowing that this was another leap forward that would have to be announced to my family. I preferred that John stayed away during this announcement; they weren't going to reject it but their response could dampen one's spirit and I didn't want him partaking in anything that would give such a sweet occasion a sour taste. Nevertheless, I took another bold step into the house expressing my excitement as I shared the latest development. They smiled and congratulated me from where they sat in the living room. If I ever did expect a warmer response, it was long before reality hit me. At that material time, a positive response was all that mattered. I gave John a call afterwards to let him know it was well received. We knew that God was doing His thing and we gave Him praise every time we successfully crossed another milestone. He had shut the mouths of several lions to give us an easier passage and we knew He would do the same with the few more lions ahead that we would have to encounter.

Good Friends are Priceless

At this stage, we had a number of things enumerated that we had to do, like formally inform key ministers in my family church including the pastors, attend a pre-marital counseling class, go for an introduction ceremony in my mom's village – a usually small cultural event set up for parents and key members of the extended families of both the future husband and wife to meet. The man's family is expected to formally make their son's intentions known to the girl's family and request permission from her family to take her as his bride. As soon as this list of activities was taken care of, we would confidently be able to fix a wedding date and get our wedding plans concluded. Incidentally, to achieve the last bit, the introduction ceremony, raising money was absolutely paramount and what we had in our accounts individually couldn't come close to meeting all the needs. A senior colleague and godly mentor, whom I respected a lot, at my workplace still gave me counsel in this regard. He said he couldn't explain why all the money never comes at once when planning a wedding, there was always something about that last minute breakthrough that was common with weddings which he experienced as well. But, he also reassured me that just the way he couldn't explain the first phenomena, the second, which is the provision that comes at the nick of time, was going to show up undoubetdly. By the time he was done with his wedding story and all he suffered before he could finally get married, I knew I didn't have a single challenge. He encouraged me to keep planning as though the money had come, that was what he did and if his could come to pass, it would all work out for me too. Another aunt and mentor whom I admired and loved so much gave me the same encouragement. She motivated me to take a step of faith and try out a few wedding dresses. She volunteered to go with me so I could have the experience of what it felt like to be getting married. It was a thrilling experience and boy did it give me a new perspective to the reality of my wedding coming to be. It was certainly a faith booster, the future became my present and I knew without a doubt that I was ready for that next giant leap. I found a specific dress that had the 'wow' factor and made me feel like a princess, I longed to buy and hide it away in my closet but we didn't have the money at that point. I could only hope that it would still be available whenever I was ready to start shopping.

So, if I wasn't getting any faith boosters and encouragement from within my household, thankfully, I found some in colleagues that I held in high esteem. John and I grew stronger with every challenge that confronted us. John was such an amazing motivator and encourager from the beginning to the very point of achieving our goal. He was and remains the wind assigned by God underneath my wings that keeps me soaring higher. The love we felt for each other had gone beyond being unshakeable; it had become a foundation upon which we asked the Lord to build His Kingdom on Earth.

Dealing With External Opposition

I can describe myself as a non-conformist. I have never had any desire whatsoever to follow a certain trend, rather, I enjoy pursuing visions that look forsaken or unpopular to people and funnily enough, my fuel has always been opposition. Once I have confirmed in my heart that what I'm embarking on is the right thing, opposition only strengthens my resolve. So, every step towards getting married to my husband gained strength with every challenge and human obstacle that stood in my way. At this stage, my mom became more supportive, even though it felt robotic sometimes and on other times it felt as if she was questioning herself to know if she needed to reduce on it. In all, I was grateful for how far she had allowed herself let go and be more accepting. I eventually discovered that what was primarily responsible for this switch was a church she went to for prayers. She mentioned that a prophet in the church told her that it was revealed to him that she was having a hard time accepting her daughter's relationship, but that it was God-ordained. She told us that she was also told to let us be because we were perfectly matched from Heaven for each other. She later mentioned another incident where some other pastor was passing by her friend's shop and began to prophesy to her friend about her. Apparently, the pastor stepped into the shop and a picture she took with her friend that hung on the wall caught his eye. He began to speak revelations concerning my relationship and how it had not been fully accepted by my mom. The pastor went as far as mentioning prophetically that I was serving in the National Youth Service Corps at that moment. It's amazing how God had to take it through this route because it was one sure approach that would help my mom keep calm and accept the reality that my relationship with John was incontestable.

Along the line, we got wind that the final pre-marital class for the year was going to hold soon and as a result, we began to make enquiries to know if that was the one we needed to attend based on the fact that our wedding was early the following year. We knew that we couldn't by any chance miss the appropriate class we had to attend if we wanted things to move according to plan. The pastor in charge was one of those who knew me from when I was a child, he saw me grow up to this point of preparing for my marriage. As much as he was happy to see us, he had to break the news to us that registrations had been closed a few days earlier. It was also the last for the year. We tried hard to contain ourselves and not look perturbed but those words gave us an immediate proportion of tension on our insides. That was definitely not what we expected to hear. It was the only counseling class left for us to attend, knowing fully well that our introduction was scheduled to be at the end of the same year and our desire was for our wedding to take place within the first quarter of the next year, year 2009.

With nothing else to do, we entreated him to find a way to include us, especially as the Pastor in charge of the enrollments. He gave it a little thought, looked at us and made it clear that it was a difficult task we were asking because he would have to bend the rules and prevail over those he had given strict instructions concerning the closing date, but, he was willing to make it happen. Before we left the church office that day, we were able to get registered and make payments for the eight-week course.

The Crowd vs God's Approval

There was some uneasiness in the air because of the body language and comments directed my way from a number of co-ministers and respected brethren in the vineyard who felt I was going to be getting married too early at 24. I knew that my decision to get married early was perceived differently by the several women of faith around me. There were those who genuinely and happily couldn't believe the 'little girl' they watched grow up before their eyes was about to get married, and there were those who wondered why a 'small girl' like me was in a hurry when women like them were still single. They were of the school of thought that a single woman is supposed to maximize her single status and become a boss of her own before settling into the 'regimented' life of marriage. From their attitudes and the things I saw them prioritize in their lives, I could tell that they felt that marriage should be the last option on a woman's list of life's accomplishments. Their choices suggested that it is a decision you make when you are done enjoying the pleasures of life on your own and on your terms, then, when you discover that things are getting a little boring and you remember that you planned to be a parent someday, you begin to look beyond yourself and welcome the idea of marriage. On the contrary, I had discovered the secret of getting married in an early age. Besides being able to have children earlier in life, one is able to move into the phase of life where they achieve more, faster. The Bible says two are better than one (Ecclesiastes 4:9-12). It also talks about being able to chase ten thousand as a pair, rather than one thousand each when apart (Deuteronomy 32:30). When you get married, you will discover that your visions and achievements alone cannot be compared to the magnificent new journey full of adventures and experiences, which result from the merging destinies and purposes of the couple, according to God's intricate plans for the marriage union.

Here I was, living my dream. I remember one of them asking me what would become of my singing ministry if I allowed myself get married so early. I was so shocked at the ridiculousness of the question that I had to ask her if marriage was ever an obstruction to fulfilling purpose. The general vibe I got from majority of them was that of disapproval of my decision and I felt an air of contempt for the choice of the husband that I made. Nobody, not a single one of them ever had a negative thing to say about John's personality or character, before me or behind my back, but they all just seemed disappointed not to have their expectation met of the status of the man I would present as my husband-to-be. It seemed as though I had robbed them of a certain excitement they expected to have. That, on its own, was enough for me to draw more strength from because all they were bothered about had nothing to do with who he was, rather, it had everything to do with his material status. If that's all people are complaining about around you, you should ask happily, "Is that all?" because you have nothing to worry about. I have always known that the opinion of the crowd never matters in crucial decisions; it is God's approval that counts. **God will always place a few unbiased people around you who will tell you the truth**. Once you can locate those people and your spirit bears witness that they are speaking God's heart concerning your situation, don't wait, make your next move as one running with God alone on his or her side.

Another place where the vibes weren't welcoming was during our pre-marital counseling class where there was so much opposition from the counselor. Initially, I felt it was being unconsciously done but after observing the counselor's consistent favorable and tender approach to the other three couples in our group and his sarcastic approach and biased disposition towards my relationship, I knew that this was no joke. His favorite couple amongst all was the one that seemed to have it all together financially. The man already had two cars, lived in a well-furnished apartment and had a professional career. It was embarrassing to watch the way he patronized the man and approved of his relationship even when we could see that he was an 'unchurched' guy just going through the motions. Everyone could see the subtle friction between the couple but the counselor chose to overlook it rather than do his job of helping them deal with their differences. Instead, he focused on my fiancé and me as if he had been assigned the duty of frustrating us out of our relationship. He didn't realize that we swallowed the indirect insults and demeaning comments patiently because we were quietly counting down months, weeks and days to our greatest heart's desire to be together forever officially. There was nothing we ever did, no comment, no submitted assignment or action was right in his eyes. At a point, he ridiculed us because John was expected to have rented an apartment where we would live and it was their duty to inspect it before the 8 weeks of counseling was over. He had not. We were still believing God for the money for that. Well, our counselor openly spoke in a debasing manner to us, giving everyone an impression that we had failed according to his standards and according to that of the administration. The class became very mentally exhausting, unfortunately, we couldn't get wedded in my mom's church without it, as such, we had to complete it. Sadly, John had to travel 936miles in and out of Abuja from Lagos every weekend for two months to attend these classes only to receive the treatment we got.

When the lady I mentioned earlier came up with her thoughts on how my getting married was going to affect my ministry, I decided to get a second opinion about what she said, not because I didn't know the truth but sometimes, some people make you want to confirm what you know by discussing with people more knowledgeable than you. I went to see a very well respected spiritual figure who runs an independent ministry in Abuja. He is also one of those who knew me from my childhood. Without giving out prior information, I asked him what he thought about marriage and individual callings of the man and the woman. Well, his response opened my eyes better and further consolidated what I had always believed in my heart. He told me that **marriage in itself is a ministry**. While a woman may believe she has her individual calling, she must also understand that by virtue of marriage, her purpose and her husband's are now merged. They will both begin to fulfill their individual purposes within a unified purpose and vision. He added a very key word of wisdom that my attention had never been drawn to. He said that there is actually a time frame when a woman is focused on childbearing and raising her children. She raises them to a certain level or age where she can find some free time again. During this period, whatever it is she feels is her ministry might have to be paused for a while – because raising those children and instilling the ways of the Lord in them is as important as whatever gift or talent she thinks she has. Believe it or not, motherhood is a ministry because those children are souls entrusted into your care for you to mould into the vessels that will transform their generation for God. Ultimately, a couple's unified purpose is the best platform for everyone's individual purpose to find expression. This is a million dollar advice that can save a lot of women the argument over self-sufficiency in marriage. When you realize how important children are to God where Kingdom agenda is concerned, you will learn to balance your ambitions to accommodate quality family time.

Several other negative comments were directed my way that I won't be mentioning for the sake of keeping this chapter summarized but when I began to feel this negativity oozing out of some people around me, I decided to visit a minister of the gospel whose ministry to the unmarried was recognized in the city. Their words and opinions left me hurt within, especially because they were people close to me and because their words seemed to linger on my mind in a tormenting way. I wasn't trying to give a thought, it just seemed to find a way to repeatedly echo in my subconscious and produce sadness, which made me know that the enemy was at work. Therefore, I decided to book an appointment to see this man of God, to hear his counsel like I did with the other Pastor I spoke to concerning marriage and ministry. I had attended a few of this Pastor's programs in the past and I trusted his good judgment to help guide me through what my response should be to all the negativity around me. When I visited his office and narrated everything to him, he made a striking statement that I can never forget. He told me that the aim of the enemy was to use those people to plant negative seeds in my mind to torment me and ultimately make me lose out on what God had started in my life, if I ever allow them take root. It was a case of mind poisoning because the mind is the battlefield. He told me categorically and with authority to stop keeping my mouth shut! He added that **the only way to fight mind battles resulting from satanic seeds in the mind is by talking, by responding aloud with the Word of God**. Every time people say something contrary to what you know God has said to you, respond by talking back and saying what you believe and what you want to see happen. When thoughts arise in your head contrary to what God has spoken to you, talk back aloud immediately. Address it with authority and speak a Scripture that counters the very thought that arose.

That settled it. I was done bothering about what people were saying and allowing the enemy use them to gain control over my thoughts. Apparently, I knew much more than I thought I did. It took focusing on the joy of knowing that soon it was going to be all over for us to get through the mental exhaustion we experienced. As if that wasn't enough, the process of traveling back and forth on a weekly basis under durex had also put John's business through so much stress. His assistant who should have stood in the gap and ran things like a loyal partner decided to seize the opportunity to desensitize a number of clients who were getting used to communicating with him whenever John was away. Consequently, his sly behavior was most presumably targeted at winning over the clients to himself, almost crashed the business.

Having successfully completed the pre-marital class, we decided to fix our wedding date for February 14, 2009. We also discussed with my mom and all agreed that it was a good idea to go officially and inform the leadership of my family church that we were getting married. Well, we made a big mistake. I'm sure John has written a bit about our encounter in his side of this book. When we left the meeting, I was wondering what had just happened. It felt like a nightmare. I couldn't believe that John was treated with such an open display of ridicule and disapproval in the most gruesome manner. Every question was in relations to what he had and didn't have, who his parents were in society and many more of such questions. At first, it felt like a normal drill aimed at gathering general information but when no further questions followed concerning his spiritual life or his outlook on life but rather he was laughed at for having an old-modelled car, for example, I understood quickly that we were not going to leave that place in the happiest of moods or with a thumbs up. We took a very deep breath as we walked out of the premises and on our return home, my parents could not believe their ears when we poured out all that was said to us.

Here we were, a few months away from our projected wedding date. It looked like everything around us was out to frustrate our plans, and we still were behind our estimated budget. Despite all that, everything had to be made to look perfect to my family who didn't have the threshold to handle the worry over financial difficulty after they had exhausted their tolerance by coming to terms with my choice to wed John. God was all we had. We had to trust Him to make a way.

(How To Know It's Her)

CHAPTER 12
The Clone Concept

Let me use this chapter to enlighten you on the deep revelation concerning the concept of clones and cloning in marriage, as given to me by God. The first cloning that was carried out in the history of humanity was carried out by God Almighty Himself in Moses' account of creation known as the Book of Genesis. The Bible recorded in Genesis 2:21-22 that;

And the LORD God caused a deep sleep to fall on Adam, and he slept; and He took one of his ribs, and closed up the flesh in its place. Then the rib which the LORD God had taken from man He made into a woman, and He brought her to the man. Genesis 2:21-22, NKJV

Now we can pause for a while and meditate on these two verses of the scripture and then somebody should please tell me if this was not a surgical procedure that God Himself just carried out. He could have picked up some dirt from the ground just like He did concerning Adam and molded it into the person of Eve, which could have been much faster and straight forward for Him in my opinion, I mean, He is God Almighty. He could have chosen to even use a different style of creating Eve, maybe from a bunch of leaves or a tree trunk perhaps. So, why did He choose to go the more complicated route, if I may say, by first putting Adam under a heavy dose of Heavenly anesthetic, which the Bible refers to as 'deep sleep', because it was going to be a long day for Adam. And then, He opened Adam up and brought out his rib, perhaps to get his stem cells from the bone, if not, why not his heart or kidney or liver or a piece of his muscle? And then He (God) fashioned a female version of him (Adam) out of it and finally took His time to stitch him back up with the most advanced 'Heavenly laser technology' that didn't leave a trace of surgery on him. My point is, God was not just trying to paint a picture of His arduous task of the long surgery on Adam and have Moses get it recorded just because He wants to show His surgical prowess, rather, there is something deeper than meets the physical eye of Bible scholars, researchers and students that God was trying to teach and that is, the concept of spiritual and divine cloning of couples.

Every man has his perfectly matched woman or let's call her 'wife', cloned to perfectly fit him and predestined together from Heaven for his life's purpose and assignment. That is why, soon after Adam woke up from the theatre of God and from the influence of the heavy dose of the spiritual anesthetic and was confronted with a very beautiful looking version of himself, he couldn't help but scream out by revelation, because it wasn't recorded that God told him what exactly he just did to him and how the woman came about. Adam said by divine revelation *"this is now the bone of my bones and the flesh of my flesh; she shall be called Woman, because she was taken out of Man"*. And then, God, who was still in His doctor's regalia, standing, watching and enjoying the dramatic romance between these two love birds, had to seal His Heavenly perfection by saying in verse 24 that *"Therefore a man shall leave his father and mother and be joined to his wife, and they shall become one flesh"*, meaning that there is already a **wife** cloned and designed for every man from the foundation of the world. Now, age differences, race, ethnicity, location and class strata are all but extras, subject to variations according to time and purpose in the destiny of each man.

For whom He did foreknow, He also did predestinate to be conformed to the image of His Son, that He might be the Firstborn among many brethren. Moreover whom He did predestinate, them He also justified: and whom He justified, them He also glorified. Romans 8:29-30, KJV

Blessed be the God and Father of our Lord Jesus Christ, who hath blessed us with all spiritual blessings in heavenly places in Christ: according as He hath chosen us in Him before the foundation of the world, that we should be holy and without blame before Him in love: Having predestinated us unto the adoption of children by Jesus Christ to Himself, according to the good pleasure of His will, to the praise of the glory of His grace, wherein He hath made us accepted in the beloved. Ephesians 1:3-6, KJV

Let me break it down more vividly. In Romans 8:29-30 and Ephesians 1:3-6, the Bible gives us a picture of our pre-existence in Christ before the foundation of the world, so, that means we were sent out on assignment to earth based on our different purposes. In addition, God, who knows clearly well that most of us are going to need a help meet or a helper comparable to Genesis 2:18-21, better still, as it is said in the New Living Translation of the Bible, *a helper who is just right for him* (note the words *'just right for him'*. Other Bible versions say *'suitable for him'*), had us cloned and paired perfectly from Heaven and then sent us out to different or same geographical locations across the Earth. **God's pairing style depends on purpose and assignment** and His decision to place us in different time zones or same time zone (talking about age gap here) also depends on the different purposes and assignments. So, you may find yourself from the U.S discovering and finding your clone or your assignment partner from Asia or, you may just be an African and your clone is divinely orchestrated from Europe to locate you in a divinely arranged meeting that you may term as a 'coincidental meeting', if you lack understanding of spiritual things.

Now this is the clause; you must do the finding, especially as the man. And for the woman, you have to pray for your clone and your assignment partner from Heaven to find you out and for your paths to cross by divine orchestration. John, what are you talking about here? Could God not just save us the trouble and make it easier for us? News Flash!! The last time He did so for Adam, He was blamed for it and so He decided to leave us the pleasure of doing the finding ourselves, which is what this book is all about.

*God said, "Who told you that you were naked? Have you eaten (fruit) from the tree of which I commanded you not to eat?" and the man said, "The woman whom **You** gave to be with me-she gave me (fruit) from the tree, and I ate it." Genesis 3:11-12, AMP (emphasis added)*

He who finds a (true and faithful) wife finds a good thing and obtains favor and approval from the Lord. Proverbs 18:22, AMP

Note the word 'true' in the Amplified version of Proverbs 18:22. You see, the sweet part of this is that God is always so merciful and gracious towards us. When we seek His face or seek Him to help us do the finding, He is still ever so readily available and happy to guide us through His Holy Spirit. He loves us too much to sit back and watch us make mistakes especially in crucial matters such as this, such as finding our clones and Heavenly partners, perfectly created from us (men) and paired with us to fulfill our life's purpose and assignments.

Now here is the danger and the big problem the world has been facing in the area of marriage since creation, the reason why the world is in a mess, why the family unit is fast becoming an obsolete concept of the sociology ideology, why divorce has become an acceptable norm even in the churches, why same sex marriage is gaining more grounds all over the world like a deadly pandemic. I want to show you the very reason why the social fiber of humanity is facing self-extinction even before the second coming of our Lord Jesus. The enemy, satan, who had always been at logger head against God's love, purpose and agenda for us humans, His creation and handiwork, has long since creation till now been devising different methods of making sure there is a heavy pollution of the human race through clone mismatching. First, the devil attempted the pollution of the human race in Genesis 6:1-4. At that time, there was so much sin on the Earth and a hybrid human race emerged through this pollution, which led to the cleansing God did through the flood, leaving an unadulterated and uncompromised family, Noah's family, consisting of father, mother and children to continue His plan for mankind. Since that did not succeed for the enemy, it became a matter of clone destruction through sexual immorality among humans such as adultery, fornication and same gender marriage. Therefore, the devil, came up with the strategy of mismatching clones in order to bring a gross disorderliness that will create, in eventuality, a colossal breakdown of the marriage institution which will inadvertently result into a cataclysmic failed society and world order, as designed by God.

Mismatching and 'mispairing' of clones in marriage has been a strategy the devil has used for quite some time now in order to create marital breakdowns and home wrecks through infidelity and through differences that come from incompatibility. This, inadvertently, results in a high rate of divorce, we see in the world today, which creates dysfunctional homes and emotionally and psychologically broken children who become susceptible to any influence, ultimately creating an imbalance in our societies and nations, and as a result, they themselves become subject to more confusion through more sexual immorality. An increase in dysfunctional family value system has eventually lead to several dysfunctional societies and nations. It's been happening and will not be slowed down or completely stopped if we do not address the heart of the matter, which is the marriage institution.

This is the same reason why God, in the Old Testament, will always instruct His children, Israel, not to take wives for themselves from amongst the idolatrous heathen nations. This is simply God's way of trying to avoid spiritual and physical pollution through clone mismatching. Our God had always been interested in raising unto Himself a holy and unblemished nation in His children. Now, this is what happens when we pick or make a choice of a spouse who is not a citizen of the Kingdom; a perfect mismatching of clones has already taken place when someone whose spirit has not been rebirthed by the Spirit of God marries a born again, Spirit-filled believer. There's going to be a big, in fact, huge problem in that marriage and even with the offsprings of that marriage, except God steps in to intervene, by His mercies. Consulting the Lord for direction does not stop at the point of making sure the person is or is not born-again. Even while picking from the fold or within the Kingdom, you need to consult the Holy Spirit who was there from the inception, when you were both being created and paired as clones from Heaven, to help you pick out your perfect partner who has been programmed from inside you since inception. Your clone's spiritual and even sometimes physical genetics, personality, choices, taste and preferences perfectly matches yours because she was taken out of you. She has always been inside of you, drawn out of you to be a perfect help and partner for your divine purpose and assignment.

Research has proven and shown that husbands and wives have similar DNA. Researchers and scientists at the University of California compared the DNA of eight hundred married couples to random couples and found out that despite the old adage that opposites attract, married couples have more DNA in common than the strangers that were paired. This means, in other words, that birds of a feather really do flock together. Have you ever wondered why couples begin to look alike over the years in marriage, which also serves as an evidence of genetic similarities at work and all together? It is a sign that an awesomely creative God greater than us created us, paired us up by first creating one out of the other from the foundation of the world and from our inception in Heaven.

When God does or shows something in His Word, He usually does it to establish the principles, the precepts and the process that guide a certain thing that exists in the realm of the spirit. An example would be His method of creation. When He spoke light, the firmaments, animals and plants into being, He wasn't only trying to show us how He created the world but He was teaching us the power and purpose of the spoken word. He made us in His image and it is a long-standing fact that all over the Holy Scriptures, we see that the tongue is the rudder that stirs our lives in the direction of whatever we speak. The book of Proverbs tell us that death and life are products of what we say (Proverbs 18:21). In other words, if God's method of creation and His choice to make us in His image reveals that He has given us power to create our world through our spoken words, then, we can see that things don't show up in the Bible just to give us a historical account; it is there to trigger us into searching and understanding why God chose to do things a certain way and how it applies to us. Now, if we also look at how God took His time to mould man from dust with His hands and breathe life into him, it establishes the fact that we are so precious to Him and that every fiber of our entire being was fearfully and wonderfully thought through and handcrafted by Him, which Psalm 139 breaks down in detail. Even though every man after Adam is born through a woman and nobody looks like dust or clay, it has been established from the beginning during creation, by the law of first mention and in the realm of the Spirit that we are all earthen vessels and our bodies are but mere dust. In the same manner, when we consider the method with which the first woman was created, we should be able to see that one of the emphasis being laid during her creation was the fact that she came out of a man. So, we can also conclude that every time a female is born, in the realm of the spirit, she was not only fearfully and wonderfully made but she was also pulled out of a man, her God-ordained life partner to whom she is a clone. In other words, she is connected to a specific man whom she's meant to meet and become one with as her husband.

In Genesis 1:27 which was also the Scripture Jesus referred to in Matthew 19:4, when He was answering the Pharisees on a question thrown to Him over the issue of marriage and divorce. It was stated clearly that man had inside of him his woman from the beginning, just as the Scriptures say that in the beginning He, God, made them in pairs. And in verse 5, Jesus further reiterated this clone concept by making it clear that a man's wife is already in existence, waiting for her second half to find her and be joined back to her so that they can become one flesh again. Let's read it together;

The Pharisees also came to Him, testing Him, and saying to Him, "Is it lawful for a man to divorce his wife for just any reason?" And He answered and said to them, "Have you not read that He who made them at the beginning 'made them male and female,' and said, 'For this reason a man shall leave his father and mother and be joined to his wife, and the two shall become one flesh'? So then, they are no longer two but one flesh. Therefore what God has joined together, let not man separate. Matthew 19:3-6, NKJV

When God gave me this revelation in this Scripture, it blew my mind. This is why God hates sexual sin such as fornication and adultery, which I will like to refer to as 'clone pollution'. You are tampering, polluting and destroying someone else's clone when you do that. The question therefore will be, what if I discovered after giving my life to Christ or after reading this that I didn't marry into the perfect will of God or what if I realize based on scriptural and spiritual principles that I am not married to my clone? Apostle Paul, teaching in first Corinthians 7:12-16, teaches on the necessity of continuance in such marriages or marital relationships, because there is a chance of saving your unbelieving spouse except it is he or she that chooses to leave you. Because the truth is, regardless of our mistakes, God hates divorce!

But not one has done so who has a remnant of the Spirit. And what did that one do while seeking a godly offspring? Take heed then to your spirit, and let no one deal treacherously against the wife of your youth. "For I hate divorce," says the Lord, the God of Israel, "and him who covers his garment with wrong and violence," says the Lord of hosts. "Therefore keep watch on your spirit, so that you do not deal treacherously (with your wife)." Malachi 2:15-16, AMP

The process by which God saves your marriage is what I would term 'clone repairing'. In other words, God by His mercies, knowing we have faltered through our mistakes, and in other cases, walked in disobedience, will still go ahead and 'repair' us spiritually, in character and physically, to make us fit perfectly for each other, eventually. The only snag here is that it is usually a more painstaking and difficult route to pass through and it will require us engaging the fruits of the Spirit as stipulated in Galatians 5:22 for the Chief Surgeon in Heaven and on Earth, our Lord Jesus Christ, to put things right and remodel us into perfect clones for each other. So, do not quit that marriage! Instead, allow the Master who created you and your spouse to perform clone repairs and re-clone you perfectly for each other. Agreeing, in beliefs about God, life, visions, money and problem solving approaches is key in making any marriage work and is predominantly found in perfectly matched clones, where, each partner's individual differences tend to compliment the strengths or weaknesses of the other. However, where a mismatched couple is concerned, the differences outweigh the similarities but through clone repairs, God is able to work on each party, by His mighty creative power, if they are willing, to begin to not only change some behaviours that their spouse does not like but to also begin to fall in love with things about them that never would have appealed to them in the past.

Based on the need for agreement if two people want to walk together, according to Amos 3:3, the Lord will repair the discord that exists in that marriage so the couple can begin to be one in thought and action. The re-cloning process can be quite a difficult phase of marriage because it requires patience, it requires wanting the marriage to work and it requires understanding that the process of birthing something new can include birth pangs. The Lord used this to give me a revelation into why a lot of marriages and homes seem to be going through quite a rough and hard time even with every effort on the part of both or either of the spouses to make it work. It involves, on God's part, a holistic re-engineering of the spiritual, behavioural, emotional and physical DNA of the couple to fit into each other.

And so, it's not strange that two Christians marry each other within the permissive Will of God and they begin to encounter challenges and differences in their marriage, experiences they didn't bargain for. And at this stage, it's only our Lord Jesus who created us that can re-clone them into a perfect fit. It's like trying to remodel a square metal peg to fit into a triangular metal hole. There will have to be a process of cutting, filing, chiseling and most likely application of heat that the two metals must go through to fit perfectly into each other. So, when you are going through difficult moments in your marriage that's not the time to consider quitting. The Lord could just be taking you through a process of re-cloning, particularly when you have handed it all to Him in prayers through your relationship with Him. **Jesus is the only third party that's capable of making your marriage work.** However, a lot can be avoided from the beginning if you seek out and determine to find your clone, the perfect Will of God for your life, especially through the help of the only best friend and truthful counselor you can ever have, the Holy Spirit. He has your best interest at heart.

(How To Know It's Him)

CHAPTER 12
A Dream Come True

In October 2008, I rounded up my youth service. We had already fixed the introduction ceremony for December and a number of the requirements had been paid for. My mom preferred to have it done in her village in Abia State. Even though we didn't think it was necessary to travel all the way to her village to do this when both of my parents were in Abuja, because usually, the choice of where the event takes place is largely influenced by where the parents of the bride-to-be live. However, we didn't mind, as long as it brought us closer to our goal. We didn't bother asking questions or suggesting otherwise, wisdom demanded that we cooperated to facilitate reaching our goal on time and keeping the process hitch free.

As we set out for Abia State in December with my dad, John and his mom were supposed to join us there from Lagos a few days later. Incidentally, she had fallen critically ill within that period and was admitted to hospital. It almost seemed as if the whole event was going to be postponed because the Ibo culture demanded a minimum of one parental figure to be there to accompany the suitor to the family home of the woman he's interested in. John needed to bring such a representative as well and we knew that the enemy was only trying to attack us because at this point, the only person that could represent his mom was her younger sister and she was outside the country. Aunty Leonie, John's aunt, was always in and out of the country because of her sensitive position as Mother Superior over a sect of the Catholic religious sisterhood. She was expected to have returned to Nigeria but for some reason, she hadn't and according to culture and tradition, there was no way a ceremony like that was going to hold without this requirement. Were we going to have to reschedule this event? Did it mean that our wedding date would have to be moved forward since this phase has not been crossed yet? How in the world were we going to get my dad to get into an airplane from Abuja to Abia state again, a man who would usually need weeks of convincing to leave his house just to visit someone within the same city, how much more driving to an airport and boarding a plane to another part of the country. He wouldn't even have the time because this trip was thoughtfully fixed during the festive season, the only free time we could maximize before his work would fully resume in the new year. He wouldn't be able to find the patience and time to make another of such trips until after a long time, perhaps the next yuletide celebration. We couldn't pass up this opportunity so, we kept praying. We knew that auntie Leonie was going to be in the country soonest and we kept looking forward to a phone call from John's mom to inform us that she had arrived. Two days to the introduction, our miracle happened. John told me that aunty Leonie had just arrived Akwa Ibom State, less than two hours away from my mom's hometown, if traveling by car. I was told that my mother in-law-to-be was overjoyed with this testimony and had been in touch with her sister to acquaint her with the ceremony. We were over the moon with the great news too. Without delay, we happily and calmly informed my mom that it had been confirmed that John's aunt would be there unfailingly, representing his mom. John had also gotten in touch with his aunt and given her the address and by the afternoon of the eve to the introduction, a station wagon vehicle carrying two reverend sisters drove into the family compound with about a dozen crates of portable water and a few other things. They greeted the family cheerfully, dropped what they brought and told them that they were all going to be around for the event the next day.

The morning of the introduction was like a dream come true. We woke up not knowing how it would go, as much as we knew that at the end of the day, we would have achieved our reason for travelling to my mom's village. We didn't know how the 'elders', my mother's kinsmen, were going to behave towards my husband-to-be. It was just that knowledge of him not being accepted fully that we hoped would not stir someone with an untamed tongue to say something offensive. In those types of ceremonies, in certain cultures where money is king, when you come with a 'suitcase' full of money and you are able to mesmerize the extended family and the 'elders' with a show of affluence, their words go beyond acceptance to almost adoration. But in our situation, anything could happen; it could be subtly said or directly expressed that the man did not meet their financial expectations, what do you do in such a situation other than swallow whatever they say and move forward. They didn't fail us. Someone had to mention that I was the daughter they were reserving for a man in a minimum position of a minister or senator in the country. I truly commend my husband for having the courage to forge forward in spite of obvious discouraging attitudes coming from my extended family members. Before the introduction ceremony, he tried to mingle with my uncle's sons and other cousins who were way younger than him. They ate together, talked together, and attended a local football game together organized by the youth of the community. I observed that their actions and gestures were calculated to make him know subtly that though they were smiling with him, he wasn't expected to get too comfortable because he had not done anything impressive. If there were an expression for giving someone a cold shoulder but also smiling and talking to the person at the same time, I would categorize the vibes coming from them into that expression. Permit me to call it friendly unfriendliness. I concluded without a doubt that he was only being tolerated. When they spoke to him, they didn't fail to pass across the fact that I was the golden goose they hoped would lay the golden egg for the family and here I was, not fulfilling that dream of theirs because he came into the picture. A lot of these encounters were enough to get any man saddened and discouraged, especially when he thinks of the fact that he will have to associate with them for a lifetime because of his connection to the woman. It takes a man who truly loves a woman to overlook actions from the woman's family, actions that are clearly geared towards trampling on his ego and personality, and still keep moving the relationship forward with a passion.

My dad grumbled all through the ceremony because of his dislike of the cultural approach Africans have to everything. He felt they just enjoy making a big deal out of simple things. A quick decision, according to him, that would require a 'yes' or 'no' answer could take days to conclude on because they would have to seek everyone's opinion first before arriving at a simple conclusion. In our case, he thought it was humiliating and absurd to put anybody through their arduous route in the name of wanting to establish that they value their daughter. I wasn't even their daughter as far as he was concerned, that was part of his anger. I remember when he asked John and me with disgust where they were when he was paying my school fees and taking care of me. "Now they appear to lay claims over Illi (the name he fondly called me) as their daughter" he said. He just couldn't wrap his mind around the traditional way of doing things in Africa.

Aunty Leonie's presence along with her usual entourage of Reverend Sisters was very comforting and a confidence booster. In the midst of all the ups and downs and the back and forths, I realize now that those kinsmen were aware that they didn't have the power to stop anything. I can bet that if they had as much as attempted to take their cultural and traditonal cross-examination beyond what they did, my dad would have spun like 'The Mask' and shown them his mafian side. Gratefully, God was in control of the day and everything went according to plan. The meeting between the two families came to a happy close and John sped off to Lagos early the next morning.

The Wedding

We had successfully crossed another giant milestone, being the Introduction. That was it! The morning was near and joy was already welling up inside of us. The need for money to plan our wedding and our future together was great but the pursuit of it looked like the least of the challenges for us to tackle based on all that we had been through and the fact that we had successfully arrived at this phase in our relationship. Left to us, we would just organize an event of about fifty people, comprising of closest family members and friends, but that wasn't my mother's idea of her only daughter's wedding. Another area we had to give attention to was the requirements from my family church. They had a checklist of things to be done by an intending couple before they tied the knot. While sorting that out, we also needed to get our wedding rings, my wedding dress, John's suit, search for where we could order an affordable cake, choose and book the caterer and several other things that had to be budgeted for which gave us a lot of brain work to do. But none was compared to the thought of our post wedding accommodation. Accommodation was another giant standing before us at this phase of our journey and only God could slay it for us. It was an important need for that matter which had to be taken care of within a given time frame. My mom also had a long list of friends and a number of groups and associations she belonged to and her major concern was making sure no person was left out. We, on the other hand, were praying for how to raise money to cater for an estimated crowd of about two hundred and fifty people, not based on our calculations but based on my mom's large network of friends, membership to a large indigenous association, other women associations and home church workers' groups. To achieve a wedding that would accommodate that number of people, we needed some good money. It was a dicey situation as well. We were still at her mercy deep within, even though on the surface, it looked as if we had all come to accept and love each other, as if we had conquered the entire situation. We wanted to please. We needed to please her. Because it was written all over the wall around us that we were able to get this far and to this phase because she decided to accept our relationship, she chose to let me have my way. The impression I was given was that she convinced my dad to let us be or else, we wouldn't have even had him on our side. That unspoken yet almost tangible impression given felt like a ticking time bomb; if we weren't careful to tread gently, quietly and with caution, we stood a chance of setting off the bomb that could hamper our plans. We just wanted to make her happy even if it meant breaking our backs doing it. We just wanted to see ourselves slip wedding rings into each other's fingers and be declared husband and wife. That was our sole goal.

If there's one thing I know, it's the fact that we planned. If you have ever been in a financial tight corner, you will understand exactly what I'm saying. When you have to work on a tight budget because of limited resources and deep inside, you're trying to accept the reality of knowing that your wedding ceremony cannot be as small as you would have wanted it simply because the number of guests cannot be reduced below a certain number no matter how much you tried, after all, they're your parents' guests and you can't tell them who they should and shouldn't invite, you'll nearly burn out like a firework birthday cake candle trying to figure out a solution to such a simple yet complex situation. It's the kind of situation you know the solution to. It's either you have more money or cut down on your guests. It's as simple as ABC and yet as difficult as dodging a bullet when the money isn't there and when you don't have control over the entire guestlist. And so, we continued to flip the plan upside down, inside out, sideways and forward to see how we could achieve much with little.

When you believe God to provide for your wedding through people's generous support because you know you have next to nothing in savings and you can't turn to your family for help, wisdom demands that you stick to the key necessities that must be taken care of and provided for at the wedding. Incidentally, John's mom was a retiree and was doing everything possible to process her gratuity in a country where corruption has made them heartless enough to act fraudulently with the benefits and of senior citizens, making retirement a living hell for them after so many years of service to the state. She hoped to support us from whatever she would receive but the bureaucracy surrounding processing its release from the governement coffers was unbelievable.

So, in such a situation, our major concerns became securing our wedding rings and dress/suit first. We focused on finding a good and affordable venue, not necessarily our preferred choice, but a location where a wedding can hold. We had to ensure there was a wedding cake and that food and drinks would be available. I had my imaginations of what the wedding favours should be but had to scrap it and go for something more affordable. Hall decorating became a secondary matter, for example, even though I visited with a well-respected and recognized decorator in the city, one conversation with her and hearing her charges for the least of her decorations brought my dreams in that regard to a halt. I wanted a spring-themed wedding décor and I knew she could make it happen with a snap of a finger. She was going to use live plants as well if I wanted but the lowest price for décor alone was equivalent to the amount I needed to put the entire wedding together. Even then, I knew it wasn't expensive given the beautiful job she was ready to do for the least of her decorations, judging by the catalogue she gave me to look through but the money was not just within our reach.

On my mother-in-law's end, she was running from one office to the other to work on her gratuity and pension, with the hope that she would be able to relieve some of our financial burden when it got paid. At this point, she was in a financial need herself and was banking on that gratuity to experience financial relief. One thing I know that kept us strong and fiercely pursuing our wedding plans was the unwavering faith we had that our marriage had been signed, sealed and delivered from Heaven and that there was a great purpose ahead of us to fulfill for our Father's Kingdom by our union. We didn't stop planning or making arrangements, we didn't stop visiting possible wedding reception locations, we didn't even stop negotiating prices of things believing that we would come back soon to aquire them, even when we didn't know where the money would come from. That was one phase of life where I understood what it meant to walk by faith and not by sight. My resolve over this marriage coming to pass was too strong for my mind to attempt conjuring fear or doubt. I believe this mindset must have thrown the devil off balance because there was no threat of his that could work on me. I mean, I was so sure that even if it came right down to being joined by a pastor and a few witnesses comprising of only our parents, because of the lack of financial resources to have the usual big wedding, which I probably would have preferred anyway, nothing was going to stop it from happening come February 14th, 2009. I wasn't hoping to call things that be not as though they were (Roman 4:17), I had taken my faith further to where I was already seeing those things in existence in my spirit and thanking God for our marriage and home that were already established in Heaven and on Earth.

If there's one thing you must bear in mind, it is the fact that all the partying and ceremony at your wedding is usually not for you. To be honest, every couple's major concern is to get wedded and move on to the next phase of a new life together but the only reason you'll find people holding big budget weddings is just for the guests' entertainment and sometimes, from the pressure and excitement of close family members whose desire that it matches up to other people's standards and expectations.

My aunt and friend, Happiness, in the youth department where I served in church was a wedding planner and at my request, she joyfully decided to help me with planning my wedding. The budget she had to work with was certainly not proportional to the number of people we informed her would be there but she understood what the issue was and did her best to work around it. Sourcing the funds was totally in our hands and our determination far outweighed the challenge. I remembered again how I longed to have a wedding with a small gathering of friends and family in a church hall beautifully decorated with flowers and then move to an outdoor reception with more floral arrangements, exquisite tables and warm string lights that give a fairy-tale like ambience. I pictured an amazing cake with a wow factor, quality food, drinks and wedding favours for our few guests but here we were planning the very opposite, and because of this, it became a matter of quantity over quality. The options we wanted were right before us but we painfully had to give them up for something less just so we could spread resources to cater for the size of the ceremony we were working towards. A few examples would be how we made contact with a pastry chef who trained in the U.S. She was based in a town just two hours away and was ready to deliver my dream wedding cake but her price was double the price we got from a church member who could ensure there was a cake at the wedding for half the price even if the appearance of the cake was no match for the one we wanted. We also had two caterers we were negotiating with who promised to deliver excellently made Nigerian dishes on our menu, on time, but we chose one over the other because of a twenty percent discount that was offered – all because there wasn't enough cash and guess what, that was the decision that created the major disaster at the wedding.

My mom discussed with me and decided to handle the traditional wedding, which was smaller and cultural in nature. She had explained the complexity of what was expected to be done according to culture and tradition and was willing to handle everything about it, knowing her kinsmen and what they expected. When she offered to finance it, we were very happy and relieved. With my uncle and his wife, a few of my cousins from my maternal side, a number of members of the indigenous association my mom belonged to, John's immediate family and a few extended family members, and a handful of guests from my family church, it made a very cute and well organized traditional wedding as Happiness, our wedding organiser, also took care of the venue set up and decoration. The interesting part was that it all took place right at my parents' doorstep so there was no need to pay for a venue. How I longed that I could quietly and happily achieve the same arrangement for the upcoming white wedding, but it was beyond us.

Our court and traditional weddings took place on the same day and we excitedly looked forward to the white wedding, which was to come up two days after, to get us to our awaited final destination of living together as man and wife. But, unbeknownst to us, things were about to take a turn that would rock our wedding day like a ship in a tumultuous tempest.

I thought that finding myself being walked down the aisle by my dad without my bouquet, which I forgot at my parents' house where I got dressed up, after hurriedly dashing into the car that whisked me away to the wedding venue so I could meet up with time was the only odd thing that was going to happen that day; I never knew that we were in for the jaw dropping shocker of our lives. While we were all seated, in the middle of the wedding service, the lights went off as the venue suffered a power cut. I wasn't very bothered because the day before, John and I had come to crosscheck everything at the venue to ensure things would roll smoothly. The air conditioners were tested, the sound system was tested, the electric generator was tested, and everything was in perfect working condition. So, the management decided to quickly switch over to this massive generator we saw them test the day before and unbelievably, it refused to come on. They tried and tried but it just wouldn't work. Everyone in the church, including the Italians were fanning themselves profusely so much that the fanning motion and sound was getting me worked up on the altar where I sat. The heat had long made people lose their patience and I could tell that they couldn't wait to jump out of the small jampacked auditorium at the sound of us being pronounced man and wife.

Talking about the hall being jampacked, the crowd of two hundred and fifty that we were so afraid of was doubled by a singular announcement made in my family church at an evening service, the night before our wedding. Everyone, I mean everyone was encouraged to be in attendance, as reported to my mom by a church member. I really can't explain why but that was the situation on ground. I couldn't understand what was going on from the altar where I was but I noticed that the seats in the hall were full and people were leaning against the wall. When I turned to look out the window, I wasn't sure if my eyes were playing tricks on me but the crowd outside seemed far bigger than the one in the choked hall. There were so many people that the venue looked like a market place.

The Reception Party

When we moved to the garden behind, where the reception party was meant to hold, even the seating arrangement, set up to seat a specific number of people, was far from sufficient. Everywhere was rowdy from the middle to the back that the banquet seating arrangement was no longer enough because of the crowd. More chairs had to be rolled out and set up in a theatre arrangement to accommodate the extras that gate crashed. Our VIP guests and honorable family friends were drowned in the moving crowd, which I believe further confused the organizers. The feeling of chaos intensified as the master of ceremony struggled to recognize those on his list and others that had to be included at the spur -of -the -moment. When he called for a member of the clergy to open the celebration with a word of prayer, no one responded. They had all left. Some of them opened up to me much later about being disrespected openely by some self-appointed ushers who spoke rudely to them. With a little research, I discovered that these ushers were church members who wanted to help manage the crowd but did so without ethics and manners and couldn't tell who was a special guest, part of the clergy or who required to be seated on the V.I.P seats. After our wedding, when John and I went over to visit the chairman of the occasion, a parental figure who voluntarily gave us one of his beautiful cars with a driver attached to it, days before the wedding to be at our service before, during and a few days after the wedding, he expressed how he was treated as well. He and his wife found themselves seated at the back, they were practically lost in the crowd. They were so kind to fuel the car for the number of days that it was at our disposal and here they were, without, at the very least, front row seats to honor them.

You'd think it couldn't get any worse than that but it did. We had already painfully accepted the fact that John's Bishop and his wife, Mama Ossai, were not coming because my family church was not going to relinquish officiating the wedding to an external minister. It wasn't a new thing in Nigeria for the bride's church to handle everything about a wedding but I guess they felt we could have made an extra effort to alter the norm, unfortunately, it wasn't in our power to do so. The pastors from my family church had also left immediately after the group pictures we took together on the altar, right after the wedding service, as it was part of their ministerial ethics to do so. Consequently, the reception party was devoid of a single pastor to pray an opening prayer when the Master of Ceremony requested for it. We were so sad in our spirits and felt abandoned at that moment. By the way, I forgot to mention that the confused Master of Ceremony I talked about earlier was not the real MC. He was engaged in the duty because the real M.C, a very good friend who volunteered, as his contribution to the wedding, because he had always done it professionally, sent a message a day or two before, that he wasn't going to be there due to a mishap. And so the confusion that came over this person hosting in his stead was very obvious because we didn't have time to run through the V.I.P list and order of events thoroughly with him.

While we tried to balance the joy of knowing our dreams had come true with everything that was going wrong and flipping upside down, the mother of all disappointments was on the way. We were okay with the sparsely decorated venue for lack of investment in that direction, we were happy to have cake even if the 'wow' factor was missing, but to think that somewhere at the beginning of the reception party, there was a sudden shut down of the sound system without provocation. That was strange. It didn't give room for a 'bride and groom dance' or any other exciting activity whatsoever. Needless to mention that the noise coming from the overwhelming crowd did not only take away calmness from the ambience but created the most disorganized appearance I had ever witnessed at any wedding ceremony. The entire situation felt irredeemable and was dumbfounding.

The expatriates, whose food came earlier because they had a separate caterer since they were not included in the plan for the basic Nigerian dishes, could not start eating because the other food catering service that was expected to have arrived long before then with the Nigerian dishes for the larger crowd and all the flatware and cutlery was not there yet. They were responsible for the provision of all the tableware for all the guests.

The delay was unbelievably real and made me laugh in shock and amazement. I couldn't believe this was happening. The entire wedding ceremony started in the afternoon making the reception party an evening event so there was no excuse why the food would delay; there was more than enough time to fit in a few unforeseen delays here and there and still make it there on time. People couldn't even have a drink because the cups to pour out the drinks in the juice packs into were on the way with the food. At some point, I lost total touch with the environment and atmosphere because I felt I had been punched in the stomach and my mouth tasted sour. The roller coaster ride was just too much for me to handle. John and I wished we could snap out of it like a horrible nightmare but it was real. The disappointment was real. The guests who left angrily without eating, some with side talks of disappointment, others without comments and some with scoffs and jibes was real as well. After all was said and done, the long awaited catering service arrived by dusk and that was also when the sound engineer was able to fix the sound system. Such impeccable timing, when more than half of the seats were empty!

Many people told us themselves, much later, that they went home with the gifts they brought; some said they forgot they had gifts in the car while others said it was because they were upset. The few that remained who were family and very close friends tried to encourage us through it, one of them said something profound that hasn't left me since then, she said '...know that the wedding is not the marriage'. Let me repeat that: THE WEDDING IS NOT THE MARRIAGE. **No matter how beautifully or horribly the wedding ceremony goes, it can never define the outcome of the marriage**. The wedding is just a one-day event to celebrate your union but the marriage itself is your life, your present and your future. If two people are not meant to be together, even if you organize the most royal, crème de la crème and the world's most exceptional wedding in the entire universe for them, the marriage will not work. Interestingly, if two people destined for each other get married in the worst possible situation, maybe a tsunami and an earthquake happen all at the same time swallowing up the entire wedding feast, they would still go on to fulfill their purpose together as designed in Heaven, with a testimony of their victory over the enemy's attacks on that special day to back it up. In other words, the trials on your wedding day does not take away from the glory ahead for you as a couple, it has the capacity, as a matter of fact, to make you step into purpose faster and better equipped. This is because your mere ability to go through a wedding disaster together without letting it hinder your vision and mission of getting married is a first passed test that proves that you are both ready to make your marriage work in any situation you find yourselves. However, your own wedding does not have to go through half of what ours went through. If God has blessed someone financially to put a beautiful wedding together, that is awesome, there is nothing wrong with that. But the mere fact that yours encounters such shaking, even after putting in the best you could into planning, is a very good indicator that your marriage is headed for greatness; because the devil and his cohorts do not fight or try to destroy something that is not a threat to them and the agenda of hell.

I know the reason the enemy found a loophole to create a chaotic event at our wedding was primarily due to lack of funds. It made us settle for cheap this and cheaper that, we settled for less when we knew where to find far better quality but for the lack of resources. Interestingly, in spite of the lack of enough funds, if we had had our way to achieve our small and close-knit type of wedding with very few guests, the funds we had would have taken care of that. To match large quantity with good quality requires lots of money and that, we didn't have. We also lacked the experience to judge the outcome early enough in the planning phase and the boldness to cry out for a change in plan to my strong-willed and uncompromising family. So, our advice would be, if you have limited resources, please don't be shy or intimidated to go for a small wedding. Do not allow family members coerce or nicely persuade you into going for something out of your budget when they are not willing or able to make donations towards helping you achieve it. Unfortunately, what parents and family members don't realize is that if they do not support their children to accomplish something as all-encompassing as a wedding, the shame, the disappointment and embarrassment is a collective one as well.

Another angle to wedding preparation that cannot be ignored or over emphasized is the need for prayers. Before you meet the right person, you need to pray. When you do meet the right person, you have to pray to scatter every plot of the enemy to stop your journey half way. When you get to the stage of preparing for the wedding, oh you have to really pray harder. The devil and his agents will not sit back and watch your life take shape and prosper. Even if they eventually realize that they cannot stop you, they will want to make the ride a living hell for you so that by the time the wedding is over, you are battered and breathless like someone who survived a shipwreck and had to swim for days through an ocean with heavy currents to find land. You won't believe the reason why. The devil wants you to enter your marriage feeling doubts, negativity, fear of incompatibility with your spouse and most certainly, the feeling of rejection from God. The enemy needs to create this negative atmosphere around you, generated by the negativity created within you, to be able to find a legal entry into your purpose-driven home.

When we were preparing for this wedding, I know John prayed much more than I ever did but looking back now, I know that I was joking thinking to myself that my prayers were anywhere close to being enough. I didn't have the depth of revelation that I have now concerning the marriage institution and how the enemy will fight dirty to destroy it so as to ensure that God's agenda and Will on Earth through mankind does not get done. Therefore, there is a need to take authority over your plans, to combat the demonic realm that wants to thwart every good thing that God wants to do in your life and there is a need to combat satanic forces working through human vessels to frustrate your efforts. Moreover, if you have observed a demonic cycle in your family line where marriage, child bearing, or divorce has been a battle for family members or people of your gender in your family tree, then you have more work to do. You will have to engage in warfare prayers to break such cycles and stop it permanently from affecting you and your children. A demonic cycle in the family is best tackled before marriage but just as we know, that the enemy keeps trying to see if he can gain grounds again and again after he has been cast out, you cannot rest your oars and feel "oh well, that has been sorted out...moving on". You must stay on guard, walk circumspectly, work out your salvation with fear and trembling and perform continuous proper "maintenance". With these constant checks through prayers, you remind the devil in the place of prayer that you have broken free from that bondage through Christ. You will have to sustain and maintain your authority in Jesus by practicing submission and obedience to His Word and keep your spirit alive by praying in the Spirit in order to stay above the enemy and stay seated in your seat of victory.

Back to our wedding reception party disaster, after all said and done and very few family and friends stayed back to clear up the venue and clean it up, the photographer was the person God used to put extra smiles on our faces. He came to us and told us to discard everything we had just been through and give him the happiest poses we could ever think of because nothing could change the fact that we had sealed our union and that we were a beautiful couple. That was so uplifting. It was already dark so we found a spot with a street light and posed away, laughing and taking those memorable pictures that gave our wedding photo album a happy photo ending.

Right after that, we walked to the car that was waiting to take us to the hotel. As I snuggled my head against my husband's chest in the back seat while he gently wrapped his arms around me, in the quietness, we realized that this was it. Our lives together had started and what we had just been through was over. It wasn't going to define us neither was it going to change the fact that we are finally happily married now with our much desired future, dreams and visions before us. As I smiled to myself constantly maintaining body contact with John, I thought to myself "We did it! We won! We got to the finish line of our goal, we actually got the victory at the end of the day despite everything the enemy threw at us". I'm sure he was thinking the exact same thing but the tranquility in our spirits made the silence between us in that deeply spiritual moment too golden to be broken. I felt the deep connection we shared that made me feel that we were transmitting our thoughts and emotions to eachother without uttering a word. We had exercised all our faith and exhausted almost all our resources to ensure our marriage materialized and we didn't want to think of the need for a house of our own that laid in wait ahead of us. We were grateful that we had secured a temporary apartment that would be available to us for a while until we found ours but this moment right here, this was a moment to hush, a moment to heave a sigh of relief and enjoy the deeply rooted love that motivated this journey and brought it this stage of materialization. We weren't going to allow foreseen and unforeseen needs ahead preoccupy us, for the next one week, at least.

TEXT MESSAGES FROM 2007-2008

Here are a few text messages out of so many that we sent to each other while we were courting, which we documented in a special book years back before discarding the phones we had back then, after they became a little too old and faulty. We particularly wrote them down so as to be able to revisit them and reminisce on those days and the experiences. Even the ringtone we personalized to each other's contacts makes us melt with beautiful memories every time we hear it today. We have to admit that these messages fans the flame of love in us every single time we find time to go through them, stirring up joy, love, passion and desire for each other and bringing back to life the sweet memories of those dating days. We decided to share some of these messages just to encourage you to preserve every precious memory you have with your clone; it's a way of preserving your love life. You'll be glad you did, years down the road in marriage.

From John to Elliana:

*Good morning honey. Just opened my phone now after charging the battery. I've never slept so peacefully in my life as I did yesterday. I actually woke up late. Felt so lazy in love, I feel so happy with the world & everybody. I now know what it means to be so fulfilled.

You're the best thing that has ever happened to me. I love you so much darling in a way I can't describe. I'll let you know my plans for today concerning my trip. Take good care of yourself. I love U... 12:02pm/ August 6th, 2007

* Hi love, can't seem to get you out of my mind...well it's good coz I don't even want to. You're just driving me crazy...Love you too much. 8:41pm/ August 14th, 2007

*You asked for it. For in a few minutes from now I Sir John the prince of (not Wales) the church of Jesus and the knight of the round table of Christ will take on you, Princess Elliana the love of my life...on a duel of the songs. Better be prepared coz something great is going to happen! Let me also remind you my darling...that beautiful braids on your beautiful face isn't going to charm me to lose coz I can see how beautiful you look even without being there. 11:50pm/ August14th, 2007

*Honey I was thinking so much of you but hadn't time to text and just when I was composing a text for you I got yours. Sweet heart thanks for believing and trusting me coz that's all I want from you. I want you to also know that love overcomes anything. To me, there are other girls/ladies/women or whatever there is and there is only just one YOU! Nobody can ever take your place in my life. Never! I love you...always, forever. Two, five, ten, fifteen, forty, sixty years to this time, even after this life when we get to heaven, I'll not stop loving you. 2:33pm/ August 15th, 2007

*Part of my dream sweetheart for us is... I have seen too many marriages and relationships that are not happy even Christian ones. And so I want ours to be a healing balm to other marriages & relationships and an example that they can indeed be a heaven on earth. I want couples to look unto us as a guiding light to happiness and fulfillment in theirs. I want God to use us to show the world what marriages and relationships should be like especially according to His own original pattern. I had looked and searched for the right person to fulfill this vision with until I found you or rather until God gave me U. 2:55pm/ August 15th, 2007

*Hello honey... I'm sorry I slept off. The level of tiredness I felt could knock out an elephant. You actually woke me up, as in, I saw you standing clearly looking so beautiful in my vision and all I was saying was I love you and actually woke up to finding myself saying it out loud. Honey, this is getting...I mean I've never felt this in my entire life before. Honey I love you so terribly I feel like crying each time I say it. I mean I don't know what life will be like without you. You are every breath that I take my love...U live in me. I'm so glad I found you. I love you so much my darling, my baby, my life, my flesh and bone, my princess, my joy, my sweetest heart, my pride, my everything...I love you just as our Lord Jesus loves(d) the church! 2:41am/ August 16th, 2007

*Just wanted to disturb you in church...anyway was just love sick...later! 7:44pm/ September 7th, 2007

*My sunshine in the day...my moonlight in the night time...the one I have wanted for all these years...my dream come true...my cuppy cake...the apple of my eyes...my most perfect gift from God...the only one that holds the key to my heart, that gives me joy. How else can life be sweeter than having you, you are a sweetener to my taste bud...every other blessing I get later on in life is an addition...U are my main, ultimate and greatest blessing from God. Howz your day going. I love you. You'll always be my baby. I will love you forever my love!!! 12:50pm/ September 13th, 2007

*Hello my honey cuppy cake…I'm thinking of words to draw, chai, we live in each other, never seen this kind of thing before. You flashed me while I was composing my text. Baby let me take you to the altar tomorrow now…I mean this is a mystery of love. As I was saying, I'm searching into the deep well of my love for you to get words…Baby pl…kai…this is extraordinary my…I love you honey, I love you Pl… 8:53pm/ September 17th, 2007

*My oxygen…my dove…what more, better gift could I ask and I got from God other than you. Baby U are all of my treasure…and I can't be grateful enough to God. just rounded up service with absolutely no concentration coz of the thoughts of U…will be spending the night @ my sister's place so we can have our biz meeting at length…can I talk to you my dove, my angel, my honey, tonight…pl….se…if I don't I won't be able to sleep…darling I'm so in love with you… 8:48pm/ September 5th, 2007

From Elliana to John:

Hi baby, you've been through a lot in the past few hours, wished I was there with you. You're not just my hero, you're an extension of Christ. I'm so happy about the progress, seemed impossible initially for you to travel. Just got your message while typing this, means we're connected in thought. In the nearest future, you won't have to look for me. I'll almost be the clothes you wear. 23:32pm/ August 20th, 2007.

Thanks for the credit, forgot to say that. Baby, I'm so glad that God never fails, He rewards His children. Sweetie, you're a reward. You possess all I could ask for. I'm a strong believer in the phrase 'Love conquers all'. I plan to go all the way with you. What a better blessing or higher peace than to know you're with the right half. I owe you one when we get married. 1:11pm/ August 23rd, 2007

**You gave me a good laugh with your Italian grammar! Baby, I love you so much too. I do believe in us. I'm positive that I'll be happy with you, that you'll be loved by all in my house and whether they accept or not, I have made my choice. I can't love you enough. Talk to you later baby, you're an angel on earth! 8:24pm/ August 30th, 2007*

**With the way I love you, I would break my rule once in my entire life to chase after a man if that man was you! This love ehn...hmmm...when we get married, this world won't know what hit it! 22:31pm, November 11th 2007*

**Baby, my passion, tesoro, sugar, harmony, melody, desire, dream come true, sexy, romantic, Rexy, high priest, my joy, peace, ministry, my sigh of relief and satisfaction... you're the best birthday gift God packaged and gave to me! I'm so loved by Him. He hears the silliest of wishes that I thought were unspiritual – because He's a true Father! I promise to love you faithfully, to be there when you need a hand and heart, to support you, your calling and vision, to express the depth of love and emotion in me for you... it's your birthday too! I love you forever! 01:13pm/ November 27th, 2007 (on Elliana's birthday)*

**My luv, when you cry I cry, when you laugh I laugh, your emotions are my emotions, your vision and destiny is where I want to be. We're so into each other and I won't allow anything come between us. Not even our own emotional high. Honey, everyone around me testifies that you're a blessing, for me you're a dream come true! Nothing can separate us from the love of God...I love you. 06:38pm/ December 18th, 2007*

**My honey, I love you so much! You don't know what your coming to Abuja means to me...I'll miss you so much. I love you right now in a* *greater measure than I ever did! Baby, please rest for me...pls! I put angels on assignment for you from this minute. No harm can come near you. You're going to Lagos to meet open doors waiting for you! I love you till the end of eternity...text you soonest! 5:37pm/ December 11th, 2007*

**Sweety my voice is so gone!...& I'm still marketing! I miss the eye contact that we make while marketing to people... I luv you so much, can't wait to see you tomorrow. You're my heart, my passion! 01:41pm/ December 13th, 2007 (During the marketing trip at Shiloh, Lagos)*

**Whatever it is that God has sent me to do in your life apart from loving you and honoring you, I'll do with my whole life... you're everything to me, I'm overwhelmed by you, you're my testimony. I love you. 11:55 pm/ December 18th, 2007*

**I love you sweetie, I'm blessed to have you as a partner, spiritual head, lover, husband, counselor. I sure can't explain the depth of love I feel today and generally for you...it's overwhelming...at night, I cried mostly because the thought of how I love you was beyond me...sweetie, the hand of God rest on you mightily today. I love you now, this weekend, next week, next month, years, years and years to come! 12:43pm/ Februaury 25th, 2008*

**Baby!!! Howz service going? I've left church. Have an outing with my folks. Just want you to know that thoughts of you gives me joy and peace!...is this how love feels?! I love you so much! I look forward to all our marriage has to offer, I'm so blessed amongst women! My mum made an interesting comment yesterday...I love you!!! 11:51am/ March 23rd, 2008*

PRAYER POINTS
MARITAL BREAKTHROUGH

These are warfare prayer points and they require that you pray them fervently with the resolve that you will take back what belongs to you by force from the hands of the enemy and a determination that you're done with disappointments and struggle as it concerns your marital life. Please find time to enjoy a session of praise and worship before commencing your prayers, it creates a spiritually charged atmosphere and shifts your prayer experience to the next level.

Prayer:

Father I thank you because Philippians 2:9-10 says: *Wherefore God also hath highly exalted him, and given him a name which is above every name; that at the name of Jesus every knee should bow, of things in heaven, and things in earth, and things under the earth.* And your word also says in Luke 1:37: *For with God nothing shall be impossible.*

1. Lord I ask for forgiveness for any sin that will hinder my prayers. Cleanse me with the precious blood of Jesus.
2. I ask for forgiveness for the sins of my forefathers back to the fourth and fifth generation. I wash those sins off of my bloodline with the redeeming power of the blood of Jesus.
3. Lord Jesus, make known to me the secrets of my inner life in the name of Jesus.
4. I break every covenant of marital failure and late marriage in my life in Jesus name.
5. I remove the hand of household wickedness from my marital life in Jesus name.
6. Every marine spirit power troubling my marital life, loose me and let me go in the name of Jesus.

7. Every covenant made against my life when I was born affecting my marital life, be undone by the blood of Jesus.

8. Let every incantation, incisions, hexes, and other spiritually harmful activities working against me be neutralized by the blood of Jesus.

9. Every evil force magnetizing the wrong people to me be paralyzed and bound in Jesus name.

10. I cancel any evil covenant I have with marine spirits and I remove my name from any evil contract by the blood of Jesus.

11. I remove the right of the enemy to afflict my plan to get married in the name of Jesus.

12. I command every strongman fighting marriage to bow to the power of God in my life in Jesus name.

13. Let the angels of the living God roll away the stone blocking my marital breakthrough in Jesus name.

14. Open my eyes Lord to see where I am going wrong and aiding the enemy with my attitude and lifestyle in the name of Jesus.

15. I forsake any personal sin in my life past and present that has given ground to the enemy in Jesus name

16. Let every dissipation of my glory as a result of sexual activities in my life be visited by God's mercy and be restored in Jesus name

17. Lord, redirect my life to meet my perfect match in Jesus name.

18. Let the evil veil that is shielding my true image from being seen be burnt to ashes in Jesus name.

19. I stand against evil spirits of fear, discouragement, worry, frustration and depression in Jesus name.

20. Let my book in heaven be opened and let all that is written concerning me begin to find fulfillment in Jesus name.

Thank you Lord for victory, I receive answers to my prayers with thanksgiving in Jesus name.

PRAYER POINTS
BREAKING SOUL TIES

Prayer:

I thank you Father for the redemptive power in the blood of Jesus. Thank you because your word says in Isaiah 49:24-26 that: *Shall the prey be taken from the mighty, or the captives of the righteous delivered? But thus says the Lord: "Even the captives of the mighty shall be taken away, and the prey of the terrible delivered; for I will contend with him who contends with you, and I will save your children. And they shall be drunk with their own blood as with sweet wine. All flesh shall know that I the LORD, am your Savior, and your Redeemer, the Mighty One of Jacob"* Your word also says in Galatians 6:17 *that From now on let no one trouble me, for I bear in my body the marks of the Lord Jesus.* Thank you Father because I have the right in Christ Jesus to be set free and to be forgiven of my sins (confess any sexual sin or covenants in your past relationships). I receive freedom and forgiveness of sin right now in Jesus name.

1. I deliver myself from every spirit of perversion that has taken control of my soul as a result of my past sexual activities in the name of Jesus.

2. I free myself from every inordinate affection that has kept me bound in the name of Jesus.

3. I bind the demonic powers that controlled my relationship with ... (mention the name of the person). I command those powers to lose their hold over my life in Jesus name.

4. By the blood of Jesus, I remove all evil soul ties, affections and relationship covenants in Jesus name.

5. I renounce all evil soul ties now and I break every hold it has had on me in the name of Jesus.

6. I flush out of my system every demonic deposit in me because of my association with ... (mention the name of the person) in Jesus name.

7. I renounce all hidden evil soul ties that are still affecting me today and command their hold broken off me in the name of Jesus.

8. I claim deliverance from any negative affection towards anyone in Jesus name.

9. Let all evil affection towards me be wiped off the mind of ... (mention the name of the person) in Jesus name.

10. I fix my eyes, my heart and my affections on the Lord Jesus from this day forward in the name of Jesus.

Thank you Lord for answered prayers, I claim my deliverance in Jesus Mighty name.

ABOUT THE AUTHORS

John Rex is the senior pastor of Voce Del Regno, a ministry headquatered in Italy with a primary vision to prepare the way for the second coming of our Lord and Saviour Jesus Christ. He is a seasoned teacher, propagating the message of the Kingdom of God with a burning passion to draw men and women alike to a life of holiness, consecration and return to their first-love, Jesus Christ. Through his teaching ministry, he is equally passionate about carefully guiding people through the process of discovering, manifesting and maximizing their God-given assignment on Earth as they passionately live out the Will of God on Earth as written in Heaven.

John Rex is also an Evangelist at heart with a mission of snatching over a billion souls from the clutches of hell into the Kingdom of God. He holds a Bachelor's Degree in Sociology. He is a prolific author, a Leadership Coach, a researcher and a passionate teacher of God's Word.

Pastor John Rex and his wife hold dear to their hearts the ministry of restoring and reviving broken homes and building more godly family units that will influence our society with Kingdom culture, using the relationship between Christ and His bride (the Church) as a model, because the marital union is a clear symbolism of what our spiritual walk with God is expected to be.

Elliana Rex holds a Bachelor's Degree in International Relations. She is an English Language teacher, a worship leader and songwriter with a strong calling towards children and the youth, to groom them into mighty men and women for the Lord. John and Elliana Rex are blessed with four lovely children.

To contact the author for feedbacks, to schedule a meeting, speaking engagement and conference, kindly call:

(+39) 3519123205

Or send an email to:

howtoknowitsherhim@gmail.com

"...that afternoon, the housemaid, who seemed to weild more authority than expected, informed us in the coldest tone immaginable that she had received a call from my mother's friend instructing her to inform us that her children were coming over from the U.K and would need the entire house to themselves. We were expected to move out before the week ran out. What were we supposed to do with such a sudden unexpected news at a point when we were still house hunting? We hadn't even exhausted the second week there and she had promised that we could stay till we found a place of our own. I would have expected my mom's friend to speak to us directly, or maybe to my mom, if it made her feel bad in anyway that things were taking a sudden and unexpected turn. But, sending the maid and worse still, the attitude of the maid, made it feel like we were being thrown out. That's exactly what it was, we were being thrown out. Indifferently. We knew that rest time was over. We were supposed to have the benefit of house hunting calmly without bothering about where to sleep but it was time to rise up again like soldiers and face this new battle squarely. If you understood our story, you'd know why my parents-in-law's house was not an option for us. And so, without hesitation, we borrowed my father-in-law's pickup truck to transport our luggage to a destination unknown.

– an excerpt from *Twelves Years After*, a sequel to *'How to Know it's Her, How to Know it's Him'*, coming out soon.

'TWELVE YEARS AFTER'

By John and Elliana Rex

a sequel to

'How to Know it's Her, How to Know it's Him'

A continuation of the journey of John and Elliana Rex after their wedding.

It is a must read for every married person as it promises to be a captivating and equipping guide and resource to help couples navigate their marriages towards their God-given purposes. In this book, couples will learn secrets to growing stronger in love through tough moments, effective approaches that make children fall in love with God from birth and how to experience supernatural financial supply, daily, as a family.

For enquiries, please send an email to:

howtoknowitsherhim@gmail.com